Before the Killing Fields

Leslie Fielding read History at Cambridge (where he is now an Honorary Fellow of Emmanuel College) and Persian at the School of Oriental and African Studies, London. He joined the Foreign Service in 1956 working initially in Tehran and (briefly) Singapore, before being put in charge of the British Embassy in Phnom Penh, Cambodia, from 1964 to 1966. His subsequent diplomatic career took him to Paris, Brussels (in the European Commission) and Tokyo. He has also been a Visiting Fellow at St Antony's College, Oxford, and Vice-Chancellor of the University of Sussex. He has contributed to two volumes of short stories, *Travellers' Tales* and *More Travellers' Tales*. He was knighted in 1988 and is married to the medievalist, Sally Harvey.

Before the Killing Fields

Witness to Cambodia and the Vietnam War

Leslie Fielding

To Bruce Anderson
for Leslie Fielding
with best wishes
Febry 2011

I.B. TAURIS

LONDON · NEW YORK

Published in 2008 by I.B.Tauris & Co Ltd
6 Salem Road, London W2 4BU
175 Fifth Avenue, New York NY 10010
www.ibtauris.com

In the United States of America and Canada, distributed by Palgrave Macmillan
a division of St Martin's Press, 175 Fifth Avenue, New York NY 10010

ISBN 978 1 84511 493 0

A full CIP record for this book is available from the British Library

A full CIP record is available from the Library of Congress

Library of Congress Catalog Card Number: available

Typeset in Garamond by Stilman Davis
Printed and bound in the Czech Republic by FINIDR, s.r.o.

Contents

List of Illustrations

Acknowledgements

The author is grateful to the Travellers Club, Pall Mall, London and to their publisher for permission to reproduce 'The Number One Twister' (p. xxv) and 'The Crocodile Princess' (p. 215) from Travellers' Tales *(Castlereagh Press, 1999).*

On page 128 the cartoon is from a now long-defunct, monthly publication in Phnom Penh, produced by people I must presume long dead, called Réalités Cambodgiennes, *dated 29 July 1966. Unfortunately I found the name of the cartoonist indecipherable, and he is unknown to me. God rest their souls.*

Foreword

The Rt. Hon The Lord Patten of Barnes

This is a wonderfully entertaining read and hugely germane to many of our present preoccupations in International Relations. As geopolitics focuses increasingly on Asia, it is instructive to be reminded of how we got to where we are today. Leslie Fielding provides us in addition with useful insights into managing the Transatlantic Relationship, and is engagingly frank about the gap between European aspirations to play a role on the world stage and what happened in the past on the ground. Those of us who worry about humanitarian interventions in dire and dangerous circumstances will also find much here to illuminate our discussions.

These days, diplomats' memoirs (latterly, Meyer and Bremer) are like falling leaves – as numerous as those of ex-politicians. And fully as self-justificatory. The refreshing thing about Leslie Fielding's book is that it is as much a *Mea Culpa* as an *Apologia*.

The author takes us back to Indo-China in the 1960s and 1970s – to America's disastrous engagement in Vietnam, and the ill-starred British efforts to get Cambodia counted out. In the event, Cambodian neutrality collapsed; the country went to war on the American side, got smashed up and ended in the grip – for four insane, genocidal years – of the monster Pol Pot. The latter was aided and abetted by that other monster, Mao Tse-tung. A quarter of the population were exterminated.

Thirty years on, Cambodia has bounced back. Times are still hard. But law and order prevail, and Western tourism, particularly to the magnificent temple complexes, is growing exponentially.

Thinking about Cambodia is, however, more than a matter of what jungle paths may still be planted with landmines and which hotel is the best value at Angkor Wat.

During the Vietnam War, successive US governments pressured the British hard to commit at least a token fighting force (the Black Watch was usually mentioned). The Australians, similarly pressured, duly came up with the goods. But the Brits resolutely declined, not only because they were already committed to the defence of Malaysia against President Sukarno, but also because they considered it to be the wrong war in the wrong place.

In this, Harold Macmillan, Alec Douglas-Home and Harold Wilson were influenced by Anthony Eden's judgements, when the latter skilfully negotiated the exit of the French from Indo-China in 1954, and made possible a fudged but peaceful solution (probably the high point of his diplomatic career). After 'free elections', North and South Vietnam would be united, inevitably under some sort of communist government (like him or not, Ho Chi Minh had come out on top). China could be relied on, in her own self-interest, to prevent the new Vietnam from getting too uppity, or from grabbing bits of the adjoining kingdoms of Laos and Cambodia, which were to remain neutral. In the end, we thought, a communist Vietnam would settle down, rather than upset the dominoes of South-East Asia.

Today – as even Henry Kissinger concedes – British judgements in the 1960s have been amply vindicated. But let me offer two, inter-related, thoughts. In the light of what has happened in Iraq (which I admit is a different story from Vietnam, and where the last chapter still has to be written), would a modern British government have had the courage to say, 'No', to the Americans, as we did over Indo-China? We know Mr Blair's answer to that. And what prospect is there that the Member States of the European Union will, in foreign policy terms, finally grow up and accept a full measure of international responsibility? This is the price of being taken seriously in Washington and of sustaining in the first half of the twenty-first century a Transatlantic Relationship generally as vital (with individual exceptions from time to time, such as over Vietnam) as that which protected us and prevailed in the second half of the twentieth. Back in the 1960s, what they call 'European Political Co-operation' did not exist, and the only non-British European voice on peace and war in Indo-China was that of General de Gaulle – far from his finest hour. Fielding's description of the French and their works at that time will make uncomfortable, if salutary, reading, in a French translation.

As to Cambodia, I would have preferred to see, in the period described by this book, more of a 'tough love' approach to Washington

from London. Fielding is, in my judgement, a touch too hard on the US (although aspects of his 'Ugly Americans' chapter undeniably ring a bell). The fact is, as he acknowledges, the assassination of President Kennedy and the health problems of Macmillan removed from the scene two remarkable Statesmen, who were prepared to listen to each other, and might have worked out another way forward. The real damage was done when Kennedy's successor, President Johnson, decided to commit US combat troops in Vietnam. However that may be, the British government, once convinced in 1963 that a Geneva Conference could well be convened to guarantee Cambodian independence, neutrality and territorial integrity, should have pressed ahead, despite US reservations. The irony was that, two years later, the US, looking for a way out of Vietnam, changed its mind on Cambodia and aligned itself with the UK. But the opportunity had passed. Ho Chi Minh had military victory over the Americans well in his sights and his sponsor, Mao Tse-tung, preferred conflict to conciliation. As far as Cambodia was concerned, *hinc, illae lacrimae*.

All this is grim stuff. Happily, *Before the Killing Fields* has many other things to offer. Students of Politics and International Relations can see how a British Embassy actually functions and how Foreign Policy is actually made, warts and all. Harvard Business School could do worse than use the book as a case study in Man-Management and Organisation-and-Method. For the tired businessman in Club Class, the author gives us raging mobs, ravishing Princesses, exotic opium dens, Oriental superstition and necromancy, bombings, shootings and even espionage.

The moral is, however, while understated, as plain as a pike staff. And I am not entirely surprised that Sir Leslie was in the end to come back to the Faith of his fathers.

Chris Patten

Introduction

From April 1964 to November 1966, I was in charge of the British Embassy to Cambodia. Initially, I cursed my bad luck. It was a formative, but also a traumatic, experience for a relatively young man (only 31 years on arrival). There was already palpably a curse upon the land, for which the future reserved terrible things.

One purpose in writing this book has been to achieve what, in contemporary 'psycho babble', could be called 'closure'. Millions were to die, primarily as a result of the ruthlessness and cynicism of Ho Chi Minh and Mao Tse-tung and of the delusions of a fundamentalist called Pol Pot. An accessory cause was the erratic political course of the well-meaning, but eccentric, Cambodian Head of State, Prince Norodom Sihanouk. The outcome was, however, also influenced by egregious errors in US foreign policy. And the British? To some degree also, there may have been serious miscalculation.

A dark shadow did indeed lie over the future of the place and people which I will set out to recapture in these pages – the misfortune of the subsequent right-wing military coup against the Cambodian Head of State in 1970, leading to civil war and foreign invasion; much worse, the nightmare which followed the victory of the Khmer Rouge in Cambodia in 1975. 'Brother Number One' and his followers were responsible, over less than four years, for the death of perhaps a quarter of the entire population, including almost all the Buddhist clergy, the educated middle-classes and any who were unwise enough to admit that they spoke a word of a foreign language.

While some of us in Phnom Penh saw bad things coming (and I myself came to suspect that the rule of Norodom Sihanouk could not endure), none of us then guessed just how bad things would be. Nobody noticed an obscure, leftist, ex-schoolteacher called Saloth Sar, later known by the world under his revolutionary name of Pol Pot.

A subsidiary object in writing this book has been to de-mystify the recondite and over-secretive business of diplomacy – to 'take the lid off' Embassy life in a way which conventional Ambassadors' memoirs have not (until Christopher Meyer's) for a general public wishing to know more of these matters. For this reason alone, as well as many others, the book has had to relate to a particular time, place and real-life drama, as experienced by one of the protagonists. The setting is the mid-1960s in Cambodia, on the cusp of peace and war, sanity and genocidal madness. Embassies have not changed enormously since then, however – save, perhaps, in ease of communication. This narrative is thus not too distant from contemporary diplomatic reality.

Inevitably, *Before the Killing Fields* is unusual in presentation, as well as strange in substance – a combination of chalks and cheeses. Violence, intrigue and the supernatural in an exotic, oriental setting are interwoven with issues of day-to-day office management, and the motivation and morale of expatriate personnel. It tells what it is really like to be a diplomat in the field when the chips are down. In my own case, during nearly three years in Phnom Penh, I found myself in turn perplexed, repelled and physically apprehensive; my health was inter-mittently fever stricken and run down. But I was also, at intervals, highly amused and even exhilarated, and always professionally fulfilled. Boring, it most certainly was not.

With hindsight, one or two overall judgements have been attempted. Yet the main aim has remained to be true to the time, the place and the principal protagonists. This is a narrative of what those who lived them still call the 'Swinging Sixties'.

The following is therefore an account of how my colleagues and I operated in a distant, tropical country; it is an account of how we overcame – or perhaps did not overcome – the problems which confronted us; it is an account of what we did, on the instructions of the British Government of the day, to help Cambodia in its efforts to remain neutral, independent and at peace in an Asia that was committed, subordinate and at war.

Alas, it is not a British success story. Our arguments did not prevail in Washington and people in London did not press them as far as (with hindsight) they certainly should have. If in 1963 J.F. Kennedy had not been murdered and Harold Macmillan had not resigned for health reasons, things might have been different. With their successors, Lyndon Johnson and Harold Wilson, the old chemistry was gone; the common ground of political judgement lost.

To the Cambodian, Chinese and Vietnamese employees of the Phnom Penh Embassy, and its young British non-diplomatic staff – especially Barbara, Betty, Andrew, Frank and Malcolm.

Also to the memory, among so many others, of Hong, Sau and Ngō, Ailsa and Donald.

Figures in Relief – Four Cambodian Cameos

Map: Cambodia and Vietnam in 1964

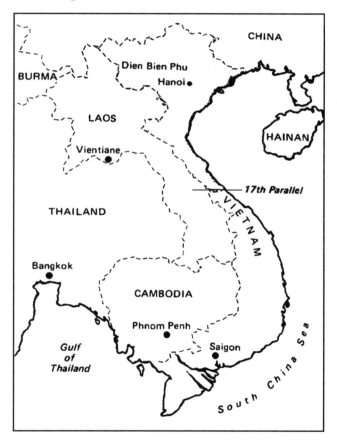

I

Mob at the Chancery Gates

On 11 March, 1964, the Chancery offices of the British and American
Embassies in Phnom Penh were attacked and partly wrecked by
organised mobs from the streets.

There had been demonstrations against the 'Anglo-Saxons' in the
past, but they had thitherto always assumed a non-violent character.
A well-marshalled crowd would troop by along the main street
shouting slogans and brandishing posters and the like, but in other
respects they had been peaceful. The immunity of the Chancery
building and grounds had always been scrupulously respected.

When the British Embassy's offices opened on the morning of 11
March 1964, it seemed as if it would be a day of demonstration like
any other. A few idlers had gathered on the pavement outside the
Chancery, but otherwise the coast was clear. The Ambassador,
having business to transact with his US colleague, departed to pay a
call at the American Embassy downtown. While he was talking in the
US Chargé d'Affaires' office, the mob closed in simultaneously on
both Embassies. A brick sailed through the window past the British
Ambassador's head and the attack on the Americans began. It was
not for an hour or two that the British Ambassador was able to force
his way out through the rioters and return to his own Embassy to
assist the Head of Chancery, John Shakespeare, whom he had left
temporarily in charge. The following is John's own account of what
happened at the British end of town from the recently published FO
papers of the period –

> A few minutes after the Ambassador had left for the
> American Embassy, a Volkswagen van covered with 'US
> Go Home' placards arrived outside the Embassy. A
> well-dressed elderly man emerged carrying a pot of red

paint and a large brush and began to paint labouriously on the pavement and the Embassy gates 'US Go Home'. As the crowd outside was still thin, Mr Higginbottom (the Second Secretary) and I went outside to remonstrate with the painter and the one policeman on duty. I told the painter that he had got the wrong Embassy and that if he insisted on painting his slogans he should go down the road to do so. With much embarrassment he picked up his pot and brush, entered the car and drove a few yards across the road. I returned to the Embassy in a fury to draft an indignant letter to the Municipality to ask them to clean up the paint immediately, but this was soon to be overtaken by events.

A squad of about twenty unarmed police now arrived in a lorry and took up positions around the Embassy compound, one at approximately every ten yards, from the Australian Chancery next door, to our Vice Consul's house in the side-street behind us. A few minutes later a procession of small children carrying the by-now-familiar 'US Go Home' and '*Perfide Albion*' placards filed past the Embassy without so much as a glance in our direction, while their teachers shuffled along behind in embarrassed fashion. As it still seemed quite peaceful, I tried to telephone the Ambassador at the American Embassy to tell him he could return without danger but was told their line was out of action.

Towards 9.45 am a large crowd began to gather in the road outside and shortly afterwards a long and well-regimented procession of young men carrying huge placards with the same slogans marched up the Boulevard Norodom from the direction of the American Embassy. They were headed by four well-dressed, senior-looking officials or dignitaries, none of whom I recognised. Thinking them to be a delegation that had come to call on the Embassy, I put on my jacket and went down into the entrance hall to receive them. But the 'delegation' did not materialise and vanished into the crowd that was now pressing up against the wall of the Embassy and brandishing slogans in a still quite good-humoured fashion. These slogans included a

preponderance of 'US Go Home' and *'Perfide Albion'*, (with *'Perfide Albino'* as an interesting variant), but also some *'L'Asie aux Asiatiques'*, *'A bas le monde libre'*, *'A bas les marchands de canons'* and one particular pearl *'Vive le Cambodge Pacifique'*. Curiously, there were no slogans inviting the British to depart among the many hundreds displayed.

The two Embassy gates, which we had hitherto left open as a sign of our confidence in the good-nature of the crowd, were now closed by the police themselves. I went outside for a few minutes to look at the crowd from the balcony in front of the Embassy. The first missile was thrown, a bottle of ink that hit the Embassy wall a few yards from my feet. I went inside as it was now apparent that the crowd was growing more hostile. A few minutes later, some time between 10.00 and 10.15 am, a brass band joined the crowd (now about 2,000 strong at a rough guess) and started to play what we took to be martial music. A Ministry of Information loudspeaker van drew up in the road opposite the Embassy; an attractive girl climbed on the roof and began to harangue the crowd. Her harangue consisted largely of a repetition in Cambodian of the slogans carried by the demonstrators. Her place was then taken by a man who did the same. He succeeded in whipping up the crowd to new heights of excitement and set them chanting frenetically in unison.

All at once and without any warning the sky was suddenly darkened by hundreds of stones and rocks hurled at the Embassy from the front ranks of the crowd (a distance of 30 yards) which fell against the walls and windows of the building with the noise of heavy hail. We closed and bolted the doors and waited for something to happen. After a few minutes the stone-throwing stopped, the crowd swarmed over the wall into the garden which they filled completely and began hammering and beating at the doors and windows of the Embassy. There must have been at least one thousand in the compound at one time, according to the Australian Embassy next door, who saw everything.

We retreated to the security zone of the Embassy, behind the grilles. I tried to telephone first the Foreign Ministry and then Prince Sihanouk's French Private Secretary, to appeal for immediate help, but the line seemed to be cut (later we discovered that it had been short-circuited by the wrecked Diplomatic Wireless Service aerial). Very soon afterwards the crowd broke into the Consular Section and began the systematic destruction and looting of everything they could lay their hands on. They started to shake, and beat against, the smaller grille with table legs and iron bars. I got everyone upstairs as it was quite clear that the sight of us only incited the mob even further. We gathered in the dark little corridor between the Registry and the Chancery Typists' Office, the only place in the Embassy that now offered any shelter against the rocks and bricks that continued to be hurled through the windows. The Registry was particularly dangerous as it had been impossible to close the shutters outside in time and large splinters of glass and rocks, many of them over six inches across, poured continuously through the window.

I decided we should burn the ciphers and succeeded in opening the strong room door unharmed. We started to burn them in the strong room but it was a slow business and in any case one could not remain inside for more than two or three seconds without suffocating, so we continued the burning in buckets under the Registry windows.

In the meantime, an ominous metallic hammering sound outside proclaimed that the rioters were hard at work on our cars. Very soon they had piled two or three together near the flag pole and were preparing to set fire to them when stopped by the police – the only effective action that I saw the police take during the whole of the morning – and that, no doubt, because of the possible danger to their own skins. However, the crowd did succeed in making a bonfire of paper, tyres, etc., looted from the Consular Section a few feet from the Embassy steps, which blazed merrily for at least half an hour so far as I could tell.

After what seemed an eternity, but what was in fact, I think, only an hour, the noise began to die down as the police and certain well-dressed, authoritative-looking mob leaders in plain clothes succeeded in persuading the crowd to leave the garden. I went outside to talk to our protectors, who stood in a little knot in the shade of a jack-fruit tree puffing at cigarettes (ours no doubt) and giggling among themselves. Picking my way through the debris and the upturned cars I went up to them and asked who was in charge. They all shrugged their shoulders and pretended not to speak French. I then addressed myself to the only one who appeared to have any authority (perhaps because he was the only one who wore a tin helmet) and said very slowly that there were some young girls who were very frightened inside the Embassy (this, I felt, was a perfectly justifiable lie) and I wanted an escort to take them to their homes. He giggled and said '*Deux heures, trois heures. Pas assez de police*', and would I mind going back inside the building as my presence there only excited the crowd. As I walked back, one or two stones were thrown, happily missing their target.

In the pause that followed we decided to complete the destruction of the cipher books and begin the destruction of all remaining top-secret and secret papers. Strangely the electricity was still working so we started the shredder in the Registry and began to feed papers into it, but the power supply failed ten minutes later.

Meanwhile, the crowd outside appeared to have grown even larger and the loudspeaker van started up its senseless cacophony once more. At about 11.15 am, the crowd pushed aside the few police at the gates and once again renewed their attack. They completed the sack of Consular Section and turned their attention in earnest to the two grilles that were still protecting us. I went downstairs to try and reason with them. The sight through the smaller grille was one of sickening destruction. Young men and boys were beating and hammering at everything still intact with table legs and iron grilles,

while older men, some impeccably dressed, sat quietly in the middle of the chaos directing the pillage. Two particularly unpleasant oafs were hammering away the lock of the smaller grille which miraculously still held. I went up and protested that this had now lasted long enough and that they were terrifying the girls upstairs. One of them, his eyes glazed with what can only be described as hypnotic hatred, shouted at me '*A bas les Américains*'. 'But we are not American', I protested. 'We are British', at which he shouted even louder, '*A bas les Américains*'. I was clearly getting nowhere, so went upstairs to rejoin the rest of the staff. I told them that the grilles below were still holding, that the crowd below seemed bent only on the destruction of property and would almost certainly not attack people (I deduced this, a little optimistically perhaps, from the fact that I had not been attacked through the bars). I said that if the grilles finally gave way and the mob started to come upstairs I would go and parley with them and ask that they let us leave the building safely in a group. The staff, for whom I have nothing but the highest praise, were magnificently calm and showed no sign of fear. In fact, the only ones to break under the strain were our Cambodian telephonist, who sat sobbing in a corner, and our Chinese Consular clerk, who stood shivering like a jelly throughout.

At about 11.45 am the noise of hammering and shouting downstairs grew louder. I went down in time to see the main grille across the front entrance slowly falling to the ground behind the weight of about 50 frenzied demonstrators. I went back to tell the staff that the grille had given way and told them to be ready to leave in a bunch directly behind me when I had spoken to the mob leaders. I emerged from our dark corridor to find the mob already half way up the stairs, pulling down the Embassy photographs as they ascended. I went towards the man who was obviously the leader and said this had gone quite far enough and would he please now let the staff leave the building. To my surprise he turned round, shrugged his shoulders to

his colleagues and started to go downstairs. I then noticed with immense relief that by now half the crowd in the entrance hall consisted of police – not that they were doing anything to restrain the crowd, but at least they were not actively breaking up the telephone switchboard, *etc.*, like the rest. At that moment too, the fire seemed to go from the crowd outside and the mob began to retreat from the building with the police beginning to push them back rather pathetically. I noticed that in the road outside there now stood a large anti-riot vehicle with 'USAID' in large letters emblazoned on the sides and police on it directing hoses at the people in the street. The crowd gradually left the garden and a few minutes later the Ambassador appeared, having come in unobserved by a back entrance that had been overlooked by the crowd.

At no time did I see any soldiers in evidence (the military only turned up at 1.45 pm to clear the crowd from the streets around the Embassy) and at no time did there seem to be more than 20 or 25 police protecting the Embassy.

The British Vice Consul's private car, after the Embassy's Chancery had been attacked by a state-directed mob in Phnom Penh (1964)

II

The Number One Twister

It was in 1965, eighteen months after my first arrival in a less than welcoming Phnom Penh. The Brits were nearly out of the dog house. The Head of State wanted to be nice.

I was invited to the Palace, where I was greeted by the sound of revelry by night – a daughter of 'Monseigneur' had just got married. Cambodia's capital city had gathered her beauty, her chivalry and her diplomacy in one of Phnom Penh's great and gracious palaces. Fireworks cascaded across the indigo midnight sky, illuminating the wide waters of the mighty Mekong River and the fringes of sugar palm trees which stood along the banks. Tropical flowers released their slow perfume upon the balmy breeze. The chandeliers shone over fair women, brave men and rotund ambassadors. A thousand hearts beat happily as the Head of State, His Royal Highness Prince Comrade Norodom Sihanouk, the former (and, as history would tell, also the future) King, dressed comfortably in an impeccable, dark-blue, silk tuxedo, conducted the Palace orchestra as they played a dance number of his own composition.

Then, a change of mood; a different sound struck like a rising knell. Hush! Hark! Was it the remote thunder of a B-52 bombing raid across the Cambodian frontier with Vietnam? Happily, that night, not so. The Prince having handed over his baton and withdrawn to mingle with his guests, and the normal conductor taking over, the band had struck up an entirely novel – even an alien – rhythm, fresh from the West; it was Chubby Checker, *Let's twist again, like we did last summer*. The elders and chamberlains froze; the generals looked to their aides; the young Cambodian lords and ladies glanced around them for a lead; the cabinet ministers and parliamentarians seemed puzzled; the diplomatic corps

hesitated politely, taken by surprise. It was my cue – my only moment of greatness, ever.

The bride happened to be quite the loveliest young woman at the Royal Cambodian Court. She was, after all, the Prima Ballerina of the Royal Corps de Ballet. I had often admired her, in traditional head-dress and costume, dancing at the head of her troupe – on one entirely unforgettable occasion it was in the open air against the backdrop of the floodlit temples of Angkor Wat. A favourite daughter of the Head of State, Bopha Devi was a royal Princess over whose petite figure and bejewelled, but diminutive, fingers the giant figure of General de Gaulle was to bow low during a forth-coming state visit to Phnom Penh. (But this moment was mine, not the General's.)

Like many intellectuals, and some theologians, I am a disco devotee. A *habitué* of Hélène Cordet's 'Saddle Room' at the bottom of Park Lane throughout the early 1960s, I was well up to speed in these matters. The Palace *soirée* had hitherto proven rather stilted, and one at which I – as a self-conscious and slightly worried Chargé d'Affaires of a mere 32 summers – had been zealously over-doing the diplomatic hard graft. In a moment of recklessness and release, I nodded briefly to His Highness this and His Excellency that with whom I had been talking in my stilted French, crossed the ballroom to the Princess and swept her wordlessly onto the floor.

After a minute of bewilderment, she caught my rhythm; after two minutes, was twisting elegantly but with enthusiasm; and after five minutes, found herself alone with me in the middle of a wide circle of spectators – some agape and agog, others smiling cheerfully, yet others (mostly the communist heads of mission) envious and disapproving.

When the music stopped, the Princess giggled and withdrew, while I struggled to recover my breath. On the MC's mike, the unmistakably regal voice of 'Monseigneur' cut through the specu-lative murmurs of the Court, declaring that Monsieur Fielding was then and there awarded the title of '*Le Twisteur Numéro Un du Cambodge*' ('the Number One Twister of Cambodia'). The orchestra broke into a ragged fanfare, and a chamberlain was sent running for a prize which the Head of State duly handed over, in the shape of a silver Cambodian cockerel in a crocodile-skin box bearing the crest of the Khmer monarchy. I bowed and withdrew with appropriate self-deprecation into the surrounding throng, where enemies offered me reluctant congratulations, friends slapped me on the

back, creeps ingratiated themselves, and two newspaper editors asked me for my view of the foreign policy implications.

Clearly, I told the editors, Anglo-Cambodian relations were henceforth to be understood as normalised. Lowering my voice for dramatic effect, I added that Royal edicts sending foreign Embassies to Coventry were rarely formally rescinded; they tended simply to be air-brushed out, when convenient. So the storyline this evening, I whispered, surely had a twist to it.

H.R.H. The Princess Bopha Devi, Prima Ballerina of the Royal Cambodian Ballet, whom the author instructed in 'The Twist'

III

Chez Madame Chhum

Dinner at the French Ambassador's is always fun: interesting and articulate people, chilled *Rosé de Tavel*. On this occasion, however, I have another, subsequent, assignation. My Cambodian chauffeur, and my huge Austin 'Princess', have been given the evening off. So in white tuxedo and black tie, I slide into my little open-top motor and move quietly away from the Ambassador's elegant Residence, into the tropical night. I head South, for the ill-lit outskirts of Phnom Penh. Most of the real estate round here is owned by *Maman Vénérée* – more correctly known as the Queen Mother of Cambodia. I park, discreetly, two hundred yards short of my objective. I stroll towards a large wooden building surrounded by trees and lit by candles and spirit lamps. Further up the un-tarmacked street, leaning against a lamp post, is a Cambodian *gendarme* – not that anywhere in the capital city is dangerous to walk at night, but nevertheless this was an outward and physical sign of Her Majesty, the Queen Mother's, inward and spiritual concern that her property should be fully respected. And, indeed, four or five black, official-looking limousines are already parked, closer to the entrance (their drivers absent, or leaning back in their seats, sleeping open-mouthed).

I walk up onto the verandah, and receive whispered greetings. First, I am ushered into the presence of Madame Chhum, whose fingertips I kiss, and who signifies to the staff that I am an acceptable guest. I shed my European clothes, wrap one of the house sarongs around my hips, order two *Trente-Trois*, ice-cold French lagers, and enquire after His Highness. As agreed, he is expecting me.

An exceptionally pretty Vietnamese girl (Madame Chhum's was said to be more than a mere opium den, although I never checked that out) leads me down a wooden corridor carpeted with rice straw, to one of the top-class chambers. Within, lying prone upon

the floor, a wrinkled Cambodian crone of advanced age (possibly even over 50) is preparing the opium with the illumination of a rush light.

First, she makes it bubble and boil, over a spirit lamp. Then, she transfers the oleaginous lump to the ceramic bowl of a bamboo-stemmed pipe. This, in turn, is passed to the Minister, himself lying prone, in a sarong, on a low bench to one side. Within the chamber, as throughout the house, there permeates the sickly-sweet smell of top-grade opium on the boil. His Highness, an *habitué*, has already consumed several pipes in the course of the evening – no doubt, he is proposing to take one more, before going home.

I myself have never found that opium (once, some years before, gingerly essayed at a *Qashqai* feast in tribal Iran) offers me anything approaching the charms of a small gin and tonic, but there is no accounting for taste. Anyway, sharing the *Trente-Trois*, we begin to talk frankly and at ease.

Yes, 'Monseigneur' (*i.e.* Prince Sihanouk, the Cambodian Head of State) has acted arbitrarily and without consultation. The Chinese have leaned on him. But the entire Cabinet, while ultimately power-less in confrontation with a *deva-reja* or god-king, nevertheless wishes to accept the latest proposal of the British Government for a peace conference. They are grateful to Prime Minister Wilson, to Mr Patrick Gordon Walker and naturally also to me. So, would I like a pipe? 'So kind, but no, thanks'.

Slowly, gently, without any manifestation of egregious emotion or horrible hurry, I withdraw, pressing my palms together and bowing, as Cambodian good manners require. Resuming my tuxedo and its accessories, I settle a grossly exorbitant bill for two beers; I once more kiss Madame Chhum's fingertips; I slip away in search of my Triumph.

Back at the Residence, free (after my final hot shower of the day) of the clinging odour of opium, I scribble some notes on the pad by my bedside table, and fall asleep. Tomorrow, at 8 am, will be soon enough to send off a cipher telegram to the Foreign Secretary in London.

IV

Friendly Fire

It happened, I was told, one sunny day in 1966 on the Cambodian frontier with South Vietnam. No diplomatic attaché was hurt, except in dignity, but certainly there was a certain amount of dry cleaning and renewal of wardrobes afterwards.

The Khmer village was a mess. Bomb craters. Slight residual smell of cordite and burning generally. Trees uprooted or chopped down by machine-gun fire. Straw huts on stilts, blown over. Farm implements scattered. Untended chickens pecking around in the mud. Dead buffaloes with distended bellies, legs pointed stiffly at the sky. A dead human or two, rattan screens flung over the messier bits to keep the flies off.

Otherwise, on the broader landscape, a tranquil and traditional Cambodian setting. – Bushy-topped sugar palms. A chequered pattern of dark-green rice fields, divided by earthen tracks and wayside ditches. In the middle distance, a line of steep-sided low hills covered with scrub. Flashes of water here and there, running along the irrigation channels. Somewhere not far away, an ill-marked international frontier. A blue sky with a few fluffy white clouds.

The day before, the village had been attacked by the Americans, more likely by navigational error than in 'hot pursuit of red hordes' (the village was apparently without military associations). Now on the scene to investigate was the International Control Commission (ICC) from Phnom Penh – Indian, Polish and Canadian diplomats, accompanied by assorted attachés from the British, French and one or two other Embassies. A column of Jeeps and Landrovers was neatly drawn up on the laterite road just outside the village proper. Altogether twenty or thirty foreign observers and Cambodian officials, all in smart civilian clothes, wandered through the village with

maps and cameras and note books, assembling material for a report on yet another 'Frontier Incident'.

Not far away, just within Vietnam, our gallant allies were still at it, in defence of democracy. There was a crump of bombs and a rising column of smoke, not too far distant. Also the sound of aircraft. One of these, a Skyraider with US markings, flew across the border to inspect, stirred by curiosity. The foreign diplomatic observers must have looked like a Sunday school outing or a Swan Hellenic tourist expedition, with their Panama hats, white shirts, old school ties, and neatly pressed, light-weight suits. The Skyraider pilot had clearly seen nothing like it before in Vietnam, or even back in Alabama or Tennessee. He'd already dropped his two bombs, but he still had some ammo left and perhaps five minutes more flying time over the area. After another circle to make sure that they really were a Viet Cong division on the march to Saigon, he straightened up, entered a shallow dive, took a bead and opened up. ZOOM, ROAR, TAT-TATTA-TAT.

Well before that racket, the Skyraider had attracted everyone's wholehearted attention, even that of Mr Bindra – the very fat and frequently quite confused Head of the ICC. The Vienna Convention on Diplomatic Privileges and Immunities appeared, there and then, more a scrap of paper than a cast-iron guarantee. The Sunday School party scattered – Brits first, being better trained and more professional – diving for cover in the village ditches. Mr Bindra was on top of the Brits, who could hardly breathe. But that suited them just fine. To either side were East Europeans smelling of BO and of cheap scent – also good protection.

The Skyraider, mission accomplished, flew off back to Saigon and (possibly) one of those tinny medals the Americans shower on their military heroes. After a few minutes, the diplomatic observers all emerged diplomatically from their various places of diplomatic hiding, brushed some of the mud off their diplomatic ducks, waved away the last of the various scents and looked around them. Mr Bindra won the Olympics – he was already almost within reach of his Jeep. The rest of the party followed at different speeds, the Anglo-Saxons affecting a nonchalant stroll. No one had been hit.

At the back of the crocodile, the voice of the Australian Military Attaché rose above the shuffle of Gucci moccasins: 'Yeah. US pilots. I reckon either they're green, or they're yella. That one was green!'

Border Incident: a snapshot taken in a tight spot at a Cambodian village close to the frontier, after being mistakenly strafed from the air by forces from Saigon

The Prelude

1

One-Way Ticket to 'Phnompers'

The DC6 was descending. Out of the vibrating perspex window, I could see palm trees standing alone or in clumps, separated by grey-brown squares of sun-baked earth. The rice fields lay dusty and parched, and empty. Here and there I made out pools of stagnant water, the blue-green depths rimmed by dry mud. Out of the flat alluvial plains arose steep conical hills covered with dark green undergrowth and scrub. On the summit of some of the hills there sat the tiled and curved roofs of tiny temples, gold and red. Dotted among the plains, other pagodas winked and glittered amid clusters of khaki-coloured, straw-roofed houses. Across the landscape the grey clouds rolled, their shadows mopping up the patches of heat and light laid down by the tropical sun.

I had climbed into the aircraft less than two hours earlier, one damp morning in May 1964, at Singapore Airport. My destination was Phnom Penh. My mission was to assume charge, for an indefinite period, of the British Embassy.

The task filled me with gloom about the present, and foreboding for the future. I had not asked for it; I did not want it; and, two weeks earlier, I had not even known that I was going to get it. Not the lobster and *vin rosé* served by Royal Air Cambodge – not even the bright smile and girlish appeal of the sarong-clad Cambodian hostess – could settle the butterflies in my stomach.

Six weeks earlier, I had been happily employed in the Foreign Office in London, tidying up for my successor the desk which I had run for nearly four years in the Western Organisations and Coordination Department, to do with WEU (Western European Union) and political and diplomatic aspects of NATO.

For three of the past four years I had also been a Resident Clerk. With three other colleagues, I shared sprawling accommodation on the

top floor of the Foreign Office. We took it in turn each night to be on call. Some evenings, I dined in tranquillity and slept undisturbed. On others, the telephone would ring in the early hours and the corridors would echo with the clatter of containers and the shuffle of boots, as messengers brought urgent diplomatic telegrams incoming from the ends of the earth. Three missionaries had vanished in the Congo; please inform next of kin. An Ambassador proposed last-minute modifications to the instructions he had received for his call on the President the following day. Our Representative at the United Nations was on the direct line (at 10 pm his time, but 3 am on my watch): a new situation had arisen in the Security Council and he proposed to act thus – did the Permanent Under-Secretary of State concur? The Prime Minister was on the line and wanted to know where the Foreign Secretary could be found that evening. A businessman was at London Airport preparing to fly off to Berlin to clinch a major contract; but he had left his passport behind in Newcastle. Tribesmen from across the border had raided a village and massacred the guard post in the Fezzan. Could the RAF Commander, Aden, call down an air strike on the retreating band at dawn, before they crossed back into neutral territory; if so, should the Hunters use rockets or only machine guns? Sometimes the Resident Clerk could give the answer, either at his own discretion or on the basis of comprehensive advice left with him overnight by a Foreign Office Department that was on the ball; more often, he had to consult speedily the senior officials concerned, get the blessing of a Minister, summon advisers into the building at all hours to cope with a complex and changing situation.

High over the Gulf of Siam, en route to Phnom Penh on a one-way ticket, I looked back on these years with nostalgia. A very junior figure, still learning the trade and usually not yet permitted to act without supervision, I had nevertheless been at the centre of things and therefore carried myself with the corresponding degree of contrived authority. People knew who I was and treated me kindly as 'one of the club'. We were dashing young blades and knew ourselves to be so. Our voices on the telephone to Whitehall or across oceans and continents were steady and confident. We were, at least in our own estimation, an elite within an elite. Not till one day we became Ambassadors, Governors and Under-Secretaries of State, and perhaps not even then, would the world ever again seem to be so much our oyster.

Inevitably, all this savour came to an end one day – I was told that I was to be posted to Singapore, where I should serve not in the UK

High Commission, but on the staff of the Political Adviser to the Commander-in-Chief Far East, in Phoenix Park. I welcomed the prospect of change. I had for some months come to a comfortable, intellectual dead-end on my desk. At the hearth of the Resident Clerks' Mess I had warmed my hands and I was ready now to depart London. My private life was without commitment. I had seen my father through the final stages of cancer. I had been unsuccessful in a proposal of marriage. It was now time to press far to the East of Suez.

The situation in South-East Asia had at that time taken a difficult turn for the UK in the shape of the 'Confrontation' policy of President Sukarno of Indonesia. Sukarno stood in opposition to the Federation of Malaysia in which the British had decided to wrap up and seal the last of their major colonial responsibilities, and in particularly strong language he expressed disapproval of the terms of reference and the outcome of the plebiscite conducted in North Borneo and Sarawak under UN supervision on the issue of whether those territories should form part of the Federation. So, Sukarno had caused an undeclared guerrilla war to be launched against his newly-federated neighbours and against the British forces committed to their defence. All this promised interesting work and some excitement for a diplomat in Singapore.

My own job brought me particularly close to what was going on in the Far East. The task of the Political Adviser – a fairly senior man of Ambassadorial rank – was to work closely with the British military machine East of Suez. As the title implied, he gave political advice to the UK Commander-in-Chief, on what the British army, navy or air force might be doing, or might be called upon to do, in the area. He had an extensive staff drawn from every relevant department and service of the British Government. This staff was to collate and sift information from all sources about what was happening, and likely to happen, in South-East Asia and the Far East.

For the latter purpose, a major committee had been set up in Phoenix Park – the so-called 'Joint Intelligence Committee, Far East', or 'JIC(FE)'. It was chaired by one of the Political Adviser's two right-hand men. (He was a Counsellor under whom I had previously served in Iran, for whom I had great respect, and who had also incidentally been awarded the DSO for his deeds with the Resistance in France during the Second World War.) I was to be Joint Secretary, with another FO colleague, of JIC(FE).

The task, although non-specialist, promised to be exacting. On the intellectual side, it would be necessary to acquire pretty quickly

a nodding acquaintance on paper with most of the countries of Asia, to know in broad terms what the political situation was in each one and which of the local problems were likely to interest the British Government. In relation to 'Confrontation', what was required was to assimilate, analyse and write up, with the aid of specialist colleagues in sub-committee, a whole mass of disparate, and sometimes unsifted, information – from night landings in Malaysia by groups of terrorists, to the structure of the Chinese underground cooperating with Sukarno in Sarawak, to the size of the last rice crop in Java. On the human side, which was almost as important, one had to be able to get on with and bring harmoniously together a wide range of personalities and allegiances. One sat round a green baize table with soldiers, sailors, airmen, policemen, ex-colonial administrators and members of the intelligence services, who were experts, or had access to experts, in everything from air-photography analysis to budget forecasting, tribal languages in Borneo and the thickness of the armour on a Soviet Sverdlov-class cruiser. Traditionally, the Secretary's post, like that of the Chairman, was filled by a Foreign Office career diplomat – in the exaggerated hope that he could write clear English, exercise talents for conciliation and keep his eye on the overall political issues. He was to see the wood rather than the trees.

I thought of that world with regret, as Royal Air Cambodge approached the thickly forested coast of Cambodia. The shore, a slender thread of silver sand and sea-foam, lay square across our path and we shuddered slowly across it at a great height. Then the wing swept up and we banked onto a fresh course. The last lap had begun. Soon I would be ejected from the ephemeral security of my strapped-in seat and made to walk the earth, hold up my head and represent my country. The cup was thrust upon me; it was now too late to refuse it.

Back in Singapore, I had been installed in my bare, cool office in Phoenix Park for only two weeks when the telegram came in from the Head of Personnel Department, 'personal for Political Adviser, priority'. Sheila Waghorn, the personal assistant to the Adviser, popped her head round my door and yelled above the noise of the air-conditioning unit that the boss would like to see me. That boss was Alec Adams, a wise old bird who knew the region well and who was fluent in various languages (including Siamese). 'They want to take you away from us, Leslie', he said when I went in. 'They want you to be our Chargé d'Affaires in Phnom Penh'. Having gathered

my wits, I stuttered my objections. I had come to Singapore to do a job that interested me, to which I felt adequate and for which I had undergone prior preparation. I had begun to learn Cantonese even before I had left London. I had already started to strike roots in Singapore. I would be no good in Cambodia. My French was not strong enough. My new car did not have left-hand drive. 'Lord, I am not worthy', etc. (I added mentally and inwardly that I was negotiating the lease on a super Singapore flat and had my eye on a beautiful girl on the C-in-C's staff who drove in and out of Phoenix Park in a white MG open sports car.)

All this (and even, I suspect, the mental and inward additions) was appraised by the pale blue eyes of the boss. His eyes crinkled. He sympathised. He wanted to keep me. He would see what could be done. So Alec Adams CMG, Political Adviser, took up the cudgels. He and the Chief Clerk overseeing the Personnel Department in London belaboured each other across the ether. All to no effect, the instruction stood. I had to go.

I quickly discovered that the Embassy in Phnom Penh had been having a thin time. For political reasons, the British Government were unpopular and the local populace had been mounting demonstrations against us. In the end, as recorded in Cameo I (page xvii), a mob of toughs, idlers and students had sacked the Chancery building, and also that of the British Council, some six weeks previously. Mercifully, no one had been hurt – although several had had narrow squeaks from flying glass and bricks. The British Council Representative (who was subsequently made an MBE for his steady conduct in the face of hysterical demonstrators) and his young family had got shoved around and roughed up. Anglo-Cambodian relations, already strained over a major foreign policy issue, inevitably took a further plunge. Our women and children were evacuated for the second time (they had already been temporarily removed to a neighbouring country; but once the streets of Phnom Penh had calmed down a little, they had returned – just in time for the second, and more violent, spasm of popular hostility). The Ambassador, Mr Peter Murray CMG, had remained cool and professional. But his good work in Cambodia over the preceding three years had been undone in circumstances not of his making and he had taken it hard at the personal level. His advice was that – one, diplomatic relations should not be broken off (we should retain our diplomatic mission in Phnom Penh); two, he himself had, however, in his own candid opinion, outlived his usefulness at the Cambodian Court, even if it

would have been appropriate (which it probably was not) to keep a resident Ambassador on there; and three, he therefore should be withdrawn quietly and the Embassy be placed in the care of a Chargé d'Affaires for an unspecified period of time. Later, after things had cooled down, it would be possible to assess the longer-term future of our mission and in particular whether a new Ambassador should be sent there. These sensible recommendations were duly accepted in London, and set in motion.

This was where I came into the picture. The normal and indeed automatic choice for a semi-permanent Chargé would have been the Ambassador's number two, on the spot, the Head of Chancery. This post was filled at that time by a First Secretary called John Shakespeare. A 'Blue Chip' diplomat (Winchester, Oxford and the Guards), loyal but independent minded, and blessed with private means – Shakespeare had every personal quality. He spoke elegant French (having once taught at the Ecole Normale Supérieure and latterly served in our Embassy in Paris as Private Secretary to the Ambassador). He wrote well (before being recruited by the Foreign Office he had served on the editorial staff of the *Times*). He had played a prominent part in organising the passive defence of the Chancery building and it was partly thanks to his own force of character and indifference to a shower of projectiles that the mob never manhandled any of the staff. ('*Vous ne passerez pas*', he said calmly to the milling rioters as he stood unarmed at the head of the staircase, barring all further access to the building.) Above all, he both liked Cambodia and was trusted in his turn by the Cambodians (he had once even acted as private secretary and general factotum on loan to the Cambodian Head of State, when the latter was paying an official visit to Malaysia).

John Shakespeare had all these qualities, but he was not physically fit, having picked up malaria. More important, he was married with three small children. His family had been evacuated and there was no knowing when they would be able to rejoin him in Phnom Penh. His young wife could not be expected to cope alone for a period of up to two years on her own.

So London decided that Shakespeare and I should do a swap. I would fly up to Phnom Penh to take over as Head of Chancery and Consul. He would take his wife and children to Singapore and settle down to the job which would otherwise have been mine. After I had had two or three weeks to acclimatise and while the Cambodian Head of State was undergoing medical treatment in the South of

France, Ambassador Murray and his wife would depart from Phnom Penh quietly, ostensibly on extended 'home leave'. At the end of that time, there would be the following courtly minuet. I was to inform the Royal Cambodian Government that it had been decided to attribute other functions to His Excellency the Ambassador, who would most unfortunately be unable to return to Phnom Penh to pay his farewells, but who devoutly trusted that this small discourtesy would be compensated by the messages of affection and farewell that I was instructed to transmit on His Excellency's behalf. Until such time as the name of Mr Peter Murray's suggested successor as British Ambassador were known and could be submitted to the Royal Cambodian Government for their high *agrément*, the Foreign Secretary had ventured to appoint Mr Leslie Fielding, First Secretary and Consul, as Chargé d'Affaires *ad interim*.

It was a neat formula – and a successful one – for the Cambodians swallowed the pill without demur and no one lost any face.

After being told of the FO's final decision on my future, I spent the next ten days in Singapore in a rush of preparation. Clothing, food, drink, household utensils and all that was cheap locally and expensive in Cambodia had to be ordered and – mercifully, in only some instances – even actually paid for. A plan was made for re-shipping my own private car – still on the high seas from England – from Singapore to Saigon and thence up to the river Mekong to the Cambodian capital. Light accompanying luggage, already unpacked, had to be repacked and unaccompanied heavy luggage diverted. A diplomatic uniform in tropical white – not required in the anonymity of Phoenix Park but *de rigueur* on state occasions in Cambodia – had to be run up by a Chinese tailor and orders sent for the immediate despatch by air of a glittering court sword, gold buttons and gorget patches and a solar topee complete with gold spike.

I continued to discharge my duties in Phoenix Park, but these were – thanks to the unselfishness of others – kept to a minimum. We happily had available, in the extensive diplomatic archives of the Political Adviser's Office, copies of most reports from all our Embassies in the area. I drew the Cambodia files for the previous two years and started to read myself in, starting at the elementary end by learning the names of the Cabinet Ministers and of the chief towns, then taking notes on how the present political row had come about, observing the judgement of the outgoing Ambassador unfold across scores of telegrams and dispatches, watching the events reach out towards a conclusion which was already known. There was no point

in being moody, once the decision had been taken, and I tried to fit myself to the die that had been cast. So I sang snatches of Italian opera in competition with the whirr and rattle of the air conditioning. My new tropical suits arrived from the Cho-Sen Tailoring Company and were disrespectfully dubbed 'Leslie's Phnompers Rompers' by the secretaries. At Singapore cocktail parties, I cultivated the nonchalance of a brave but unassuming man who was shortly to walk the high-wire without a net carrying two pelagic seals under each arm – or to be dropped by night from a low-flying aircraft into a moonless and uncharted wilderness. But the kamikaze swagger and the boyish grin of this Battle of Britain Spitfire pilot concealed sadness and self-doubt. I was inwardly a tiny bit scared.

Just before I set out for Phnom Penh, I was given my final briefing by Edward Peck, the Assistant Under-Secretary of State responsible for Asian and Far Eastern Affairs at the Foreign Office (later to become Sir Edward Peck GCMG, High Commissioner in Kenya, and Ambassador to NATO). I had known him professionally when I was Resident Clerk – our paths had crossed once or twice over urgent telegrams about Indonesian 'Confrontation', or Laos, or Vietnam, or some other crisis which pulled him into the Foreign Office late at night or at weekends. On one very rough night, we Resident Clerks had even put him up in our spare room and given him breakfast the following morning. It so happened that Edward Peck was paying a flying visit to Singapore. The Political Adviser asked me up to meet him over a drink one evening before we all went on to Flagstaff House, to dine with Admiral Sir Varyl Begg, the British Commander-in-Chief.

The Political Adviser's house was one of those magnificent dwellings built by the Raj years ago, to the sole specification of comfort in a hot climate before the introduction of electric fans and air-conditioning units. Surrounded by close-cropped lawns and towering, well-watered trees, it stood tall and four-square, with a first-floor drawing room cavernous and open to any breeze that might blow. As I hopped out of my taxi, I met that curious hush that falls in the tropics as the sun goes down. I had arrived early and recall that I listened guiltily to my soft foot-fall, as I crept up the staircase onto the first floor. The silence was broken by a clink of ice in a glass. There in the twilight stood Ted Peck, cheerful and reassuring. 'Here comes the Chargé', he said. Then: 'You're early'. I replied something like, 'Always be at the place of parade five minutes before it is due to begin'. With youthful pomposity, I added 'and diplomatic

etiquette requires that this rule should extend to receptions given by one's Ambassador'. I identified, with a bow, the Political Adviser, who had just appeared, still putting the final touch to his bow tie. Ted Peck shook his head sadly and said that I'd need to do far better than that at the Cambodian Court. We all three sat down in the traditional chintz-covered armchairs. 'Leslie, we want you to go to Phnom Penh to be a sort of postman between Prince Sihanouk and Her Majesty's Government. Not the foggiest idea when we shall be able to send a new Ambassador. So you may have to play at postman for some time. Maybe also play at being an Aunt Sally for the locals to throw things at. Look after the staff. Don't worry too much about Embassy bricks and mortar: let the Cambodians burn the Chancery down, if they insist. Think of the flattering headlines at home: "Chargé faces mob".' Then Peck, Adams and I got down to business and we talked earnestly for nearly an hour.

So much, then, for the why I came to be a passenger of Royal Air Cambodge. The aircraft was making its landing approach, steadily losing height over a countryside in which I could now distinguish buffaloes, carts, people, even dogs. Occasional toy buses and cars ran like beetles along the roads beneath. I could see that many of the houses stood on stilts, presumably as a precaution against floods in the rainy season and rodents in the dry. We sank lower still, sailed over some palm tree tops and the back yards of a hamlet and then dropped neatly onto the concrete airstrip. The propellers roared in reverse. We taxied over to the terminal and I spotted, standing slim and smiling on the apron, a figure who could only have been John Shakespeare. The engines were silenced, the jet of cool air over my head diminished and then cut out. Down the cabin, as the big doors were flung open, blew a gust of hot air with a reek of fuel and tropical vegetation. It was 1 pm on 16 May 1964. I was 31 years and nine months old. Time to shape up and show some stiff upper lip.

But before I can carry this narrative further forward (on page 51), I need to sketch in some of the wider background. History is crucial in Indo-China, so I will next give a brief account of Cambodia's past interaction with the outside world, and describe the awkward juncture at which the Kingdom found itself at the time of my arrival.

The Place and the People

2

Travellers to an Antique Land

A thousand years ago, the Cambodian Empire ruled supreme in South-East Asia, under the aegis of a mystical, semi-divine monarchy. By the mid-nineteenth century, the game was up – the nation was reduced to a few hundred thousand in number; the Kingdom was about to be split up and absorbed by two more dynamic and aggressive peoples, the Vietnamese and the Thai. France saved Cambodia from extinction, through the Protectorate. Once France had withdrawn, defeated, from Indo-China in the mid-1950s, the pressure was on again. It is still there today.

Part of the setting to this book therefore has to be historical. The military and political dilemmas of the 1960s in Cambodia, and the peculiar *numen* of the then Headship of State, can only be fully grasped by reference to the country's and the Kingship's past.

Although younger than Egypt, Cambodia is still an 'antique land'. The principal stone monuments which stand in the forest at Angkor were built over nine hundred years ago; the brick towers at Sambor Prei Kuk have withstood the sun and the rain and the thrust of tropical vegetation for thirteen centuries; the early civilisation of Cambodia dates from the dawn of the Christian era; and primitive man scattered his crude stone axes across the Indo-Chinese peninsula well before 12,000 BC and back into the Great Ice Age.

Indo-China, as the name implies, is the meeting place of Indian and Chinese cultural influence. The two cradles of life and centres of political power in the Indo-Chinese peninsula are the Red River delta in the North (now part of Vietnam) and the Mekong River delta and its fertile and watered hinterland in the South (now shared between Vietnam and Cambodia). Of these two poles, the Northern fell early beneath the tutelage of China, while the Southern was open to India. The Chinese invaded the Red River delta in the

second century BC and annexed to their empire the Annamite barbarians who lived there; successive Chinese dynasties controlled the region down to the tenth century AD. In the Mekong delta, Indian influence was asserted by more peaceful means. Traders and religious teachers began to arrive in this area not long after the time of Christ. There are references in Ptolemy's *Geography* to places whose names were of Sanskrit origin all along the coasts of Indo-China. The Indians profoundly affected the thinking of the indigenous peoples with whom they were in contact, giving them a cultural framework within which to develop their own political, artistic, legal, religious and social ideas. Hindu and – later – Buddhist beliefs came to Cambodia in this way and were adapted to Cambodian usage; so, too, did the concept of the god-king (see pages 17 and 24).

The earliest Hinduised Kingdom in the Southern delta was known as Fu-nan (the word, appropriately enough in Indo-China, comes from the Chinese). Fu-nan was a collection of principalities under loose suzerainty; it was founded in the first century AD and endured for five hundred years. As a maritime and commercial state, it sent embassies early on to India and China; its craftsmen in glass and gold and silver, its weavers of cotton and brocade found distant markets for their goods. Roman medals, a Sassanid effigy, and engravings inspired by Hellenistic art have been dug up on the site of one of Fu-nan's ports and merchant centres. One of its kings – Chandan – may even have been of Iranian origin. It was, by the standards of the earlier Indo-Chinese past, a cosmopolitan and outward-looking state. In the sixth century, however, Fu-nan was attacked by its former vassal state, Chen-la (another Chinese name). This inland neighbour was to become the dominant power for the next two or three hundred years. The people of Chen-la were the first Khmer, and they spread their dominion far and wide – North into what is now Laos and West into what is now Thailand. From this period too dates the name Cambodia – or, rather, Kambuja, deriving from Kambu Svayambhuva, the founder of the Khmer dynasty. It developed in many ways. Architecture improved: temples of brick and stone rose up to replace those formerly of wood. Trade continued to prosper: Arab and Persian merchants began to appear. The Kingdom proved turbulent, however, and fell apart, divided by civil strife into Northern and Southern centres of power – Chen-la of the land and Chen-la of the sea. Matters went ill for a time, and Chen-la of the sea had to submit to the suzerainty of Java. It was not until the ninth

century that the Javanese were cast off and the Khmer Kingdom reunited.

Thereafter, Cambodia entered upon a period of greatness which was to last until the fifteenth century. The Khmer Empire spans the corresponding period in the West which extends from the creation of Charlemagne's empire to the fall of Constantinople, in England from Egbert to the Wars of the Roses. At the zenith of its power, this empire embraced not only what is now called Cambodia, but also the whole of Thailand, most of Southern Vietnam, half of Laos and the Northern sector of Malaya. Already considerable architects, the Khmer were to build the great temples for which they have since become justly famous – including Banteay Srei (950–60), Angkor Wat (1120–50) and the Bayon of Angkor Thom (*c*.1200). The arts flourished: libraries and schools were set up, roads and rest-houses and hospitals were constructed; agriculture expanded and intensified – the land was drained and irrigated, and then given over to rice production in the populated areas along the Mekong River, around the 'Great Lake' of the Tonle Sap and in the area of the Royal Capital.

Both Hindu and Buddhist notions of religion had long co-existed, but the state cult was at that stage Hinduism, specifically the worship of Shiva. It was from Indian ideas that the Khmer concept of kingship emerged, the notion of the '*deva-raja*', the god-king. The *deva-raja* was the sum of all authority, ultimate judge of all disputes, upholder of law and order within, and defender of the realm without. He was a god on earth, an intermediary with Indra, and the other celestial beings, assuring thereby the fertility of the soil, the abundance of water and the general prosperity of the Kingdom. The Khmer capital with its royal temple reflected the universe in miniature. Facing the East, oriented four square by the points of the compass, the temple expressed the seasons of the sun. The broad moats around the temple represented the ocean which surrounded the earth. Just as the gods dwelled on the heavenly mountain at the centre of the world, Mount Meru, so a temple-mountain of soaring terraces was constructed in the Khmer capital on earth with a sanctuary at the summit to contain the symbol of the king's divinity.

This greatness did not last. Its strength was sapped from within by social and religious changes. It was cast down from without by invaders. The Thai and the Annamites harassed the country and hemmed it in, until a greatly enfeebled Cambodia was on the verge of national extinction by the mid-nineteenth century.

The Thai hit Cambodia first. A collection of Southern Chinese peoples, they had been slowly infiltrating down into the Indo-China peninsula in small numbers since the end of the first millennium AD – part of a slow but general population drift from North to South which had peopled the area in preceding ages. Initially Cambodian vassals (some of them served in the royal army), they set up kingdoms of their own in Thailand and Northern Malaya in the twelfth century AD. Their southward and westward penetration was accelerated by the Mongol invasion of China. In the fourteenth century, the Thai turned Eastward and began to wage steady war against the Khmer empire. They sacked Angkor on three successive occasions. The capital was abandoned; the Cambodians shifted South and East; the great Khmer epoch came to an end, not with a bang but a whimper.

Changes were in any case already overtaking Khmer society from within. Hinduism came to be supplanted by Buddhism of the Lesser Vehicle, hieratic concepts giving way to a more personal view of religion. The classes and casts of Brahmanism and early court life began to break down. The people, depleted by wars and exhausted by the burdens of empire, neglected the irrigation works and also left the big temples to decay and be overrun gradually by the jungle. Only the kingship remained to hold them together and link them directly with their past. Dynamism gave way to passivity and then the search for mere survival.

Successive waves of soldiers of fortune, merchants and missionaries arrived. In the sixteenth century, the Portuguese came and then the Spanish. In the seventeenth century, the Dutch and French came. But they made little impact and trade languished. The Thai continued to be troublesome. They had already, in 1593–94, taken and briefly held the new Cambodian capital at Lovek. They now began to claim general suzerainty. But so also did a new enemy – the Annamite. This other people, the Vietnamese as they are called today, were of distant Chinese origin and they were to prove the most expansionist of all Cambodia's neighbours. They had already begun, in the fifteenth century, to press Southward from the Red River delta, along the narrow coastal plain on the Eastern seaboard of Indo-China, and down towards the Mekong delta region. By the early seventeenth century, they were beginning to settle in the delta and had established (1623) a trading centre at the then Cambodian village of Prei Kor (later called Saigon and, today, Ho Chi Minh City). For the next two hundred and fifty years or so, Thailand and Annam struggled for control of Cambodia, each encroaching further on

Cambodian territory and cutting her off more and more from the sea. Of the two, Annam was the more ruthless and land-hungry, reclaiming the marshes, driving the Khmer Westward, quickly settling Annamites everywhere in the delta.

The crisis came in the mid-nineteenth century: after the annexation of Cambodia's Northern provinces by Thailand (*c*.1800) and a major effort by Annam to 'Vietnamise' what was left (*c*.1834–40). Crowned in 1846 by Thailand and Annam, King Ang Duong, founder of the present Khmer dynasty, sought desperately to free himself from this dual vassalage. In 1853 he appealed to Napoleon III for French protection, without success. But in 1857, the French launched an attack against Annam and, with it, a process of colonisation. Once the French colony of Cochin China had been set up in the South, French soldiers and diplomats naturally began to look with a different eye on Cambodia. Both strategy and economic interest dictated the Franco–Cambodian Treaty of 1863, establishing the suzerainty of France. In 1884, Cambodia became a French Protectorate and, in 1887, joined Tonkin, Annam and Cochin China in the Indo-Chinese Union.

Under French protection, Cambodia was able to survive, live quietly, enjoy a measure of prosperity, come to terms with the modern, Western-oriented world and finally to struggle for and to achieve her independence. The defeat of France in Europe in 1940, the Japanese occupation of Indo-China, the growth of new political ideas, the militant communist rebellion of the Viet Minh, all threatened the hold of France upon the Indo-Chinese Union in the years that followed the Second World War. A treaty of 1949 granted the first concessions of limited, domestic sovereignty to Cambodia. The campaign for national independence waged by the then King (Norodom Sihanouk, who was a central figure then as in my time in the country) was rewarded with success in September 1953, when control of the police, judiciary and army passed from France to Cambodia. With minor subsequent adjustments, the country was free. Its independence was recognised at the international conference to preside over the final liquidation of the former French empire in Indo-China. This conference was held in Geneva in 1954, under British and Soviet-Russian Co-Chairmanship.

After this somewhat breathless canter across a couple of thousand years, let us turn back to near the beginning to hear some travellers' tales. We saw that the first two Kingdoms bore names which the Chinese had given them. And it is to China that we owe almost all that

we know of what Cambodian society was like before the arrival of the Europeans in Asia.

Direct diplomatic contact between chronicled and chronicler was established in 243 AD, when Fu-nan sent an embassy to China; and the Emperor sent a mission to the Fu-nanese court in the period 245–50. The first direct Chinese eye-witness account of the country reads thus:

> There are walled cities, palaces and dwelling places. The men are ugly and dark-skinned, with frizzy hair; they go about naked and barefoot. They are straightforward of character and there are no thieves among them. They devote themselves to agriculture ... in addition they love to engrave ornaments and to do carving. Many of their eating utensils are of silver. Taxes are paid in gold, silver, pearls and perfumes. They have books and archives and other such things.

Fu-nan reached its apogee of power at the outset of the sixth century, under King Kaundinya-Jayavarman. After an exchange of ambassadors had been effected with the Emperor of China, an imperial order of the day acknowledged the King as living upon the edge of the ocean and as governing the distant countries of the South. But, within a hundred years, Fu-nan had been conquered by Chen-la, its Khmer neighbour to the North.

The conquest of Fu-nan was completed by King Ishanavarman, who is believed to have reigned from 616 to 635. He set up his capital, called Ishanapura, near the great lake in the heart of his Kingdom; and, true to tradition, despatched two embassies to China. The stone statuary and brick temples of the new Kingdom, and a few religious inscriptions in old Khmer, show us a civilisation still much influenced by India. Buddhism fell into decline. The Chinese pilgrim Yi-tsing, who travelled through Chen-la towards the end of the seventh century, wrote sadly that 'the law of the Buddha once prospered and spread; but today, a wicked king has destroyed it utterly and there are no monks left at all'. On the other hand, fortified by royal patronage, the Hindu cults flourished – notably that of Harihara, a divinity represented by statues of Vishnu and Shiva joined in one body.

The Chinese annalist, Ma Touan-lin, tells us that King Ishanavarman held public audience at his court on every third day, seated upon a couch under a rich canopy. He wore a red cotton sarong and fine white robe, leather or ivory sandals, gold earrings and a crown heavy with gold, precious stones and pearls.

> Those who appear before the King touch the ground
> three times with their foreheads at the foot of the steps
> to the throne. If the King calls them and commands
> them to mount the steps, they kneel down with their
> arms crossed clasping their shoulders. Then they sit in
> a circle about the King to discuss the affairs of the
> Kingdom. When the audience is over, they kneel
> again, prostrate themselves and withdraw. More than a
> thousand armed guards wearing breastplates are drawn
> up at the foot of the throne, in the chambers of the
> palace, and at the gates and in the cloisters.

Ishanavarman died childless. The dynastic rivalries which followed
led to the division of Chen-la into two parts around the year 710.
Chen-la of the land, comprising the mountain country to the North,
lived isolated, independent and aloof for a century or two, before
being again incorporated into the Khmer Empire. Chen-la of the sea
fell into disarray, carved up by feudal rivalries into five petty prince-
doms, and for a time was subjected to the suzerainty, as already
noted, of the kings of Java, whose fleets raided the coasts of Indo-
China between 767 and 787 AD. A Khmer inscription briefly records
this sad submission. An Arab writer of the early tenth century gives a
less laconic account of what happened. Soleiman the Merchant
begins by placing Cambodia as 'the country that exports aloes'. A
good Muslim, he notes with approval that 'all debauchery and all
fermented liquor are forbidden' to its inhabitants. He then tells the
story of a Khmer monarch who one day evinced the desire to see the
head of the Maharaja, King of Java, brought to him on a plate. The
Maharaja got to hear of what was afoot and decided to act first.
Under cover of a pleasure cruise among the islands of his Kingdom,
he mounted a sudden attack up the Mekong River, seized the palace
and decapitated the unfortunate Khmer. Once returned to Java, the
Maharaja had the head washed, embalmed and sent in a jar to the
new King of Cambodia.

> From that moment, the kings of Cambodia, every
> morning when they get up, turn to face the direction of
> Java, bow down to the ground and humble themselves
> before the Maharaja in order to bear him homage.

Chen-la of the sea was freed from the Javanese by Jayavarman II,
the first of the great Khmer Kings, who reigned from 802 to 850.

Making every effort to unify the country, he brought to an end the troubles of the previous century. A Khmer inscription relates that a Brahman 'expert in magic sciences' was 'asked to perform a ceremony of such a nature as to make it impossible for this country of Kambuja to owe allegiance to Java, and of such a nature as to make possible the existence of one absolutely unique master on earth'. Jayavarman II formalised the cult of the *deva-raja*, conceiving himself the incarnation of Shiva. On a hill-top dedicated to Indra, the King of the gods, a *linga* was set up and consecrated, symbolising the royal power and divinity. A few decades later, between 889 and 900, the city of Angkor was founded by King Yasovarman I. A stone inscription of his day records that 'the earth which he protected was bound by the frontier of China and the sea'. An era of great brilliance was thus inaugurated. Over the next three to four hundred years, the Khmer Kingdom reached the zenith of its power and the Khmer people the height of their inventive genius.

Quite the fullest account of the life and customs of the ancient Khmer comes down to us from the last days of Cambodia's glory, shortly before the onset of her long decline. In 1285, King Jayavarman VIII sent tribute to the Mongol Emperor, Kublai Khan, acknowledging his vassalage. Ten years went by and King and Emperor changed. The following year, there appeared at Angkor an Ambassador from China, despatched by Kublai's grandson and successor, Temur Oljaitu, to Jayavarman's son-in-law and successor, Shindravarman. One of the diplomats on the staff of this Chinese mission, which spent nearly a year in Cambodia from 1296 to 1297, was a young man called Chou Ta-kuan. The extensive notes which he took of what he saw around him have survived. Chou's account seems to be a generally accurate one. His description of the great, walled city, the language and dress of the people, and the structure of their society tallies with what we know from other sources; some of the customs and feasts which he attributes to the Khmer of his day still have their counterparts in the life of modern Cambodia.

The society which he describes is complex. Below the King, there are the princes and high officials, each with his prescribed dress and privileges; and then the common people, artisans and farmers, lording it over their slaves. There are taxes and some form of annual census. The economy is quite elaborate: a large-scale (mainly rice-based) agriculture; a brisk import and export trade in a wide range of natural and manufactured products; a national infrastructure of roads and rest-houses. Religious and social customs have their

prominent place, governing people from birth to death, regulating the decencies and meting out justice, celebrating the seasons and the New Year. The Cambodians keep documents, which 'are read from left to right, and not from above to below'. The scribes write with chalk pencils on parchment dyed black. Then there are the elaborate palaces, where 'long colonnades and open corridors stretch away, interlaced in harmonious relation'. The dwellings of the commoners are thatched with straw, bare of furniture and equipped with a mere handful of pots and pans; for 'the men of the people ... possess no tables, benches, basins or buckets'.

What was it like to be a stranger at Angkor, seven hundred years ago? Sailors and traders, the Chinese seemed to have enjoyed themselves. Noting that in Cambodia it is the women who take charge of trade, Chou writes that his compatriots tend to lose no time on arrival in getting themselves a mate, since her commercial instincts will be a great asset. He observes that the people of Cambodia are very simple. On seeing a Chinese they bow low, or even throw themselves to the ground, calling him Buddha. He regrets that 'an increasing number, however, are learning to outwit the Chinese and are doing harm to a great many of our countrymen who have visited here'. He also feelingly complains that when the Cambodians see a Chinese using lavatory paper, they jeer at him and indicate their unwillingness to have him enter their homes. (The Cambodians preferred to wash themselves with water.) Nevertheless, the trade must have been worth these indignities. Chou admits

> Chinese sailors note with pleasure that it is not necessary to wear clothes, and, since rice is easily had, women easily persuaded, houses easily run, furniture easily come by and trade easily carried on, a great many desert to take up permanent residence.

In his accurate and painstaking description of the royal palace, Chou Ta-kuan writes

> Out of the palace rises a golden tower, to the top of which the ruler ascends nightly to sleep. It is common belief that in the tower dwells a genie, formed like a serpent with nine heads, which is Lord of the entire Kingdom. Every night this genie appears in the shape of a woman, with whom the sovereign couples. Not even the wives of the King may enter here. At the

second watch the King comes forth and is then free to
sleep with his wives and his concubines. Should the
genie fail to appear for a single night, it is a sign that the
King's death is at hand. If, on the other hand, the King
should fail to keep his tryst, disaster is sure to follow.

This curious legend illustrates the importance for the prosperity of the
Kingdom with which the *deva-raja* was invested. As we have seen
earlier, he was the intermediary who linked heaven to earth. By the
fourteenth century, Buddhism had effected a major come-back in the
country, and had, in the form of the Lesser Vehicle, largely supplanted
the Hindu cults with which the era of empire had been ushered in. But
the person of the King remained hedged about with divinity. The god-
king's authority and magnificence were everywhere on display. Chou
tells us how foreign ambassadors were invited by the King to enjoy the
spectacle – of fireworks and all – at the festival of the New Year. This is
his description of a royal procession:

When the King leaves his palace, the procession is
headed by the soldiery; then come the flags, the
banners, the music. Girls of the palace, three to five
hundred in number, gaily dressed, with flowers in their
hair and tapers in their hands, are massed together in a
separate column. The tapers are lighted even in broad
daylight. Then come other girls, carrying gold and silver
vessels from the palace and a whole galaxy of ornaments,
of very special design, the uses of which are strange to
me. Then came still more girls, and the bodyguard of the
palace holding shields and lances. Following them came
chariots drawn by goats and horses all adorned with
gold. Ministers and princes, mounted on elephants, are
preceded by bearers of scarlet parasols, without number.
Close behind come the royal wives and concubines, in
palanquins and chariots, or mounted on horses or
elephants, to whom are assigned at least a hundred
parasols mottled with gold. Finally the Sovereign appears,
standing erect on an elephant and holding in his hand
the sacred sword. This elephant, his tusks sheathed in
gold, is accompanied by bearers of twenty white
parasols with golden shafts. All around is a bodyguard of
elephants, drawn close together, and still more soldiers
for complete protection, marching in close order.

And, finally, this is Chou's description of a royal audience:

> Every day the King holds two audiences for consider-
> ation of affairs of state. No list or agenda is provided.
> Functionaries and ordinary people who wish to see the
> Sovereign seat themselves on the ground to await his
> arrival. In the course of time, distant music is heard in
> the palace, while, from outside, blasts on conch-shells
> sound forth as though to welcome the ruler. I have
> been told that at this point the Sovereign, coming from
> nearby, contents himself with only one golden palan-
> quin. Two girls of the palace lift up the curtain with
> their slender fingers, and the King, sword in hand,
> appears standing in the golden window. All present –
> ministers and commoners – join their hands and touch
> the earth with their foreheads, lifting up their heads
> only when the sound of conches has ceased. The Sover-
> eign seats himself at once on a lion's skin, which is an
> hereditary royal treasure. When the affairs of state have
> been dealt with the King turns back to the palace, the
> two girls let fall the curtain, and everyone rises. From
> all this it is plain to see that these people, though
> barbarians, know what is due to a Prince.

The Cambodian court in the 1960s, though the external appearances were mostly modern enough, was far from westernised and
something of the spirit of the past lived on in the ceremonies and
general protocol. As a foreign diplomat in Phnom Penh, I chuckled
and nodded in recognition when I read Chou Ta-kuan, as if I had
been there with him. Had I not seen something like it, only the week
before, at the Palace and in the company of the Head of State?

In due course, there followed centuries of steady and increasingly
serious Cambodian decline. The abdication of King Jayavarman VIII
in 1295 marked the close of an imperial epoch. If he reigned in prosperity, he also ruled in mediocrity. The last of the great builder kings
– Jayavarman III – had died some eighty years previously. Not for
seven centuries were the Khmer to see again a national leader who
approached him in brilliance. The Empire they then possessed,
stretching far and wide across the Indo-Chinese peninsula, was to
shrink to a shrivelled enclave on the banks of the great lake and the
lower Mekong. By the sixteenth century, Cambodia ceased to play a
role of any importance in South-East Asia; her power was at an end.

During this period, the little outside testimony we have derives from a handful of Europeans. These men were missionaries and merchants: buccaneers and soldiers of fortune operating vaguely under the imperial banner of their homelands. They came initially from Portugal and Spain.

By the 1580s, Portuguese priests and adventurers were installed at the Cambodian court, learning the language and seeking the favour of kings. Treatises had been written on the rivers, the resources and even the irrigation systems of the Kingdom.

They were the first Europeans to clap eyes on the ruins of Angkor. According to the Portuguese chronicler, Diego de Conto, these ruins – abandoned a hundred years before, overgrown by the jungle and forgotten by the Khmer – were rediscovered around 1550 by the King of Cambodia while out elephant-hunting in the forest; the beaters came across ruins and the King gave the order to five or six thousand men to cut back the vegetation, revealing the whole city of Angkor; struck with admiration at what met his eyes, the King decided that the site should be reoccupied. Diego de Conto's *Chronicle* recorded, of Angkor Thom, that

> This town was square, measuring a league along each side. There were four principal doorways and another which served the royal palaces. The town was surrounded by a broad moat the waters of which never change their level. Over the moat there were five bridges corresponding to the five gateways already mentioned, each of them twelve feet across. They were built on arches, out of dressed stone of astonishing size, possessing fretted stone parapets like marble, with a fine very well-made [stone] rope on top, astride which stand, at regular intervals, giants made of the same stone, quite remarkably sculpted with the hands holding the said rope ...

Of Angkor Wat, he wrote

> At half a league's distance, there is a temple called. Angar, built on a fine open flat site. This temple is one hundred and sixty paces long and is of so strange a construction that it cannot be described with the pen, any more than it can be compared with any other monument in the world. The central portion consists of

four naves. The roof over their highly decorated arches rears up into a very lofty pointed dome, made up of numerous columns, which are worked with all the refinements which human genius can conceive.

In the wake of the Portuguese and the Spanish came their rivals, the Dutch. Between the Spaniards and the Dutch, the seventeenth century was to see a bitter struggle for position in Phnom Penh. It was a cruel period, in which the Annamites were beginning to press hard against the eastern frontiers of Cambodia, while civil wars divided the Kingdom from within with a savagery comparable to that of the English Wars of the Roses. Kings and princes died in battle; a regent was assassinated on a hunting trip and his grandchildren (so one of the Dutchmen relates) flung into prison and fed on roasted strips of their own flesh. The Dutch were sometimes in favour at court and at other times cold-shouldered and threatened. Gerard Van Wuysthof records that all went well under King Ang Non. But this affectionate sovereign was done away with in 1642. The Dutch tried to get on with the usurper, sending an emissary to congratulate him on 'having been victorious over those who had sought to deny him his lawful rights'. But the new King was suddenly converted from Buddhism to Islam and consequently turned against all Christians. In 1643, Pierre de Rogemortes, the representative of the Dutch East India Company in Phnom Penh, and some of his men were massacred. This blow, and the manifest inability of the Netherlands to avenge it, despite the despatch of a few ships from Batavia, was to sound the knell of European prestige in Cambodia for two hundred years. The Dutch managed to secure a treaty in 1665 granting them a monopoly in the trading of pepper, skins, bone and ivory. But it led nowhere.

Meanwhile, in 1775, the Emperor of Annam had won the right to appoint a mandarin to advise the King of Cambodia. By the 1820s, after a hundred years or more of steady territorial encroachment by the Annamites, and several sanguinary military campaigns, the Emperor had delegated all military and civil authority over Cambodia to the Vietnamese governor in Cochin China. In the mid-1830s, colonisation had been taken a step further by the appointment of three Vietnamese mandarins with authority over all Cambodian ministers and officials and with the task of carrying out the virtual Vietnamisation of the country, even to the point of seeking to change the name of the capital from Phnom Penh to Nam Viang. A popular revolt against this universally detested policy brought Ang

Duong to the throne with Siamese military support in 1842. The Vietnamese were defeated and obliged to recognise the new ruler as King of Cambodia. But the twin suzerainty remained. Ang Duong was crowned King by representatives of both Siam and Annam in 1846.

The hour of France in these conditions was not far distant. In the mid-nineteenth century, the French knew little of the country they were soon to bring within their fold. Only a handful of missionaries and traders had visited Cambodia since the first of them had ventured there two hundred years before. The missionaries had met with repeated failure and there were long periods in which the French Church left the Khmer well alone. But in 1848, after some sixty years of abandon, a further group of missionaries arrived who were to achieve, if not pastoral, at least political successes. They were well-received at court. King Ang Duong was desperate for outside help against the Thai and the Annamites. The priests could possibly help him find the patron he needed. It was a French bishop who wrote out the letter which, in 1853, Ang Duong decided to address to the Emperor Napoleon III of France. The letter asked for the Emperor's protection and assistance in regaining the provinces he had lost to Vietnam in the region of the Mekong Delta.

Ten years were to pass before France was to act decisively on this request. Potential interest in Cambodia grew, following the Franco-Spanish landings in Cochin China in 1858 and the subsequent establishment of a French colony there, whose westward flank needed to be secured. The British too, upon whom the French traditionally kept a wary and jealous eye, were active in the region; in 1858 an Englishman had explored Cambodia; and in 1860 the Royal Geographical Society had given a French explorer funds to do likewise (what Anglo-Saxon condescension and cheek!). But up to, and even beyond, the signing of an agreement in Phnom Penh in 1863, the government in Paris still hesitated. They did not want to offend Great Britain (which was nurturing a position of influence in neighbouring Siam); their attention was distracted by developments elsewhere (notably the beginnings of the Mexican adventure); and they were not open to missionary eloquence (having already resisted Spanish pressure to intervene in Tonkin in 1862–63 to support the uprising of a pro-Christian pretender). French popular sentiment favoured prudence and continued to do so for some years to come. Francis Garnier was later to complain (in *Voyage d'Exploration en Indochine 1866–68*) that public opinion

is completely uninterested in distant questions. Deprived of this vigilant guide, which nevertheless operates effectively in other domains, our diplomacy has been incapable of establishing what one would call an overseas policy. For three-quarters of a century, our Consuls and our Chargés d'Affaires abroad have been living on a day to day basis, unable either to identify an aim or to pursue it with that tenacity and economy of means which has made the fortune of England.

It was presumably therefore no surprise to the Consuls and Chargés d'Affaires when, in February 1863, the French Minister of the Navy, Chasseloup-Laubat, sent from Paris reticent and obscure instructions about Cambodia to the French Admiral and Governor in Saigon, instructions which ended with the imprecation that, while French interests were not to be compromised, it was 'necessary for the present to avoid committing ourselves to any new enterprise.'

These instructions were to be conveniently overlooked. France was served in Indo-China in the nineteenth century by a succession of outstanding leaders of men, among them the dashing naval officers Doudart de Lagrée and (the already-mentioned) Francis Garnier. To these men and those who served with them, explorers and administrators and fighting dare-devils rolled into one, France was to owe the creation of an Indo-Chinese Empire. In Cambodia, the protectorate was established not by the metropolitans but by the men on the spot.

Turning a blind eye to Paris, on 11 August 1863 Admiral Benoit de la Grandière signed with King Norodom, at the latter's request, the treaty under which the Emperor of the French granted his protection to Cambodia. Paris didn't like it a bit. But in an eloquent despatch to the Minister of the Navy six weeks later, La Grandière flung every argument into the balance to justify his action. The future, the very survival, of the new French colony in Cochin China was intimately tied up with the Kingdom of Cambodia. La Grandière added (with, it seems to me, tongue in cheek),

> Your Excellency will not be unaware that it is uniquely from there that we obtain the 7–8,000 head of cattle which are indispensable to us. Is it not to be feared that, if, under too cautious a policy, the Kingdom of

Cambodia were to be abandoned to hostile influences,
our cattle supply might be cut off ...?

We do not know whether the nutritional argument was decisive, but
the fact remains that the treaty was ratified in well under a year – in
April 1864.

To start with, all did not go too well with the new Protectorate
nor with the King that it protected. For twenty years, there were
sporadic uprisings and manifestations of discontent up and down
the country, fomented both by the jealousies of his dynastic rivalries
and the exasperation of those he misgoverned. France was in the
uneasy position of possessing power without influence, and French
administrators in the field chafed with an increasing impatience to
intervene directly in the running of the Kingdom. Administrative
reforms were introduced by royal decree in 1877 but quickly
became a dead letter. The Governor in Saigon, Admiral Lafont,
wrote to the King to urge that the decrees be taken up. The list of the
Governor's criticisms was long.

> Many individuals, being implicated in theft, insolvency
> and even crime, get themselves issued with documents
> from senior mandarins, Princes and also Your Majesty's
> wives, certifying that no-one is entitled to pursue them
> without having obtained the prior authorization of the
> Protectorate .... This state of affairs is not compatible
> with justice in a civilised country.

But complaints and warnings remained without effect and in the
end the French felt compelled to resort to direct action. On 17 June
1884, King Norodom was made to sign a convention which turned
Cambodia, in fact if not in name, into a virtual colony of France. He
lived on, ageing and in eclipse, until 1904. His power was further
circumscribed in 1897 by a decree conferring the government of the
Kingdom upon a Council of Ministers, to be presided over by the
French Resident in Phnom Penh.

Cambodia was never to become the top French favourite in
Indo-China. The apple of their eye (possibly because of the beauty
of the women) was probably Tonkin. The Cambodians were
looked down upon, as past their sell-by date and racially inferior
to the Vietnamese. Writing in 1875, a Frenchman (E. Aymonier)
was to say that 'no people offer so striking a contrast than the
degenerate Khmer of our days, with the Khmer of a past such as is

revealed by their grandiose ruins'. Apathy, indolence, decadence
were indeed words constantly on the lips of the foreign observer
in Cambodia during this period. Bouinais and Paulus assured
their readers (*Le Royaume de Cambodge*, 1884) that the Cambodians

> are perhaps more inter-bred than other neighbouring
> peoples with the aborigines, due especially to their
> having kept up the ancient tradition of taking aborigines
> as slaves. Should some part of the state of decadence in
> which we find them, and which tends to reduce them
> to a savage state, be attributed to this gradual infusion
> of the blood of savages into Cambodian veins? We think
> so. And the ease with which the Cambodians take
> refuge and live in the forests like savages would appear
> to justify this point of view!

But a more balanced view of the natives was set out in a survey of
Indo-China published in 1884 by Charles Lemire:

> The Cambodians are extremely lazy and content with
> little, asking only to promenade their idle leisure away in
> the sunshine. But they do not deserve, like the Annamites
> do, the reputation of being rascals and cowards. Although
> they live for the most part in squalor, they are cleaner
> and take more care of their appearance. … They have a
> natural pride which is more a virtue than a vice, because
> it is a great source of self-respect. They grant their chiefs
> the deference which is their due and expect to receive
> the same tokens from their inferiors. Thus they remain
> attached to the habits and native dress of their country,
> and custom has the force of law among them.

Auguste Pavie, then a junior official, described in 1881 having
seen the King in procession:

> Two hundred elephants, rolling the ancient seats,
> gilded or black, which they support, carry the King and
> the princes under roofs of scarlet bamboo screening,
> and pass like a parade, filled with women of the harem
> and with dancers half-naked beneath their veils. They
> disappear with the horsemen, the carriages, and those
> on foot, in a cloud of dust …

Etiquette at court was strict. The French Resident in Phnom Penh, Jean Moura, describes it at this time as follows:

> At audiences of the King, the princes, mandarins and other dignitaries stay couched on their knees and elbows, the hands pressed together and held up on a level with their faces. The King for his part is raised up on a dais, sitting like an Indian idol with his legs crossed on a throne or divan. When he enters or leaves the audience chamber, all those present prostrate themselves three times. Nobody may talk to the King unless His Majesty has first addressed them. Those seeking a favour prostrate themselves as he passes by and indicate by their salutations that they desire to speak or to submit a petition.

Punishment for the slightest misconduct within the Palace was liable to be severe for Cambodians in Norodom's day. The King sometimes beat people to within an inch of their lives. Delaporte recorded that, when he was passing through the capital on his way back from Angkor, he saw the blood-stained heads of four young women of the harem hung up outside the palace. They had just been executed by a firing squad for infidelity. Accepted as part of the natural order of things by the Cambodians, who would no doubt have been astonished if their monarch had behaved otherwise, such events naturally tended to disconcert the Europeans and move them to harsh judgements.

If the French were censorious, however, it was perhaps in part due to the isolated and difficult life they led. Throughout the nineteenth century, apart from a small and rootless garrison of soldiers and sailors, there was never more than a handful of Frenchmen in the country. As late as the 1890s, there were only ten Provincial Residents in Cambodia. In Phnom Penh itself, Governor General Doumer noted around 1900 that there were scarcely half a dozen businessmen. A visitor of that period recorded the presence of 'a mere score of French men and women in residence of exile' at the Water Festival ceremonies in Phnom Penh. The country was not particularly healthy: malaria and other fevers were wide-spread, dysentery was a killer of the white man, so too were typhoid and cholera. Roads did not exist: there were merely tracks across the plains and forests and narrow paths through the jungle. Travel was by elephant or horse, or by means of a primitive, two-wheeled cart

drawn by oxen or water buffaloes. In April 1864, even the redoubtable Doudart de Lagrée complained in a letter to his sister,

> these last few days I have had so many hours on an elephant that I can no longer sit down. One hour on an elephant is the equivalent of three hours on a horse.

Of their daily work, we can imagine easily enough the lives that the officials led, as judges and administrators, counsellors of Kings and cajolers of princes and mandarins. The business community is more elusive but seems to have been raffish, with a full quota of 'cards'. One of them persuaded the King that his glory and renown required that an equestrian statue of His Majesty should be set up in Phnom Penh. The merchant, who was to earn a very fat fee in the process, went back to France and picked up a statue of Napoleon III on the cheap just after his abdication. He sawed off the head and had it replaced with a new one that was carefully modelled on the royal features taken from photographs. It proved a great success in the Cambodian capital, where it was installed in the forecourt of the palace. Another businessman of the period fitted the armchairs and sofas of the royal drawing room with hidden musical boxes (no doubt regardless of expense) which played when the unsuspecting guest sat down. The Governor General noted that, when three or four visitors sat down together, three or four separate tunes would be played simultaneously, to the ravished delight of the royal hearing.

As for the capital itself, where most of the French community lived, it was little more than a village, and not always a savoury village at that. A fastidious and young diplomatic attaché on the staff of Doudart de Lagrée has left us the following description dating from 1872:

> The town of Phnom Penh, whither the King has just transplanted his capital, announces its presence from afar by a great pyramid built on the top of a little hill. Phnom Penh is no more than a pile of huts built of planks and bamboo, most of them raised off the ground on piles, round which the dogs, pigs and chickens live on top of each other in conditions of intimacy which give rise to more than one kind of inconvenience for the inhabitants.

By 1900 or so, however, the town had admittedly undergone embellishment, acquiring a Hôtel de Ville, a Customs and Excise Office, Ministries of Finance and Public Records and Works, new

stone houses, new commercial districts, even the beginnings of a new harbour. But life was to continue in the same sleepy way, until the outbreak of the Second World War. The defeat of France at the hands of the Germans in Europe in 1940 did not end French administration in Cambodia, but it did create confusion and sap morale. In 1942, when Germany's ally, Japan, over-ran South-East Asia, French Indo-China was shaken to its foundations. The French were allowed to continue to run Cambodia until shortly before the end of the war; but under the hegemony, and at the sufferance, of the Japanese. The Thai, neutral in the World War, but ready to profit from Cambodia's weakness and French impotence, occupied areas of Cambodian territory in the North-West.

French power was restored throughout Indo-China following Japan's surrender in 1945, but was never to be the same. The Thai were obliged to give back the provinces they had seized, in North-West Cambodia. But, in Tonkin and Annam and later in Cochin China, the communist Viet Minh were to challenge France and finally defeat her in 1954. The French pulled out. Cambodia, already granted full independence in 1953, emerged into the modern world far from well-equipped for survival.

And this is a good point at which to bring this historical survey to an end. The next chapter picks up the tale of quite a different traveller – myself.

3

Cambodia in the Sixties
– The Quest for Security

What kind of Cambodia did I discover upon my arrival, one hundred years after the establishment of the French Protectorate and ten years after that Protectorate's final withdrawal?

Outwardly, it was a pleasant, increasingly populous land – one enjoying peace and a small measure of prosperity and sustaining a society that was deeply traditional, yet open in the main to necessary change. But I also found myself entering a country on which the shadows were closing.

The contrast with the Cambodia of 1864 was striking. Where the population had been under a million, it was now seven million and rising. Where the national territory had barely covered 100,000 square kilometres, it now extended to over 180,000. The French Protectorate had brought peace and with it modest trade, some economic development and a degree of social betterment. The Khmer had done the rest: since national independence they had been successful in further pulling the country up by its own boot-straps. None of this amounted to a re-awakening of the ancient Khmer Empire. But the modern period nevertheless appeared, on the surface of things, to be one of national stability and renewal, in which every Cambodian had the right to take pride.

About a third the size of France, Cambodia was bounded to the North by Laos, to the West and North-West by Thailand, to the East and South-East by Vietnam, to the South and South-West by the Gulf of Siam. Half of it was thick, tropical rain-forest, a quarter empty savannah, the remainder clear and cultivated land. The capital city of Phnom Penh had a population approaching half a million, and the country as a whole was dotted with populous little towns. The population was largely rural, growing rice in the alluvial plains, or living as fishermen along the edges of lakes and rivers. Water was

everywhere – in the Tonle Sap (an inland sea covering 10,000 square kilometres in the rainy season), in the numerous rivers, in the rain clouds which deluged the country for half the year during the South-West Monsoon. Communications in the empty or inimical three-quarters of the Kingdom were sometimes difficult. But a railway ran from the capital as far as the Thai frontier; there were 1,400 kilometres of navigable waterways on which plied a lively sampan and steamer traffic, while lorries and buffalo carts rumbled from village to village and town to town over the colonial network of roads. Sizeable ships sailed up the Mekong from Saigon as far as the capital, while larger ocean-going vessels could use the new national port of Sihanoukville in the Gulf of Siam.

The economy was essentially agricultural. Some 80 per cent of the arable land was given over to rice production. The chief exports were rubber, rice, cotton, tobacco, maize and timber. The chief imports were oil and petrol and the kind of machinery and manufactured goods which the country could not make for itself. But a start had been made with the laying of a modest industrial base. Factories opened up in the 1960s to make cement, textiles, glassware, jute sacks, plywood and rubber tyres. Vehicles were assembled from imported parts and the bodywork made locally. Dams were under construction both for irrigation and the generation of hydro-electric power. Tourism was a growing industry.

The climate was damp for some of the year and hot for almost all of it. This carried with it the usual diseases. Public health was improving, but the infant mortality rate was high and general life expectancy was short – perhaps between 30 and 40 in some country districts, although the national average was claimed to be 44.

Racial minorities existed: mainly Chinese and Vietnamese, but also Malay and disparate groups of tribal hill-peoples. But the great majority – perhaps 85 per cent – were ethnic Khmer. Racial admixture across the centuries had produced some wide variations in physical appearance. But an average Cambodian was bronze-coloured if a town dweller and dark, coffee-coloured if a peasant constantly exposed to the sun. The Cambodian male would be short to medium in height, muscular and well proportioned. He would have a broad head, a small, flat nose, black (often wavy) hair and oval-shaped eyes. The Cambodian female was handsome, in a robust, sensual fashion with long black hair and neat, sometimes delicate, features.

The language spoken by the Cambodians – not too complex in grammar or syntax, but hard for a European to pronounce – was an

ancient South-East Asiatic tongue. Their neighbours, the Vietnamese, Laotians and Thai, all spoke tonal languages which betrayed their Chinese descent. The Cambodians spoke something quite different. To my untutored ear, it sounded primitive and harsh, with a monotonous, clipped and staccato quality modified only by a slight rising inflection at the end of each sentence, and by a rhythmic style of delivery. However, once I had got used to it, I found the Khmer language eloquent and emphatic; and, when I could speak a very little myself, I used to enjoy wrapping my mouth around the words.

Politically, Cambodia was a Kingdom without a King. The throne was vacant. The Royal Palace was occupied by the Queen Mother, who was endowed with the title of 'Symbol of the Throne', but who, in fact, neither reigned nor ruled. Instead, the powers of the monarchy were invested in her son, His Royal Highness Prince Norodom Sihanouk – commonly referred to as 'Monseigneur' – who had formerly been King, and was now the 'Head of State'. The singular events which had led up to this situation were the legend of the land. Norodom Sihanouk had been crowned King of Cambodia in 1941, at the age of 19. Almost immediately, from having led (on his own admission) an idle and somewhat rakish life, the young King began to concern himself actively with politics. Once Indo-China had been liberated from the Japanese at the end of the Second World War, he turned his thoughts toward the ending of the French Protectorate. After a dramatic and sometimes single-handed conduct of what was later called the 'Royal Crusade', the young King's efforts met with success. But after independence had been achieved, the burden of the Kingship became oppressive to him. The ceremonial obligations and the divinity which hedged about the crown led Norodom Sihanouk to abdicate in March 1955, in order to devote himself more completely to political life. The Cambodian monarchy is elective – the occupant of the throne being chosen by a select council of notables from among the male descendants of the founder of the then royal dynasty. After the abdication, this 'Council of the Throne' chose Sihanouk's father to be King in his stead, while Sihanouk himself, retaining the title of Prince, became also Prime Minister. When his father died, the decision was taken to leave the throne vacant, and in June 1960, Prince Norodom Sihanouk was elected to be Head of State. He had become a King without a crown.

There was thereafter, of course, a notional Prime Minister, chosen by the Head of State, and a cabinet of ministers. The Constitution laid down a system of parliamentary democracy and there was a

National Assembly, to which the cabinet was nominally responsible, but this was for show. The real power lay elsewhere. A popular gathering, called the National Congress, took place twice a year, usually in the presence of the Head of State, the full cabinet and both religious and other notables of all kinds. There, people asked questions, formulated suggestions and criticised the Government's record; and the cabinet was obliged to take seriously the decisions of the Congress. There was also the national, political movement called the '*Sangkum Reastr Niyum*', or 'Popular Socialist Community', which claimed to group together people of almost all shades of political opinion and from all walks of life. It had been created by Sihanouk in 1955 to counteract the factions and fissiparous trends of national political life in the period immediately following independence. Its statutes declared that it was not a political party, but in practice it was designed by Sihanouk to put an end to political parties, unite the nation round the throne and harness the populace to the tasks upon which the survival and prosperity of the Kingdom depended.

However, above all else and over the national destiny presided the 'Monseigneur', the Head of State, dominating the institutions of state and exerting leadership in almost all fields of Cambodian endeavour. Prince Norodom Sihanouk held popular audiences at which grievances could be laid before him for settlement; he took the chair at working groups of his ministers and officials; he travelled constantly up and down the country, visiting even the remoter settlements; he regularly addressed the nation over the radio and at mass meetings; he wielded a pick or shovel from time to time at the sessions of manual labour in which the bureaucracy (and the foreign diplomatic corps) were expected to take part; he inaugurated new buildings, factories, schools, hospitals and other modern developments; he instructed the small standing army of 30,000 men to devote much of their time to public works such as road and bridge building; and generally he galvanised everyone into activity in a hot country where things would not always get done if left to themselves. In addition, as Head of State, Sihanouk received distinguished foreign visitors, paid official visits abroad, and spent time with the diplomatic corps in his own capital. No one in the Kingdom worked a longer day than he did.

Almost as influential in its way as the apparatus of state was the apparatus of religion – Theravada Buddhism of the Lesser Vehicle. Each village had its pagoda. The monks in their saffron robes were

seen everywhere, walking barefoot in the cool of the morning seeking alms. These men were justifiably held in great respect by the people, since the personal standards which they set were high. Devout, learned and kindly, they exercised a benign and fruitful influence over the society which supported them. They were often, in the smaller hamlets, the only school teachers; they acted as conciliators, lawyers and sometimes even as doctors; everywhere their advice was persistently sought and freely given on most aspects of the life of the individual and of the community.

The picture which Cambodian society presented to outsiders in the early 1960s was therefore one of stability and freedom from turbulence. In general, there seemed to me to prevail a remarkable passivity and conservatism, a principal feature of the national character being what Western sociologists (perhaps in something less than complete comprehension) have termed affability, discretion and a certain amiable inactivity. Many Cambodians appeared satisfied with a life in which there were for the most part no extremes of wealth and poverty. Eighty per cent of the population were countrymen. Land was abundant, housing no problem, and locally-produced food, clothing and other simple necessities easy to come by. A sense of order prevailed in Cambodian village life. Buddhism had inculcated over the centuries a gentleness, a system of spiritual values and a lack of emphasis on material needs, throughout a now settled but formerly warlike and acquisitive populace. Associated with this religion, and accepted almost as firmly, was the monarchy. Prince Norodom Sihanouk effectively enjoyed something not far from the status of a Khmer *deva-raja*. His relations with the people at large, who knew him as *Samdech Euv* ('Prince-Daddy') were affectionate and, in their way, intimate. I myself, once I had got my bearings, began to suspect that Sihanouk's unquestioned pre-eminence was beginning to decline from its former peak. But his political ability and personal standing were still great by any standards. If Cambodia, under the Prince, was a guided democracy led by an enlightened despot, the country was nevertheless not uncomfortable with itself.

This was not to say that everything in the garden was lovely. I soon became aware of economic and social problems, and external political tensions, which together posed a serious threat to the national way of life in the longer term.

The inherently medieval Cambodian economy was emerging into the modern world – agricultural methods were being gradually improved; a modest industrial complex planned and slowly

executed; a handful of technicians painfully trained and even more painfully set to work. Modern educational and health facilities were being developed; the existing network of communications expanded.

Under-developed countries which have newly gained their independence are usually inclined, for natural, human reasons, to set out to run before they can walk in economic terms. Cambodia, spurred on by her Head of State and assisted by a ruling class attracted to the glitter and luxury of a Western-style consumer society, was no exception to this rule. A substantial trade and payments deficit had become a regular phenomenon; direct foreign investment, never massive, had tailed off; productivity and growth had lagged. But government expenditure had cruised on, ambitiously.

To their credit, the Cambodian Government were showing some sign of recognising their plight and of seeking a remedy. But, sometimes, they misread things and made mistakes. Draconian measures were to fail to serve their purpose in the domestic budget, which remained in deficit. Almost everyone had adequate food, clothing and lodging; and the upper crust continued to enjoy most of the amenities of a Western way of life. But the important American aid programme had been abruptly terminated by the Cambodian Government, for reasons of foreign policy. Other foreign aid continued to flow, but was not an adequate substitute. Unwise measures of nationalisation and the state control of trade followed. If the overall picture was one, by Asian standards, of relative prosperity and achievement, things were nevertheless starting to turn.

The social problem was essentially one of the expectations of the young. There had been a population explosion. In the 1962 census, approximately 45 per cent of the populace was aged 14 or less. A major effort had been made to educate the rising new generations, of whom by 1968 over a million were at school. Because of the lack of suitably qualified staff, and perhaps also on account of the conservative academic tradition which the Cambodians had inherited from the French, the emphasis of much of what was being taught was insufficiently technical or vocational. Making the children of peasants literate and outward looking at the village primary-school level was useful; but teaching them Descartes at the town *lyceé* was not. Large numbers of young Cambodians were turned out, scorning manual labour and life on the land, but for whom there was no room in the urban bureaucracy where they anxiously sought place and preferment.

The external political tensions stemmed from the rise of communism in South-East Asia generally and from the war in Vietnam in particular. They became more acute, year by year. They eventually brought Cambodia to her knees. They were what most preoccupied me from my arrival and kept me busy until I left.

Basically, Cambodia just wanted to be left alone. Prince Norodom Sihanouk was the originator and executor of a policy of neutrality intended to avoid commitment to any of the parties to the Vietnam war but conducted with sufficient flexibility to enable Cambodia to come to terms with the victors, whoever they might be. Cambodian neutrality was not a political concept, but a pragmatic survival policy, dictated by the rawest and most primitive of national instincts. The Cambodians constantly sought guarantees and protection – guarantees for the Kingdom's independence and territorial integrity within existing frontiers, and protection against any who might attempt to put such guarantees in question. Various means were explored to this single end in the mid-1960s. None of them yielded satisfactory results.

In 1962, and again, with increasing urgency, in 1963 and early 1964, the Cambodians had asked that the Geneva Conference which had endorsed the Kingdom's independence in 1954 should be convened again, some eight to ten years later, under Anglo-Soviet 'Co-Chairmanship', to agree upon further and more specific guarantees. After a period of considerable hesitation, in which they saw greater hope in direct negotiations between Cambodia and her immediate neighbours, the British Government announced in December 1963 that they supported this proposal in principle. But the Foreign Secretary pointed out to the Russian Co-Chairman and to the Cambodian Government that there were still serious difficulties in the way of a new conference. He appealed for restraint, while attempts were made to overcome them. The communist powers, for their part, pronounced themselves in favour – no doubt in the expectation that such a conference would make an admirable public platform on which to pillory American 'aggression' and 'imperialism' in Vietnam. Because of this, and perhaps also through fear that to go too far to uphold Cambodian neutrality and to appease the apparent anti-Westernism of Cambodia's rulers would be bad for morale in embattled South Vietnam, the US Government and their closest allies in South Asia decided against a Geneva Conference. The proposal accordingly fell to the ground.

The British were made to share some of the blame for this. The Cambodians argued that the UK ought to have dismissed the objections and gone ahead to convene the conference, thereby facing the dissidents with the brutal choice either of turning up to make the best of a bad job or of being roundly denounced in their absence. The Brits felt that they could do nothing of the kind. The Co-Chairmanship carried no special powers, whether of persuasion or of compulsion; the British Government was an honest broker, not a Conference 'Sergeant Major'. As a British White Paper in December 1965 later put it,

> Neither Her Majesty's Government nor the Soviet Government as Co-Chairman had the authority severally or jointly to require attendance at a conference; they could do no more than issue invitations, a step which would be useless unless the governments so invited were agreeable.

This the Cambodians would not or could not believe. In a communiqué issued in Phnom Penh in February 1964, the Cambodian Government said that they could not 'remain indifferent in the face of this hypocritical sabotage of the international conference that has been asked for'. In March – as described earlier, in Cameo I– a mob attacked and wrecked the British and American Embassies in Phnom Penh. In a broadcast statement expressing token and insincere regret for this orchestrated incident, Prince Sihanouk nevertheless claimed that the attack reflected 'the legitimate exasperation of Cambodian youth at the repeated humiliations inflicted on their country by the Anglo-Saxon powers'.

The position outwardly adopted by the Cambodian Government was indeed not easy, at first sight, to reconcile with a status of genuine neutrality in the habitual Western definition.

Thus, a visitor to Phnom Penh at that time would quickly have sensed a one-sidedness in the public information media. The press was subject to informal but effective official guidance, and for the most part scrupulously toed the Government line. There was no real freedom of day-to-day public debate. Western press material, even of a factual nature, with the sole exception of *Agence France Presse* cables, rarely found its way into print. Voices from the Soviet Union and Eastern Europe were also audible, but only in the background. The foreground seemed to be reserved to the utterances of the Royal Cambodian Government and of the Peoples' Republic of China,

each of which professed to speak in full harmony with the other. Information and cultural activities by Western diplomatic missions were heavily circumscribed. The US Information Service in Cambodia, formerly an ambitious organisation, was operating almost on a care-and-maintenance basis; its vacated headquarters stood gutted, painted with 'Yankee go home' slogans and alive only to the sound of rats' feet over broken glass. Measures of nationalisation were being applied to the economy which threatened to compromise existing trading links with the West; foreign banks had already been pushed out and Western oil companies were operating under risk of expropriation. As already noted, American economic aid had been rejected. Cambodians were forbidden to have social contacts with the British and Americans, whose governments were subject to daily public abuse. Economic and military aid had been demanded of, and had to some small extent been forthcoming from, the communist bloc. Therefore, far from presenting a picture of neutrality, Cambodia gave the appearance of occupying a position on the left of the non-aligned group of nations.

Nevertheless, this impression, deliberately fostered for presentational reasons, was not to be taken entirely at its face value.

Behind all Prince Sihanouk's policies lay a perception of the utter weakness of his country. He saw himself set about by traditional enemies. Thailand had not disgorged her last land grab until 1947. Laos still maintained on paper a claim to the Province of Stung Treng. To the East were the Vietnamese, whom Sihanouk feared the most, for they had posed a serious threat to Cambodia, right up to the days of French colonial intervention. The average Cambodian disliked and distrusted them. In the fifteenth century, the Annamites had actually overthrown and virtually extinguished a nation – the Cham – of similar racial origin to the Cambodians. Sihanouk constantly referred to their fate when discussing his eastern frontier with visiting journalists and resident diplomats, including myself. He seemed to see the Vietnamese as more ruthless, talented and industrious than the Cambodians, as a people pushed by their ambition and by their own population pressures towards the rich, under-populated and under-developed Cambodian rice-lands. Cambodia had no effective armed forces – and no friendly neighbours in an Indo-Chinese peninsula torn by political dissension and military upheaval.

So Sihanouk had early on formulated certain, long-term assumptions which were to guide most of his subsequent actions, and

which emerged clearly from his numerous public utterances. They explain much that will emerge from later chapters of this book. These assumptions were – first, the power most seriously to be reckoned with in the future was China. In the middle and long term, and perhaps before then, the whole of Indo-China would become a sphere of Chinese influence. Second, the Chinese, even in their present militant mood, were not bound on military conquest and territorial annexation; they would be content to exclude Western influence and to assert their own; eventually (who knew?) they might one day even become prosperous and conservative; if he stepped softly, therefore, Cambodia might survive the ascendancy of China in Asia and even benefit from it. Third, Sihanouk reckoned that the United States of America were shortly to be subjected to humiliation and defeat in South Vietnam, and to lose all direct influence in the area. Fourth, Vietnam would be united, before very long, under communist rule; but communism, far from mitigating, might merely make more formidable than ever before, the traditional expansionist threat from the East – unless the Chinese, not wishing the dynamic and ambitious Vietnamese to get too big for their boots, were to set limits to the latter's hegemonic ambitions. Fifth, Cambodia's only hope of national survival was, therefore, while looking for a *modus vivendi* with the Vietnamese communists, to rely on Big Brother China to keep Vietnam in check.

At the same time, Sihanouk considered communism inappropriate as a political and social creed for the Cambodian people. At home, he had kept the socialist, so-called Khmer Rose on a tight rein. He had also, through his hatchet man, the Minister for National Security, Kou Roun, viciously repressed the Khmer Rouge (driving some of them – including the future Pol Pot – out of the political system in Phnom Penh and into the remote jungle *maquis*, where revolutionary attitudes and activities were to take root and flourish). The Prince proclaimed in his speeches, and evidently believed, that the strict regimentation, harsh application to ceaseless labour and general lack of *joie de vivre* which he had witnessed with his own eyes in communist China, would be profoundly repugnant to the carefree Cambodian national character, and conflict with religious and monarchical traditions. Nor did he profess to any delusions about the friendship which the communists offered. In one speech, he said:

> The communists are deceitful to us and we are to them
> … the day that they are not interested in our country, I

> will no longer be able to deceive them and ask for their
> aid. They will refuse to give me aid and will whip me or
> devour the Cambodian people.

The Prince was therefore striking a tricky balance. He had felt it
necessary to depict the Americans as enemies and potential aggressors.
But he did not wish the US to disappear altogether from the scene. In
an interview with *Le Figaro* during a state visit to France in June 1964,
he made it clear that, although the Americans ought to leave Indo-
China, they should remain in Thailand and the Philippines, and
anywhere else where they were welcome. Otherwise, 'neutrality
would be impossible, because equilibrium would be broken'. To help
maintain this equilibrium, he was making the most of his long-
standing but newly enthusiastic friendship with France, and of the
modest support of the Soviet bloc. He claimed to have issued to the
army, in 1964, strict instructions that no assistance was to be given to
the Viet Cong. If he appeared unfriendly to the UK, this was because
he saw us as wilfully obstructing the re-convening of the Geneva
Conference of 1954.

In mid-1964, on my arrival in Phnom Penh, it was still the Geneva
solution which he sought – a conference which would, in endorsing
Cambodian neutrality and setting a formal seal on its present frontiers, bind as closely as any written agreement could, the Governments of North Vietnam and of China. The Prince would have liked a
new Geneva Conference to be extended to cover the whole of Indo-
China (except North Vietnam, which he considered irremediably
communist). 'I consider', he declared, 'that now is the time to apply
a diplomatic and political solution in making South Vietnam, Laos
and Cambodia a buffer zone effectively separating the communists
from the West'.

Nevertheless, the big question in the minds of all diplomatic
observers in Phnom Penh was whether Cambodia's policy of
neutrality, however admirable in theory, could succeed in practice.
My own initial judgement, from which I never departed even in the
better times which were immediately to follow, was that the prospects, whether short-term or long-term, were rather poor. In
September 1964, I concluded a dispatch to the Foreign Secretary
with a young man's metaphor. I wrote that Cambodian neutrality
had reached a turning point. Cambodia was now free to pivot like a
weather-cock. The winds of change would, I continued, determine
the direction which she finally faced; but, in the end, the North-

Easter (blowing from Hanoi and Beijing) could dash her to pieces. So wrote the youthful Chargé d'Affaires. In the event, within ten years, something like that was what actually happened.

Such was Cambodia in the 1960s: for the foreign observer, a worrisome but also a fascinating country and one which could not fail to engage the sympathy of any Westerner of good will. Before we take a stroll into the shadows (and ultimately, towards the 'Heart of Darkness'), it deserves to be said that this was then also a society in which, with a little organisation, it was agreeable for an adequately remunerated foreigner to live.

Phnom Penh was a pleasant city. Sited at a confluence of waters where the Tonle Sap met the Mekong and the Mekong split into two branches and ran South to the sea, it was a thriving commercial centre, its Chinese and Vietnamese quarters throbbing with activity. The central part of the city was adorned with fine buildings and monuments; it was grouped round the gilded and curved roofs of the royal palace and the conical shrine on the little hill which gave Phnom Penh the name it bore. The broad streets of the residential quarters were lined with the smart new apartment blocks and houses of the post-independence era, or with the cool, spacious, whitewashed, thick-walled villas of the French Protectorate – in one of which it was to be my privilege to live. Smooth lawns and banks of bougainvillea embellished the city. Umbrageous tropical trees shaded the pavement where one walked.

It was, as my French friends still remember it, '*Phnom Penh de la Belle Époque*'.

H.R.H. Prince Norodom Sihanouk, Head of State of Cambodia, on an informal excursion to the provinces with the Diplomatic Corps (author, second from right in dark glasses)

Re-Organising the Embassy

4

Starting Again, From Scratch

To resume the personal narrative of the young British diplomat, interrupted on page 11, the atmosphere at Phnom Penh airport was courteous and I sailed through customs and immigration with the minimum of formality. The city, too, seemed calm as we approached it along the highway and drove into the shade of its tree-lined streets. (Somehow, I had been expecting 'aggro' – or at least a shaken fist.) I was taken by John Shakespeare straight to the Residence of Peter Murray, the Ambassador, with whom I had been invited to stay. It was a large house, shaded by palms, in the heart of what had been, before Cambodian independence, the *chic* French quarter. The villas and gardens, set back from the broad streets, had period charm: slightly decayed, but built for comfort, in the secure and unhurried years between the two world wars. 'H.E.' and his wife greeted me correctly, but with just a hint of inner reserve. (I already knew Murray, from my previous job in London – he had been a middle-ranker in the Delegation to NATO, and I had been his 'desk' officer in the FO in London.) Shakespeare and I sat down to lunch with them and straightaway entered into local realities. The handover had begun.

After a week, Shakespeare flew off to his new duties in Singapore. Three weeks or so later, after holding the traditional party to celebrate the Queen's Official Birthday, the Murrays, too, departed. I watched the aircraft rise up and set course to the West until it had passed out of hearing and of sight. It was a moment of intense loneliness – one in which inchoate forebodings reared and twisted on the fringes of consciousness. No one in Cambodia knew, apart from me, that the Ambassador would not be returning. I drove back to the Embassy to transmit the ritual telegram to London.

> The Ambassador left Phnom Penh on 25 June. I have
> accordingly assumed charge. Fielding.

The Embassy to which I returned that day, and for which I was to
be indefinitely responsible, was passing through a difficult and
demoralising period. Spirits were, for the present, reasonably high.
Siege conditions, and the menace of mob action, had had an exhilarating effect; initially, they induced the staff to give of their best. But
it was now three months since there had last been serious rioting.
The top men had gone; others were going; the remainder were
faced with an uncertain future and a great deal of hard work in
finally clearing up all the mess and ensuring 'business as usual'.
Everyone had rather taken a beating and there was a *fin de siècle*
feeling in the air. The UK staff were getting a little on each other's
nerves – there were the beginnings of a cynical, if not slip-shod,
attitude about the place. Morale and efficiency would fall soon,
with quite a bump, if energetic steps were not taken and fresh,
personal leadership not asserted.

The difficulty was to know, not what to do, but where to start.
Answers had to be found quickly in handling staff cuts, re-prioritising
work, repairing riot damage, tightening physical security, re-organising
public relations and generally finding an Embassy style appropriate
to unprecedented, new, local and political conditions. I will describe
all of this, because much of it relates to what the general public never
see, yet what makes serious professional diplomacy possible.

The biggest single difficulty arose from shortage of staff: the
Embassy team was in the process of being cut to the very bone. No
one quite knew how or even whether it could continue to do the
job expected of it. At the beginning of the year, the Embassy had
been at full strength. It was not a large team – on anything like the
scale, for example, of the Americans or French, to say nothing of
the multitudes of Russians and Chinese who were in town. But it
was a balanced unit, suited to the task which it was expected to
perform.

At the apex of the pyramid had naturally stood His Excellency the
Ambassador Extraordinary and Plenipotentiary, responsible to the
Foreign Secretary in London for, and exercising control over, all that
was done in His Excellency's name and under Her Britannic
Majesty's Embassy's roof. A Counsellor in rank (the equivalent of an
Assistant Secretary in the Home Civil Service), he was looked after by
an experienced shorthand-typist with the title of Personal Assistant.

He carried, in addition to his ambassadorial epithets, the title of Consul General. (The Embassy was too small for these titles to be divided between two men, and the duties of Consul General were in any case nominal; but there were advantages in international law in retaining the consular attribution.)

Next followed the Head of Chancery, a First Secretary in rank (the equivalent of Principal in the Home Civil Service), who carried the concomitant title of Consul. As the Chief of Staff of the Embassy, he had to turn his hand to a wide variety of supervisory tasks, but his main concern was with the diplomatic work of the mission – in a word, with day-to-day relations with the Cambodian Government. When the Ambassador was absent from the country, it was the Head of Chancery who acted as Chargé d'Affaires. In effect, he was the Number Two of the Embassy.

The Embassy also counted a Military Attaché, a Lieutenant-Colonel in rank, assisted by a clerk-cum-typist. In the hierarchy of diplomatic missions abroad, the attachés from the armed services rank with, but after, the diplomatic officer who normally acts as Chargé d'Affaires. They are full members of the Ambassador's staff and are under the Ambassador's authority. But their specific duties are assigned to them by the Ministry of Defence, to whom they report.

After these three gentlemen, had come two Second Secretaries, one political (whose chief task was to follow the internal politics of Cambodia in such depth as he could) and the other commercial (who helped British businessmen, bankers and would-be exporters, and reported to the Foreign Office and the Board of Trade on the local economic, financial and commercial scene). Two years previously, there had even been a third Second Secretary, responsible for relations with the local press, who had run a separate British Information Office, downtown. But this last, and his workers, had been axed in a routine economy drive. The Head of Chancery had been made responsible for some of the work, but most of it had been simply discontinued, or left to the separate British Council office in Phnom Penh.

The five men (Ambassador, Head of Chancery, Military Attaché, the two Second Secretaries) had constituted the diplomatic staff as such. They were supported by more junior British staff who discharged executive or clerical functions.

There was thus also a Vice Consul, who dealt with passport and visa matters and kept an eye on administration. In the latter capacity, he was assisted by a senior clerk who also doubled up as the

mission's Accountant. To keep order in the files and papers in the registry, and to cipher and de-cipher confidential telegrams, was another clerk with the imposing title of Archivist. To transmit and receive telegrams in morse by radio through the ether between the Embassy and the Foreign Office was a member of the Diplomatic Wireless Service. Three female secretaries completed the home-based team.

Nominally on the Ambassador's staff, but in fact resident elsewhere, were a Naval and an Air Attaché (a Captain, RN and a Group Captain, RAF – both based in Bangkok) and a Civil Aviation Attaché (based in Hong Kong). Each visited Phnom Penh once or twice a year, whenever business required his presence.

Separate from the Embassy, but for whom the Ambassador was a father figure, was the Phnom Penh branch of the British Council, with three lecturers responsible for the teaching of English and the projection of British culture. A similar, parental relationship existed between the Embassy and two or three British experts who were working for the Cambodian Government but paid by the British Government under the latter's modest programme of Technical Assistance or under the auspices of Voluntary Service Overseas.

By June 1964, this pyramid had been well and truly 'shrunk'. The Embassy and its appendages were cut back, so as to ensure only a minimal presence. The Ambassador, the Commercial Secretary and the Second Secretary (Political), the Accountant and three typists, simply disappeared. Even the British Council office went down from three to two. The exodus was then complete. New, drastically limited, objectives had to be assigned to the skeleton crew that remained.

Then there was the problem of what to do about the Embassy's premises. The mob attack on 11 March 1964 had been directed initially at the 'Chancery', a large two-floor villa on one of the main streets of the capital which had been converted to serve as our office block. Most of the ground floor, serving as the commercial and consular offices, had been trashed. The first floor, where the Ambassador's office was located, had been damaged. Eight private motor cars belonging to the staff, which had been standing in the grounds, had been wrecked. On my arrival, two months later, most of them were still there, on the Ambassador's express instructions. The idea was to embarrass the Cambodian Government and give international press photographers something to show for their expenses.

Naturally, some effort had been made to put things in order. The windows and doors were back in. The walls had been crudely

patched and roughly whitewashed. The grounds had been more or less tidied up.

The British Council library and offices in another part of town had also been trashed, and the flat occupied by the senior lecturer, looted. Here, too, an attempt had been made to restore order and decency. But the library had been destroyed.

Finally, routine, day-to-day relations with the Cambodians hardly existed, in the normal sense of the term. The British Embassy, like the American, had been placed 'in Coventry'. For the word had gone out from 'the top' (*i.e.* from the Head of State himself) that it would henceforth be treason for a Cambodian citizen to attend social events given by the 'Anglo-Saxon' Embassies, or to receive 'Anglo-Saxon' diplomats in their own houses.

This edict did not mean that we were never spoken to by, or allowed any contact whatsoever with, Cambodian people. British diplomats were allowed to call on government officials in the latter's offices, and the Ambassador or Chargé d'Affaires still received invitations to ceremonial and social occasions organised by the Cambodian Head of State. But, in practice, the Brits saw all too little of the people.

The Queen's Birthday Party in 1964 was attended by only one Cambodian – an official from the Ministry of Foreign Affairs specially designated for the purpose. None of the others who had been invited was brave enough to put in an appearance; a few had felt able to acknowledge receipt of their invitations and convey their regrets at being unable to attend. At cocktail parties given by other Embassies, and even at the occasional state reception, Cambodian guests, always in any case a little shy, proved anxious to avoid mixing with the 'Anglo-Saxons'. This reserve, tinged with anxiety, extended to the intimacy of our own offices. No Cambodians came to the Chancery, except to ask for a visa to Hong Kong; few even dared venture back to the British Council reading room, where they had formerly been so numerous and where they were perfectly entitled to go, given that the British Council and its staff did not strictly fall within the ban. For some months, I myself saw only on a regular basis the Buddhist monk who was attempting to teach me Khmer, the gardener at my house, and the locally-engaged office staff in the Chancery. The latter comprised only a clerk/translator, a telephone operator, one or two drivers and a handful of orderlies, messengers and cleaners, who had mercifully been permitted to remain in our employ.

Battered, cold-shouldered and much reduced in size, the Embassy's circumstances were therefore, all in all, far from encouraging. I had begun by speeding the departure of those who had lived through the bad times: they had done their bit and should be permitted honourable release, taking with them memories which had no useful place in the new order. What was wanted was to pull out of the line the battered battalion which had stood its ground but was in need of recuperation and re-equipment, and to replace it by fresh troops.

The newcomers were chosen individually and with care both for their efficiency and for other qualities – more personal but not less important – which would enable them to face up to the challenge and to fit in harmoniously. They were a collection of 'characters' and I took some pride in them. It was certainly a smart ship, even if more a corvette than a frigate of the line. In relative terms, and with regard to the tasks conferred upon us, it was more efficient and cost-effective than many.

Lt. Col. F.G. Robson was the new Military Attaché, arriving not long after me. He was ten years my senior and this was his first experience of Embassy life. Yet he and his wife slipped quietly into place and were to become a much-needed source of strength, both in and out of the office. A Gunner, he had fought in the Second World War and – in the Malayan emergency – had secured valuable experience of Asian conditions. Sadly, Felix Robson had also shattered an ankle when his Auster aircraft crashed in Malaya, and was to walk with a slight limp for the rest of his life. Consequently he had been transferred from the Royal Artillery to the Intelligence Corps. He made a most professional soldier-cum-diplomat in Phnom Penh, where he got to know a lot of people, travelled widely and penetrated in his Landrover or in aircraft of the RAF and even helicopters of the Cambodian Air Force into the remotest corners of the Kingdom. He wrote clear and shrewd reports.

A second key man was the new – higher profile – Vice Consul. Michael Laidler spoke fluent French, having served previously as Vice Consul in Dakar, where he had also acquired a French wife. He had entered the Foreign Service as a Branch B (*i.e.* an Executive Stream) member, straight from school, and had done consistently well in various assignments. When he left Phnom Penh, he was to be promoted to Second Secretary rank and thereafter moved steadily up the tree. I looked to Laidler to be my civilian Number Two, to get about in the city and make himself known at the Ministry of Foreign

Affairs, and also to take temporary overall charge, whenever I might be absent on business trips to surrounding countries. I would be demanding more of him in terms of responsibility and enterprise than one would normally require of an officer of his rank and seniority. I decided that he should therefore get diplomatic cover. With the agreement of the Foreign Office, I notified him to the Cambodian Protocol Department as a diplomatic Third Secretary as well as Vice Consul. He filled his appointment, and fulfilled my expectations, very well indeed.

My own job was to conduct the political side of the Embassy work, to take such decisions in other fields as could be not be delegated and to supervise the working of the Mission as a whole. Lt. Col. Robson's task was to liaise with the Cambodian armed forces and observe developments of defence interest in the country. Laidler issued visas, supervised the administration and shared with me the handling of commercial and press work. But we three were the visible portion of an iceberg of which the greater part fulfilled routine but essential functions beneath the surface. The mission totalled eight UK-based staff. The remaining five comprised an archivist-cum-cipher officer, an accountant-cum-assistant-administration officer, a clerk for the Military Attaché, a secretary for myself, and finally a telegraphist and wireless operator. Each of these was a first-rate person. Three were hard-headed Scots; the rest were (like me) mostly just English. Later, we were to be reinforced by an army Captain as a Cambodian language student. This was the team we fielded, until a new Ambassador arrived two-and-a-half years after his predecessor had left.

The machine was highly flexible. Spouses, for example, when they were allowed back, helped out in the Chancery whenever they could. The officials, as far as was possible, took care to know each other's jobs. Alone was the communications wizard – in his tiny box-like room, loud with the shriek of static from electric storms or the boom of a band (often the Beatles) from London, crammed with black boxes, dials and flashing lights, with his earphones clamped firmly over his head he grappled dedicated, but unaided, with his duties, sending or receiving by morse code. If he wanted a few days' leave, or traffic became especially intense, help-mates from his own skilled and professional mafia were flown in from outside.

We were not bureaucratic. It would have been perfectly possible, in fulfilling to the letter every written rule and traditional procedure, to pass the greater part of each day in self-regulation, with only the

briefest of glances out of the window at the capital and the country which lay around us. But this would not have made sense, nor – to give them the credit – was it what the authorities in London expected of us. We were free to exercise our own judgement and set our own priorities. It was, for example, often a necessity to reply to routine enquiries that, for lack of back papers, the precedent or background was inaccessible but that the commonsense answer seemed to us to be X or Y. These were, substantively, by no means always bad replies.

Labour-saving expediency went hand-in-hand with a refusal of time-wasting formalities. Wherever possible, I dictated correspondence in final form, rather than make my secretary prepare successive drafts, a routine dear to most of my meticulous, Diplomatic Service contemporaries. It may have done my professional reputation marginal harm for my letters to have gone out in something less than the form which might have been theirs with more spit and polish. Yet I thought it no bad thing, for the image of the Embassy in Whitehall, to appear a little rough-and-ready and to eschew the normal clerkly frills.

Our communications were also stream-lined. Naturally, we kept our diplomatic wireless facility. But we cut back the diplomatic bag service. This was, in those days, the main channel of communication between a post overseas and the Foreign Office. It was secure – carried by a resourceful and alert 'Queen's Messenger' and never leaving his sight on the journey. It was rapid – it travelled by air, so that mail from even the remotest post was never more than a day or so in transit. It was flexible and capacious – one could shove in a combination lock that had got jammed and needed expert repair as well as bundles of despatches. We had been accustomed to send and receive such a bag once a week. Henceforward, we were to do so only once a fortnight.

The general cut-back in Embassy activities required, among other things, the virtual closing down of the former commercial and press sections. The latter was already almost non-existent, since the earlier axing of our downtown information office. But from information departments in the Foreign Office and from the Central Office of Information in London, we still received a range of films, books, pamphlets, periodicals and ready-made articles on this or that aspect of British life, all for release through the public media in Cambodia. My predecessor had been able to put some of this to use. I could not. So we slashed almost the whole range.

The chief function of my re-organised, residual press section was to watch the local press and occasionally to issue a press bulletin. These were necessary tools of the Chancery – the ability to keep a close eye on all that was being said and to put a British view across rapidly and in writing. We ourselves read anything published in French. The Cambodian-language and (of less interest but not uninformative) Chinese-language press were scanned by our local staff, who produced summaries of editorials on subjects in which I had indicated my general interest. As regards our Embassy press bulletins, I drew up a shortish distribution list, comprising top Cambodian personalities in politics, economic life and the press world. I sent out a mere dozen or so press bulletins in my time, heralding the arrival of important British visitors or setting out British Government policy on a point of major interest. I kept the texts brief and the subject matter factual, to stand a better chance of being read. They were always cast in a French as elegant as my translators and I could contrive – there was already too much material put out by the foreign Embassies which deserved, on literary grounds alone, to end up unopened in the waste-paper baskets of the capital.

Routine commercial work had also had to go by the board. I felt less happy about this, but we had nobody with the time or training to cover the duties discharged by the outgoing Commercial Secretary. Nor was there at that point much useful work to be done. Trade with the West generally was not doing too well, for purely economic reasons. More than that, we Brits were in the dog-house politically and this inevitably told against us, not so much in reducing the volume of what existed – a steady turn-over, then worth about a million pounds a year, remained remarkably unaffected – as in virtually ruling out the possibility of netting fresh contracts in the face of hot competition. Furthermore, the import and export trade had just been nationalised and put into the hands of a corporation of the Cambodian Government calling itself the National Import/Export Company. Contracts and orders had therefore to be awarded, or approved, by the Government. Political and personal preferences lay elsewhere, notably in trade with the ex-colonial power, France.

This was why the decision had been taken, before my arrival, in consultation with the Foreign Office and the Board of Trade, that the Commercial Section should be closed. We did not, however, give up the ghost completely. The Vice Consul and I briefed British exporters and salesmen on their infrequent exploratory trips to Phnom Penh. And we made a special effort behind the scenes (we

always avoided the appearance of overt British Embassy support, which was likely to be counter-productive until Anglo-Cambodian relations had improved) for the very few men who took the market seriously and stood a real chance of success.

Later on, when conditions were ripe, the balance was restored. On my recommendation as I was leaving, a Commercial First Secretary was added to the team who also doubled up as Consul. This put trade promotion and the protection of British subjects and interests neatly and logically together on the plate of a qualified specialist.

The physical security of the Embassy and of the staff was an ever-present concern, throughout my nigh-on three years in Cambodia. But it demanded a special effort in the first few months. Our defensive dispositions really mattered and they had to be got right, before anything serious could be attempted.

The basic question was how to give adequate physical protection to our secrets. All governments have them. All major powers go to considerable lengths to guard them. Embassies, despite their 'extra-territorial' status in international law, being no more than militarily undefended offices in a foreign country, are always a weak link in the security chain. Physical violence can be directed against them by rioters. Agents of a hostile power can seek to pick locks and open combination safes at dead of night, so as to gain access to secret ciphers and classified documents. If they know their business, these agents will try to operate privily, so that their target remains unconscious of their attentions and the Government concerned unalerted to what has been 'blown'.

But the immediate task in Phnom Penh was to guard against further mob action. On 11 March that year, demonstrators had not made a serious attempt to seize the Embassy's archives, perhaps because their main object was simply to beat the place up. Nor would they have succeeded in the few hours available to them, short of using extreme force in breaking down the strong-room door or walls and blowing open the safes and other metal containers within. The papers with which they had bestrewn the lawns were the unclassified archives of the Consular and Commercial Departments and of no interest to anyone except ourselves. Nevertheless, it had been a close-run thing. The events of that day had posed a serious threat to document security and inflicted a severe ordeal on the defenders.

I therefore decided to reduce yet further our holding of classified material. But paper is surprisingly difficult to destroy in bulk and with speed. In the yard behind the Chancery, during successive late

afternoons, when the sun had ceased to burn too fiercely, we incinerated the contents of hundreds of files. We worked in shifts, with everyone giving a hand in the flames and smoke and drifting ash.

The remaining material I decided to keep in the window-less strong room, stowed away in the four or five safes of modern design. All were explosive hardened and had highly sophisticated combination locks. In addition, I obtained through the Security Department at the Foreign Office two gas masks and several of the latest tear-gas bombs. These were to be used to seal off the strong room and registry in an extreme emergency. We thought their effluent, which was quite unbreathable without the protection of those masks, would linger for at least a day in the building, whatever the weather conditions or counter-measures.

A further urgent precaution concerned fire. The usual appliances were in disarray and had to be overhauled and re-deployed within the building to guard against a new, theoretical contingency: a fire from below, fought from above by staff who were trapped. It was one more chore for my by now semi-exhausted staff. But it had to be done – and done quickly, with the Chargé d'Affaires visibly lending a hand and leading from the front.

While all this was going on, I gave fresh thought to our evacuation plans. If the Embassy were again attacked, or law and order were to break down in the capital, it would be necessary to withdraw the Embassy staff entirely, together with the last of the tiny British resident community. Fortunately, it was largely a question of overhauling what already existed on paper. I had already looked over the plan held by the Commander-in-Chief Far East at Phoenix Park. Our people would ideally fly out by civil airline. If these lines were to abandon all flights, and the RAF could not fly in from Singapore, then we would form up a land convoy and drive out by road to Bangkok, or south to the sea in the Gulf of Thailand to be picked up by the Royal Navy. All this would naturally require the acquiescence of the Cambodian authorities, who could, if they chose to do so, hold us prisoners by force. But I did not expect them to do this; indeed, if we had to go, I felt they would probably be glad to see the back of us.

It was one thing to check over a piece of paper but quite another to be sure that the physical means and the state of training existed to carry our plans into execution. The new Military Attaché and I therefore plunged at once into comprehensive local planning. We selected two rallying points in the city where our people could assemble in

the event of serious disturbances. One was a large house on which we held a lease within a stone's throw of the Head of State's palace in the smartest and most modern quarter of town; we considered this the safer option. The other was the Ambassador's Residence at the other edge of town, close to the French Embassy and the top international hotel (the Hotel Royal); the latter could be used for a final dispersal, if the Residence itself was threatened. Canned provisions were available, jerrycans for petrol, three Landrovers and a small truck. (Admin clerks in London wanted me to sell two of the Landrovers on the grounds that they had become 'above establishment' following the run-down in our numbers; but I told them to get lost.) I shuffled our rented accommodation and concentrated the juniors in two blocks of flats, shared with other foreign nationals, in a quiet district off a main road, adjacent to the house of an important Cambodian minister. I got the Foreign Office to supply two walkie-talkie sets, to link the two assembly points and allow communication between the first and last vehicle of any land convoy which we might want to get moving. I also had up my sleeve a portable high-frequency transistorised wireless set with which we could communicate with the Foreign Office, if the main transmitter in the Chancery building should be destroyed. It was no bigger than a schoolboy's satchel, with a manual mini-generator to match. Finally, we went over our plans with other allied Embassies who might also be obliged to conduct an evacuation. I then designated the Military Attaché as the Embassy's 'Evacuation Officer', to be responsible for the execution of these plans under my overall direction.

At this point, I drew breath. As regards the security of the Chancery, I had a primitive but effective defence against further mob violence. If I had advance warning of a major attack, I would, having destroyed what classified material I needed, lock up the whole Chancery and withdraw all staff. The absence of white faces from the upper windows would also – on past experience – reduce the provocation to the crowd without. But if we got caught, the Military Attaché and I planned to send everyone else out over the improvised fire escape (a scramble from a balcony to a roof top and down a drain pipe), lock all the safes and steel doors, press the plunger on those sinister black canisters, and finally grope our way out in our gas masks.

It was a comfort to think that at least we had a drill of our own in the event of trouble. But, over the months which followed, the physical security of the Chancery continued to be a problem that

nagged and worried at the back of my mind. Walking in at the door in the morning, riding by the building late at night, I would re-appraise the layout. I used to put myself into the shoes of a clandes-tine 'Cold War' enemy, and think what extra precautions I could take. Where would he seek entry? How long would it take him to pick the padlock, crack the combination? Would he have placed a miniaturised microphone in a dusty drawer of my desk? Who owned the adjacent buildings and who did or could occupy them? There was the villa down the side road in which some junior staff from one communist Embassy lived. Two hundred yards along the main road was the Embassy of another communist country. There was that empty house on the corner. What were the angles of incidence for telephotography? Could they photograph from a distance the docu-ments that crossed my desk in the course of a working day – if I had forgotten to draw the specially supplied security curtains? The local architect who held the plans of the Chancery – did he also do work for a hostile Embassy? The Vietnamese workmen who came to fit a new door here, re-plaster a ceiling there – were they coolies or did they seem better-educated? As I slept, would someone be photo-graphing page by page with a mini camera and shielded flash that Top Secret study of the Soviet missile complex round Hanoi, the Secret list of Cuban agents East of Suez or the Confidential analysis of the last rice harvest in China?

In fact, I was rarely ever sent, and I certainly never ever held for more than a few hours, anything like such material. The 'need to know' principle was carefully applied by the Foreign Office and full account was taken of the strength, or otherwise, of my security. A visiting technical inspector had been all over the building as soon as my initial dispositions had been made. On the rare occasions when particular, highly sensitive, secrets needed to be imparted to me or my staff because of their immediate operational relevance to our daily tasks, the authorities invariably preferred us to pop over to Singapore, Bangkok or some other secure point in order to brief ourselves. I recall on one occasion flying down to my old haunts in Phoenix Park, to see the evidence for the allegation then being levelled in certain US quarters that the Viet Cong had established rest camps, supply dumps and other logistic facilities in inaccessible areas of Cambodia near the Vietnamese frontier.

Nevertheless, I continued to patch and improve and re-build, as funds were made available from London and inspiration and energy was forthcoming. The walls and ceiling of the strong room were

strengthened with reinforced concrete. A canopy of similar material was inserted above the ceiling of certain offices, to prevent rioters lifting the tiles on the roof and descending through the plaster. The grille doors had steel plates welded on the back to prevent stones being hurled through the bars at the defenders. Riot bolts, strong and readily shot across, were fitted here and there. Bars went into undefended windows on the first floor; steel shutters, rolling horizontally on a wheeled track, were built into the Registry windows so that staff could carry on with their duties unmolested in the event of attack; padlocks were replaced by new designs; keys and combinations were changed; riot alarm-bells and a state-of-the-art, anti-intruder device were installed.

Surveillance also was tightened up. The premises, already electronically 'swept' to check for listening devices, were further screened and tested at intervals by visiting teams of specialists. The Chancery was watched and visited outside office hours. I continued my predecessors' arrangement whereby the male members of the staff took it in turn to visit the Chancery through the night and over the weekends, at irregular but frequent intervals, to check that all was in order. I carried out similar independent checks of my own, at all hours. Several times a week, especially when returning from some late-night party in the early hours, I would drop by to see that all was well. In addition, the building and grounds were under casual surveillance at all times – a member of my staff lived in a bungalow adjoining the offices at the back, another later occupied a house closely overlooking the front of the offices and grounds from across a narrow side-street (when it had fallen vacant, a communist Embassy approached the owner – but I got in first), while reliable, Cambodian ancillary staff lived in quarters adjacent on the further side.

I conclude, on the new order of things, with a word about 'panache'. For the first six or seven months, we avoided any unnecessary local expenditure, on the grounds that the Embassy might have to be withdrawn completely at any moment. By Christmas, however, it had become clear that the status quo might last indefinitely. Therefore, the time had come to smarten up.

The Residence was due for a face-lift and was repainted. New curtains, carpets and awnings replaced those faded and rotten with tropical mildew; old furniture was repaired or replaced. The small garden, lately neglected, was tended again. A brightly-painted, cast-iron representation of the Royal Coat of Arms and a flag pole went

up over the main entrance. A medium-size, ambassadorial flag, its white stripes dazzlingly new, fluttered in the bright sunshine.

In the Chancery grounds, the wrecked cars parked under the trees were finally removed to the breaker's yard. The last of the brickbats and broken glass were picked out of the soil and a beautiful and extensive garden began to take shape; flowers of all kinds sprang up in well-tended borders, surrounding a new *pelouse anglaise* (English lawn – not normally a feature of French-style premises). The Chancery building too, like the Residence, was restored, re-painted and re-equipped. Pictures went up again in corridors and offices, and another Royal Coat of Arms over the entrance. New khaki uniforms were issued to our messengers, sweepers and other menial staff. In the dead centre of the front lawn, the flag pole was lowered, re-painted a glossy white, fitted with a new pulley and hoist and raised again to carry another new national flag.

Finally there was the problem of the Ambassadorial Austin Princess, which had seen long years of arduous, tropical service and not-less-arduous servicing, and which was beginning to cost more in repairs than it was worth. We dared not take it out of the city for fear it would break down catastrophically. This was my one failure, in the great face-lift campaign. A new vehicle, with air-conditioner, had, in the normal course of replacement routine, been ear-marked for us before I arrived on the scene. After the 'events', it was decided to postpone shipment and, by the time the coast was definitely clear for delivery, the machine had been sent to some other Embassy. But I was not to be deprived, at least for use in the better-paved streets near the Embassy, of a vehicle which had become a living legend in the capital – huge, black and bug-eyed, it reared its lofty roof, rusty chrome and blistered paintwork over the heads of all other traffic; and was considered by *le tout Phnom Penh* to be vastly superior to the French Ambassador's Citroën or the Soviet Ambassador's Zim. So London agreed to supply new tyres and shock absorbers, and to meet the cost of a re-spray.

5

Labour and Leisure, New-Style

So, we had slashed and re-shuffled Embassy staff; we had fixed 'security'; we had re-ordered 'admin'; we had generally smartened the place up again. But what did the residual diplomatic Mission actually do? This chapter deals with the steady tramp in the Chancery treadmill – and also with how we relaxed.

A major task was routine reporting to the Foreign Office. The normal centre receiving these reports was the South-East Asia Department (SEAD), headed by a Counsellor, supported by two Assistants (both senior First Secretaries). These three men handled a wide range of regional questions. Above them, for the really big issues, sat an Under-Secretary of State, who dealt with business affecting the entire South-East Asian, Far Eastern and Pacific scene. Under them were a handful of juniors, in what was called the 'Third Room' of the Department, to each of whom was allocated responsibility for a country or a small group of countries within the field with which SEAD was concerned. This gave me a 'desk officer' who devoted all his time to us in Phnom Penh and to one other post in the area (Bangkok).

In putting a letter about developments in Cambodia into the diplomatic bag, I therefore had the choice of addressing it by name to any one of four officials: the Under-Secretary, the Head of Department, the relevant Assistant Head or the specialist in the Third Room. In practice it did not matter much which I chose, since the letter would be circulated to whoever needed to see it, and carefully perused in the Third Room before being acted on or filed away. When I used the bag, however, I usually wrote direct to the desk officer, for two reasons: first, to keep him personally involved – he was a key figure, with modest but appreciable executive authority, from whom it was obviously sensible to get the most; second, in

order to keep my powder dry – one would want the full attention and personal sympathy of the seniors whenever things came to a crunch, so one did well not to pester them too much on more routine matters.

But the pivotal official was the Head of SEAD – for me it was a Counsellor called James Cable. (Seven years later, I was to find myself his Number Two on the Policy Planning Staff – the FCO 'think tank' attached directly to the Permanent Under-Secretary of State and Head of the Diplomatic Service.) He completed his service as Ambassador and KCVO in Finland, only to complete a PhD at Cambridge in his retirement. James and I had our occasional differences over policy towards Cambodia, but I recognised in him both intellect and professional integrity. He was balanced and imperturbable under pressure. He always listened carefully to whatever I had to say from Phnom Penh, and when he disagreed, he explained why, promptly and fully. He was certainly an expert on Indo-China – he had been present at the Geneva Conference in 1954.

Then there were our major and more formal reports, in the shape of 'Despatches', addressed through the bag from me to the Foreign Secretary. Sometimes, they would be analyses of the local situation – such as 'Domestic Political Discontent' (reporting that Sihanouk's regime was safe in the short term, but insecure in the longer term) or 'think-pieces' recommending policies which the British Government might pursue – such as 'The Future of the International Control Commission' (proposing a reinforcement). Sometimes, they might be descriptive of an important local event – *e.g.* 'The State Visit of General de Gaulle' or 'The Indo-Chinese Peoples' Conference'; or they might consist of routine briefing updates – like 'The Annual Review for 1965' or 'Leading Personalities in Cambodia, 1964'. Such Despatches would by no means all be read by the Foreign Secretary personally. This would depend on whether South-East Asia Department thought it worthwhile to submit the Despatch to him with their comments, or on whether the Private Secretaries of the Minister took their own decision to pass it on, for information (they combed through a mass of background material each day, aiming to pick out what was most urgent or interesting) and, in any case, on whether The Great Man, amid all his other tasks and worries, actually found time to look at it. I wrote only a dozen major Despatches while I was serving in Phnom Penh. Even this was more than would be expected from a small post, in 'normal' circumstances.

But circumstances were not normal in Cambodia. Almost all Despatches from Phnom Penh were, in the event, printed on the Foreign Office presses for a wide circulation throughout Whitehall and to other overseas Embassies. For three of them, I received an appreciative personal comment from the Foreign Secretary of the day (R.A. Butler, Patrick Gordon Walker, Michael Stewart) and on one – my 'Farewell Impressions' – from the Prime Minister (Harold Wilson). This was indicative, not of the timeless quality of my prose, but of the degree of political interest then taken at 'The Top' in London in what happened to Cambodia.

Finally, there were our diplomatic cables. We used them to conduct a dialogue with 'The Office', whenever we needed urgent instructions or they needed to know quickly what was happening in Cambodia. Naturally, there had to be a self-denying ordinance at our end – if one sent too many telegrams on insufficiently important or urgent matters, one would lose the attention of one's audience and court a rebuke. So I tried (not always successfully) to keep them down in number and in length. And I also usually cultivated the habit of setting out the gist, the very barest essential of the message, clearly in the first paragraph – what is now called the 'executive summary'. This meant that harassed junior officials and pre-occupied senior people could see at a glance what the telegram was about. There were dangers in this trick: it could result in oversimplification or give too journalistic, even sensationalist, a flavour. Nevertheless I knew for myself, from my days as a Resident Clerk, how frustrating it could be to Ministers and Under-Secretaries, always very busy and sometimes without specialised background knowledge of a given country or issue, to have to wade through pages of learned description and measured comment before getting to the bottom of what the originator of the telegram really had to say.

Fully as important as reporting on the Cambodian scene was the transaction of business with the Cambodian authorities – for instance, over the renewal of an Anglo-Cambodian Civil Aviation Agreement or the payment of compensation by the Cambodians for damage done in the riots, or the preparation for the abortive Peace Conference, of which more later. In a lower key, the Embassy would often be instructed by the Foreign Office to pass to, or seek from, the Cambodian Government information on a range of international issues. We might want to notify them of a new ratification to the Load Line Convention, of which London was the repository, or to enquire how Cambodia intended to vote on the South-West Africa

issue at the United Nations, or to discuss the financing of the International Control Commissions in Indo-China. We might be asked to take up something on behalf of a British colonial administration – or of an independent Commonwealth country which had no mission accredited in Phnom Penh (say, Malaysia).

It was enough on some occasions simply to send in an official *Note Verbale* to the Cambodian Ministry of Foreign Affairs. These grave and courteous documents began with a presentation of the Embassy's compliments to the Ministry and with a declaration of the honour which the Embassy had to refer to the issue concerned, and ended by seizing the opportunity of renewing to the Ministry the expression of the Embassy's highest consideration. Whenever possible, however, I preferred to take action by calling directly on the Cambodian Minister or senior official concerned. Where the issue was complex, on which I wanted to be sure that what I said had been properly understood, I would leave behind with my interlocutor what was known in the trade as a '*bout de papier*' – literally, a 'piece of paper', which summarised the facts or arguments I had endeavoured to put across, and which I invariably couched in French. Usually, however, where the Cambodians were well briefed, or if the subject was a politically delicate one, an oral exchange of views did the trick nicely – where appropriate, outside the office on a one-on-one basis.

We also maintained appropriate contact with the other foreign diplomatic missions in Phnom Penh. With the more serious among them (including, for example, the discreet but unfailingly helpful Japanese), we had news to swap, interests in common. What, however, with hindsight, was sadly lacking, at that early stage in the history of the European Union, was any attempt whatsoever at what is now called 'Political Co-Operation' – regular meetings between the Heads of Mission of EU Member States, to share information and attempt to reach a policy consensus. As it was, I found myself largely on my own, at least where my European colleagues were concerned – although I worked hard on the well-placed and usually well-informed French.

Naturally, I made myself generally available to leading pressmen from both inside and outside Cambodia. And I tried to keep open house, socially, at the Residence to a cross-section of people in a range of employ and various walks of life. This gave me the 'feel' of what lay behind the headlines in the day's papers, or of what lay in the hearts of men that was not declared upon their lips. In principle,

I accepted all invitations out and I was, by definition, present – to see and be seen – at all official and state occasions in the capital.

The small British community, too, had a claim on my time, as did any visiting British businessmen. They could come and see me whenever they wanted, in the Chancery or at the Residence, to discuss their personal scrapes or professional pre-occupations or conditions of life and trade in Phnom Penh. Passports had to be issued or renewed and records of births, marriages and deaths kept scrupulously up to date. In my consular safe there reposed a Royal Warrant, authorising the Consul or Consul General of the day to solemnise matrimony – a right and duty which, beyond the confines of the British Isles, sea captains and consular officers share with ministers of religion. On one happy, and early, occasion in Phnom Penh, I was to act under this Warrant to marry two of my flock.

But I have strayed from the precincts of the Chancery, with the air-conditioner rattling away and the palm trees swaying beyond the window. In those soothing office surroundings there was a lot of paperwork to be done that by no stretch of the imagination could be invested with glamour yet by no stroke of the pen relegated to others.

Thus the monthly Embassy accounts, however well presented by the Accountant and however carefully vetted by the Vice Consul, had to be checked again by me and signed on the dotted line to that effect. I was ultimately accountable to Parliament, and indeed the British tax payer, for how the money was spent.

Another necessary distraction was that of staff assessment. Confidential reports on the performance of each UK-based officer were required at annual intervals by the Personnel Department in the Foreign Office. They had to be carefully drawn up, to ensure that they were as fair as was humanly possible; and each required a frank private interview with the individual concerned.

I come, next, to the Embassy at play. It was the other side of a single coin. In crisis conditions, people will almost always rise to the challenge and for lengthy periods work quite excessive hours. But they will also need to let off steam and must sometimes be helped to do so. How does a Head of Mission make this possible without acting as a 'Red Coat' at a Butlins holiday camp?

'In this establishment, gentlemen, we work hard – and we also play hard.' I had heard this said to me on various occasions in my younger life: at schools, colleges and military gatherings before arriving in Cambodia. I was never greatly enthused by such declarations. I did not

mind working hard, but had my doubts about being instructed to
'play hard' – it did not sound pleasurable and I suspected had all too
much to do with hard kicks in the rugby scrum, or a four-minute
mile or leaping over armchairs in a dusty Officers' Mess in a pair of
tight 'patrols'. I used to endure all these things in their day and now
look back on them with a certain sense of achievement – I was, for
example, in the First XV at school. As Terence wrote, 'I count
nothing human foreign to me'; yet my heart was usually elsewhere.

In Phnom Penh, we did in fact work 'hard' and play 'hard' quite
naturally, without exhortation or self-consciousness. And the play
was necessary for the work. As Marius once said (Sallust, *The
Jugurthine War*):

> I shall not make my soldiers go short while enjoying
> the best of everything myself, nor steal all the glory and
> leave them the toil. This is the proper way for a citizen
> to lead his citizens. To live in luxury oneself while
> subjecting one's army to rigorous discipline is to act
> like a tyrant instead of a commander.

The principle is a sound one: to get the best out of people on
parade, by ensuring that they are reasonably happy off parade.

It applies particularly, within the Diplomatic Service, to posts
where for one reason or another – climatic, sociological, political or
even linguistic – normal life as we know it in Britain is impossible,
where it is difficult to get to know and to mix with the local populace,
to travel about freely, or to find suitable distractions outside office
hours. At such posts, boredom is liable to set in all too quickly, and
a host of evils can follow at boredom's heels, if remedial steps are
not taken. People become apathetic in the office and depressed
when they go home. They may start drinking too much and falling
out among themselves, nurturing inbred resentments and insane
vendettas. Little things assume disproportionate importance and an
inward-looking community develops into a snake pit. If there is
menace in the air, that menace seems all the heavier. If there is bad
company about, then some people will gravitate towards it. During
the 'Cold War', such conditions could be an ideal background for
operations by the KGB or other hostile intelligence services, whose
agents might seek to recruit members of British Embassies by
befriending the lonely, beguiling the gullible and blackmailing the
imprudent and indiscreet. For good security, as well as for workaday
efficiency, good Embassy morale was of the essence.

In almost all British diplomatic missions, large or small, the task of watching over all this was normally delegated by the Ambassador to his Adjutant or Chief of Staff, the long-suffering and omni-competent 'Head of Chancery'. The latter was usually responsible, under the Ambassador, for the tone of the Embassy and the general welfare of the staff. In Phnom Penh, this exercise in what the soldiery called 'man-management' fell in theory upon me alone. In practice, however, I was greatly helped by the Military Attaché and especially by his wife. The latter fulfilled the requirement, which all such communities have, for a sort of female 'father-confessor', someone approachable and with just the right combination of the qualities of *grande dame* and plain good old *mum*.

We inherited much from our predecessors. The previous Head of Chancery had been sound on welfare, and had put the case for it squarely to me during our handover. I invented and improvised as I went along; I quite soon produced a pattern well-suited to the tastes of the new team and to the changed conditions in which we operated. What in effect was laid on was an active community life both indoors and outdoors, to match the cracking pace set during the working day.

Nevertheless, there was one unspoken rule: there was no 'jollying along', no heavy pressure to 'join'. If the individual chose to get on with some knitting, to read a book, or simply to snooze away a short afternoon, that was perfectly acceptable to the rest of us. In this respect, Embassy life was, to misapply a phrase from the Book of Common Prayer, 'a service of perfect freedom'.

There was much party-giving, and party-going. Outside my more jaundiced moments, I naturally enjoyed this. People were relaxed. I got to know another side to them, other than that presented to me in the rush and tear of working hours. I liked to have my staff regularly to my own house, sometimes for lunch and a gossip, sometimes to cocktails for the British community as a whole, sometimes to a buffet supper and dancing to Françoise Hardy or Charles Aznavour in the cool of the night. Occasionally, if there was something personal to talk over, or if I thought the individual might want to weep on my shoulder a little, I would fix up a quiet *tête à tête* in one of the bistros in town. The Military Attaché did likewise. So too, on a smaller scale, did the Vice Consul. The staff gave their own parties to which we were often invited and at which I was scrupulous to put in an appearance, whenever business permitted – at Scottish dancing sessions, ping-pong competitions and home film shows.

Then there was Holy Church. There was no Anglican priest in Cambodia; the Bishop was based in Singapore and the nearest clergyman (an American Episcopalian called Tad Evans) in Saigon. But this did not deter us. We had a portable altar and we used to bring in the priest from Saigon every month or two. Usually the service was held in the drawing room of the Ambassador's Residence, specially decked out for the occasion with hassocks and candles and lace and flowers. Despite having been in earlier days a keen High Churchman, and even a potential candidate for Holy Orders, and despite subsequently becoming, ten years later, a pious Anglican 'Reader', I was at that time a lapsed, non-practising Anglican. But I still thought well of the Church. The fact was that Protestant members of my staff and of the outside community were keen on having a service and used to turn up regularly in good numbers when there was one (the Roman Catholics attended the local churches of the French missionaries). I gave this exercise my full support. Afterwards, there was always supper for anyone who cared to stay and of course every opportunity for anyone who had problems to talk privately to the priest. As far as I knew, none of my staff had any major problems of a kind which needed 'ghostly counsel and advice'; but I always liked the idea of having a real father-confessor on hand, to do anything which Mrs Robson or I could not.

There was quite a good yacht club in Phnom Penh and an even better sports club with a large swimming pool and numerous tennis courts. There was also a pool at the Hotel Royal which those taking lunch there could use. But the clubs were expensive to belong to and the hotel was often crowded. I therefore acquired, for the Embassy's use, a house-boat on the river. Having shipped in a fibre-glass dinghy from Japan and a powerful outboard motor from Singapore, we were in the water-skiing business. The scheme was a great success. The house-boat was essentially a boathouse for the dinghy. But there were also rooms to change in, a storeroom and – most useful of all – a long wide verandah shaded by a banana-leaf roof, with wicker chairs where we could sit and watch the fun. I gave a farewell official luncheon there for a dozen or so Cambodian guests in the greatest of style, the Embassy silver winking on the white tablecloth and a portable, but muted, gramophone playing music by the band of the Royal Marines in the background. The boat and the house were guarded and maintained by a Cambodian Muslim from the minority Cham; he and his wife and children lived on a little boat

moored beside us. I used to exchange greetings and devout expressions with him in Arabic (a language of which, however, he in fact knew only enough to say his basic prayers) and one day I presented him to his astonishment (he could not read) with a copy of the Holy Koran. He was a general favourite with us. I doubt that he survived Pol Pot.

When we tired of the river, there were always expeditions to be made into the countryside. Most of the staff had small cars of their own and those that did not, had no difficulty hitching lifts. In the rainy season, we would take the official, long-wheel-base Landrovers. I used to like going to the site of some ruined temple of the era of the Khmer Empire. Once, with a visiting *Daily Mirror* pressman, we went far North, to Sambor Prey Kuk, an enormous site lost in the jungle and accessible along the last stages of the route only by a narrow laterite track running through the forest. The trip took a long day, there and back. I still have a photograph of us all, standing on the steps of one of the ruins in the angular attitudes of Oriental dancers (see page 92). Food and cans of frozen beer came tumbling out of ice boxes. After lunch, we wandered for an hour or two among the weed-grown, jungle-festooned temples, feeling alien yet (as almost always in Cambodia) not unwelcome. The solitude beyond our immediate circle was intense. We rarely, if ever, met foreigners at such places. It takes mad dogs and Englishmen ...

My other main contribution to the Embassy's human welfare was in making it possible for staff to take regular breathers outside Cambodia. If you live in a lighthouse, the time comes when you need to row hard for the shore. Each of us took his or her turn with the diplomatic bag, which had to be carried to and from Bangkok once a fortnight. This gave the escorting officer the inside of three days to see the sights, buy things which could not be found in Phnom Penh, eat Walls' ice-creams and see an American movie. On leave proper, Hong Kong (a shopper's paradise) and Singapore were accessible by direct flight from Cambodia. After 12 months *en poste*, the Government would pay a fare home to the UK for a leave of absence of up to six weeks. This was decent recompense for the climate and conditions of work, but it posed administrative problems – it meant that, even with everyone's leave neatly staggered, we were all too often one short. Yet no one is indispensable and we mostly muddled through without having to call in a spare body from London or from a nearby post to fill the temporary gap.

I should mention here the infrastructure of daily life. Accommodation was important. I did my best to ensure that it was fully up to standard. This had not always been true in Phnom Penh. Western-style houses and flats were not many, and the city itself was far from large. The influx of foreigners – diplomats, United Nations representatives, businessmen and aid personnel – in the years following national independence, and also the growth of the economy, had touched off a cheap housing boom and caused whole suburbs to spring up in the surrounding marshes. So housing was often quite tight, rents were high and the richer Americans had inevitably taken the pick of the market. Around 1964, however, this market was mauled by a bear. American aid had been cut off and the supervising personnel sent home the previous year. After the attacks on the US and UK Embassies, diplomatic personnel began to thin out. Finally, the Americans were kicked out altogether. Prices dropped, villas stood vacant and we took the opportunity to terminate leases on sub-standard property and to put the staff into accommodation of good quality and – as already mentioned – well-sited from the point of view of security.

Then there was the food problem. The Phnom Penh market was good in its way (plenty of adequate beef and pork, for example) but limited and, as regarded anything imported, enormously expensive. We were too small an Embassy to run a commissary or shop of our own. So we grouped together to place joint orders for drink and canned goods to be shipped in from Hong Kong. For butter, bacon and lamb, we had to resort to the expensive solution of having it flown in frozen from Singapore – by that time, because of the intensity of the fighting in South Vietnam, few refrigerated ships still sailed up the Mekong. In the Chancery, there was a monster deep-freeze in which, carefully labelled, everyone kept what was his; the Military Attaché and I (we both had a bigger consumption, because of the scale of our official entertaining) shared another deep-freeze at my Residence. All these supplies came in duty free, so in the end no one was too badly out of pocket.

Health, too, was a vital factor in morale. Cambodia is a tropical country: hot, humid and not far from the Equator. It was tiring to work hard in, initially at least, until one grew acclimatised. There were bugs. In the period preceding my arrival, the Embassy had had the bad luck to pass through a seedy patch. The Head of Chancery had gone down with malaria and the previous Military Attaché had been sent home to the Hospital for Tropical Diseases with a nasty

microbe in him after only six months' service. Various people, including the Ambassador and the Vice Consul, had been laid low with bouts of dengue fever and staff were affected by a crop of minor ailments and afflictions. There was little to be done about the incidence of such evils: this was the normal toll in a hot and steamy climate. However, I was worried. With its now-skeleton staff, the Embassy risked on occasion being put right out of business. In fact, the run of bad luck ended and we got away, in my time, virtually scot-free. Admittedly, we were all fitter and younger. Nevertheless because most of us found ourselves travelling at some point or another (on official business or snooping for intelligence) away from the beaten track of civilisation and out into frontier districts, deep forest and remote savannah where the medical troubles often lay, I saw to it that we all took serious prophylactic medical precautions as well. Health discipline was tightened up and the rules rammed down everyone's throats. Water had to be thoroughly boiled, before it was drunk; people had to take anti-malaria pills when going outside Phnom Penh and to take care what they ate in wayside restaurants. The Treasury doctors sent me out through the bag a set of the latest pills for everything and I saw these were readily available from the Vice Consul's office. The anopheles, malaria-bearing, mosquito did not infest the city; but to keep at bay his non-noxious but still painful brothers, I bought a spraying apparatus with which the Embassy gardener regularly went over the Chancery grounds and the gardens of Embassy houses and flats.

So much for the welfare problem and how we tackled it. As I later realised, I probably molly-coddled people too much, in the fashion of the Welfare State at home, and of everything that has ceased to breed hard Englishmen. I may also have been too paternalist about it, playing the role of the gracious squire. But though the decisions were mine, their execution fell to all of us: it was essentially a group endeavour to look after ourselves and make the most of things. That Edwardian hero and delightful arch-imperialist, Lord Baden-Powell, used to say of the hardships of campaigning in Ashanti or the North-West Frontier that any fool can be uncomfortable. We saw to it that we were not. There was, for me personally, a further consolation. I knew my staff well, their weak points and their strong. Without, I hoped, the appearance of interfering in their private lives, I knew more or less how they lived and who were their friends; I felt reasonably confident that no one was letting the Embassy down or likely to get into a major personal scrape that could be avoided. In any case

they achieved the results that I wanted, in and around the Chancery: I did not grudge any of them their full meed of pleasure, off duty.

To conclude this chapter, I set out what a typical day looked like under the new dispensation.

At six, then seven, I listen to the news in French on Phnom Penh radio and in English from the BBC's general overseas service; then drive across town to arrive at the Chancery well before eight. The first thing is quickly to scan the local morning newspapers and any overnight inward telegrams from the Foreign Office. There follows a brief morning meeting with the Military Attaché and the Vice Consul, followed by the dictation of one or two letters for London: administrative, commercial or political. These go straight into the confidential bag for London closing at 10.30 am. There is a smell of sealing wax and a clerical and secretarial bustle in all the offices: there will not be another bag carrying classified mail for a fortnight. The Military Attaché, having debriefed on yesterday's frontier incident, sets off to see a senior Cambodian General. The Vice Consul chairs another meeting in his own office. My own immediate desk-work finished, I ride off just before 10 am in the Austin Princess, flag waving, to pay a call on the Soviet Ambassador: when can a reply be expected from Moscow to the Foreign Secretary's latest message, and what does His Excellency himself think of the prospects for a new peace conference? After three quarters of an hour's Soviet disinformation and sophistry, the time comes to take my leave and move on to the Cambodian Ministry of Foreign Affairs, where I have an appointment with the Secretary General. I have thought out carefully what I want to say. In the cool of his office, I begin to say my piece – moderate in phrasing, with the employment of indirect allusions where to say a thing directly and brutally would cause offence. The Secretary General replies in the same gentle, oblique cipher. We each get the other's message. The tyres of my car turn in the hot gravel and I ride off through the city again, bright and burning in the sun overhead. At noon, I am back at my desk, drafting a telegram for London, which I pass to the clerk for encryption and thence to the wireless operator.

I lunch with some resident businessmen in a bar downtown, doing most of the listening and trying not to drink as copiously as they. After all, they have their long siesta before them, while I still have half a day's work to do. I am back at the Chancery soon after it reopens at 3 pm. There is some administrative work to be got out of the way – with the help of some strong coffee from my secretary to

keep me wide awake. The Military Attaché and I report to each other the outcome of our respective morning calls. The Japanese Coun-sellor calls at 4.30 pm, by previous arrangement, to talk shop and to pass over some very interesting information received from his contacts up-country. I return the compliment, with my own hot news. Most of the staff go home at 6 pm to shower and change into clean dry shirts and dresses before coming round for a beer with me at the Residence at 7.30 pm. I hang on an extra half an hour in the Chancery, in case the late-afternoon wireless contact with London yields any urgent incoming message. Fortunately, it does not; but I have meanwhile not wasted my time, having telephoned a news-paper editor to ask whether the next morning's edition will be carrying an Embassy announcement I have sent him.

I drive back shirt-sleeved to my house in my open Triumph, feeling the breeze cool the damp spot between my shoulder-blades, watching the streets and shops come alive again in the shadows of the early evening. My (Vietnamese) staff are there to open the gate and I rush upstairs and straight into a hot bath. I wiggle my toes and think for five minutes; then soap off the sweat, shower, towel down and slip into the ruffled shirt and light-weight tuxedo which will be required later in the evening. I hear voices and footsteps on the terrace below and come down to find my staff already arriving for that cool drink. Cool it is, with the moisture forming round the outside of the glass; and down it goes, helped on its way with a handful of salted cashew nuts. We sit around and relax and gossip and someone plays the gramophone. Then the lads and lasses troop off to their dinners.

The Austin Princess crunches up the gravel drive at 8.30 pm and at 8.45 pm I leave for the Palace. The sun has set two hours before and a dark-blue, velvet sky is overhead. The lights are winking among the trees at the edge of town as I approach. Someone opens the door of the car and I walk solemnly up the steps, incline my head, shake hands with the Head of State and his Consort and move off to mingle with the other guests. I side-step two notorious bores and try to trap a VIP. But I am frustrated in my turn, so I plan an ambush for later and turn to the Minister of Industry, to talk about our new contract for a jute-mill. Later, I come across the UN Special Representative, appointed by U Thant to attempt to mediate in the dispute between Cambodia and Thailand. We stroll out onto the balcony beneath the stars for a private chat until we are driven in again by mosquitoes or a violent display of fireworks in the grounds

below us. The evening rolls majestically onward. There is a buffet supper and dancing and half a moon sailing over the dark mystery of the landscape. My driver yawns his way home with me at 1 am, while I jot down on a slip of paper what I need to recall of such business as I have been able to transact. In bed at last, I set the alarm for 5.50 am.

Not all days were as full of deeds as the one I have just described. Others were much fuller. Sometimes I used to shut myself off from all but the very minimum routine chores and just read or wrote or thought in a fleeting oasis of calm – clearing my 'pending' tray; sorting out some new ideas; sketching the outline of a despatch on a blank piece of paper. A good time for undisturbed ratiocination was one of the two weekday afternoons when the Chancery was closed for business and my staff were snoring away their lunches or water-skiing on the River Bassac. Naturally when I couldn't stand the sight of another official document, I chucked in the hand and joined the others on the river.

6

Learning to be an 'Ambassador'

Building a secure Embassy was, if tedious and time-consuming, at least not too difficult. Nor was the improvisation of a new, office routine and the oversight of staff welfare and morale. But finding my own professional, diplomatic feet as Head of Mission (and establishing my own personal style of engagement with the Cambodians) took longer, and proved harder. Nevertheless, from shortly after my arrival, I felt it in my bones that, before very long, we should be called on to take the diplomatic initiative. In the event, as recounted in the following five chapters, the Embassy was indeed to move over once again to the offensive. So there was much more to be done, if the Brits were to become fully 'fit for purpose'.

I launched myself into an immediate crash programme of intensive study. I read everything I could lay my hands on, about the history, customs, religion and politics of Cambodia. Public libraries did not exist, or were denuded and unhelpful. But there was quite a good little library in the Chancery, much of which had been left untouched in the riots. I exchanged books with friendly foreign colleagues; others were ordered (via the diplomatic bag) from the ever helpful Foreign Office Printed Library. I scanned the latter's monthly list of new accessions for whatever was fresh from the publishing houses.

Then there was the press and radio. Each day, I skimmed through all the local newspapers. With particular care, I read from cover to cover the daily bulletin in French of the official Cambodian press agency, the *Agence Khmère de Presse* – thirty to forty invaluable pages of government declarations, speeches and miscellaneous official assessments. In addition, I received from London summaries and translations of the more important public speeches in Cambodian delivered up and down the country by the Head of State and

simultaneously broadcast by the Cambodian radio; these speeches, admirably frank and mostly addressed, in a down-to-earth manner, to provincial and rural Cambodian audiences, were a useful complement to what I already knew about the country and its leadership and what was going on. There were instructive differences between what the Prince had actually said and what the *Agence Khmère de Presse* elected to translate into French and publish in the official bulletin a day or two later. Naturally, I listened to the French-language radio myself whenever I could, so as to be a few hours ahead of what would subsequently appear in print. I listened to the Cambodian-language broadcasts occasionally, whenever I needed to know the 'tone' in which the news was read, or the mood in which the Head of State was delivering a speech (my Cambodian was never good enough to tell me a great deal more).

On that last point, having spoken fluently the language of the land (Persian) at my previous Embassy post abroad (Tehran), I was at the outset rather worried about the problem of communication in Cambodia, where the local tongue was completely unknown to me. I soon found, however, that the only basic necessary chore was to bring my French up to scratch. Happily, I had had a very solid, if purely academic, grounding at school and university and a more hands-on, vernacular, exposure during one long summer at the Sorbonne. I had also been using French in my previous job in the Foreign Office (both NATO and WEU were bilingual international organisations). This stood me in good stead in Phnom Penh where, ten years on from the end of the Protectorate, the French language continued to be the effective *lingua franca* for foreigners and Cambodians alike. Today, after so many upheavals, French has all but disappeared from Cambodia. But, in the 1960s, it was much used in the higher reaches of the Government machine, particularly at the Ministry of Foreign Affairs. Almost all written communications between my Embassy and the Ministry were in French and every Minister and official spoke it fluently; indeed, I myself never met in those days a Cambodian who had no notion at all of the French language.

It would have been unwise and arrogant, however, to have ignored the Cambodian tongue completely. I accordingly taught myself what I could glean from an American grammar book and I took enough lessons to gain a smattering. This was, I would add, not at all out of pedantry or political correctness. The structure of a language can tell you something of the thought processes of those who speak

it. It was good to be able to establish some primitive verbal contact in the vernacular with the people around me. This usually brought broad grins to Khmer faces. With the ice so broken, one could then continue in French. Finally, I have never felt fully at ease, when foreigners can talk twenty to the dozen at me, or over my head, without my being able to catch even one word of what they are saying. If someone has to be uneasy, I prefer it to be the other fellow who can never be sure how much I may, or may not, have understood.

Upon the foregoing – admittedly mostly bookish – foundation, I tried to build up my 'feel' for Cambodia by direct observation and personal contact. I talked to Cambodians whenever the sanctions imposed on the Embassy permitted them to talk to me; I formed nodding acquaintances with people at receptions and dinner parties; I attended local weddings and funerals; I mixed as best I could with the local jet set in the night clubs; I went to see the rare but instructive Cambodian movie.

There was also another possible meeting place with top Cambodians – an establishment known simply as *La Mère Chhum*. (See Cameo III on page xxix.) It was a high-class opium den and bar, operated discreetly in a cosy villa on the edge of town. The house itself was said (by the Cambodian who introduced me to it) to be in the ownership of the Queen Mother and therefore to enjoy 'protection'. However that might have been, old Mrs. Chhum included Cambodian aristos, ministers and senior officials among her clients. But not normally foreign diplomats. The place initially served quite well to break the ice and put me on the map with the movers and shakers. But *La Mère Chhum* was not to prove too productive, professionally, and I dropped it, gratefully, when contact became much easier. But I went there less than half a dozen times, for a very expensive beer (not, of course, for a pipe) and a chat, sitting in the smoky shadows with *Votre Altesse* or *Votre Excellence* or *Mon Cher Monsieur* or whatever VIP happened to be around that evening. The setting was picturesque, even exotic – and something like it might have featured in Francis Ford Coppola's film *Apocalypse Now*.

Then there were the various ceremonial and State occasions to which, as the Head of a Diplomatic Mission, I was always scrupulously invited and at which one could see and get to know the Grandees of the Kingdom. My predecessors had handed down to me a large indexed note book in which, in alphabetical order, had been stuck photographs, culled mostly from the press, of most of the leading figures of the realm. Over this, and the associated file

index of potted biographies, I bent my head in the Chancery, amending and bringing it up to date and trying to form at a distance the impressions which, in those early and difficult days, it was not always easy to gather at close hand. Drawing inwardly on this material, I would sit observing the scene at State openings of Parliament, at the Water Festival ceremonies or the Rites of the Sacred Furrow, at Banquets at the Palace or Committees of Welcome at the airport in honour of a visiting Head of State. To begin with, the Cambodian Big-Wigs looked very much alike to me. Indeed, I was still sometimes at a loss to place someone, even after two years and more on the job.

Phnom Penh was where the action mostly was – seat of the Government, site of the throne and centre of all decisions. Yet within the limits of the time available and the practicality of the route, I would also get out into the country to see what it looked like and what the people were doing. The Foreign Office in London did not like me to leave the Chancery for more than a day or two at a time, unless there was a very good reason (like the examination of something contentious and intriguing up-country), or I could assure them that all was quiet in the capital. They preferred to have – and I accepted the point – their Chargé d'Affaires at the end of the telegraph (telephonic links did not then exist, let alone video-conferencing, as today), to avoid nasty political surprises. Yet I covered, little by little, whether on my own or with colleagues or visitors, or as the guest of the Cambodian Government, much of the country that lay beyond the gates of the capital city, and felt the more confident for it.

Whether in the town or in the country, there was frequent opportunity for a Head of Diplomatic Mission to meet the Head of State, His Royal Highness Prince Norodom Sihanouk. He would throw supper parties and 'dances' in his private palace, at the edge of town. The Cabinet and top brass and social élite of Phnom Penh would be present, with the Diplomatic Corps usually also in attendance. The Prince would chat informally among his guests and occasionally gather a group round himself to talk politics. He would also take us with him on some of his provincial excursions, planting trees, opening hospitals, factories or model farms, inaugurating a stretch of new road or railway line, or celebrating the completion of a dam. The Prince spoke in French with the same engaging frankness on such occasions as in his Cambodian-language broadcasts to his people and we all learned much about his plans and problems. He once said to the French and Russian Ambassadors and myself,

> There's no need for intelligence services in this
> country, gentlemen, because you have me. I will tell
> you all you want to know – let me be your Govern-
> ment's secret agent in Cambodia.

All this was rich fare for a hungry diplomat. But it called for a grain
of salt, some careful sifting and the accompaniment of reliable
collateral material. So, I kept my ears open for the news around
town. Initially, I sought out the opportunity to talk things over
casually with anyone who would fall in with me, from French restau-
rateurs and bar-tenders (invariably pretty much in the picture with
the latest personal gossip or scandal) upwards, playing the ignorant
newcomer card for all it was worth. I benefited from the local knowledge and understanding of Khmer ways possessed collectively by the
French community, among whom I cultivated a cross-section of
acquaintance, and also benefited from the much smaller band of
Commonwealth and American residents – less confident in their
judgements than the French, but not always less perspicacious. I
rarely passed up the chance to discuss the situation with both the
more serious among the local, foreign pressmen and their grander,
visiting international colleagues. The latter, whenever they flew in to
do some serious on-the-spot reporting, were on the whole an impressive bunch. There was always also the occasional low-life hack, out to
grab a headline or earn a cheap giggle from his readers with a hostile
or waggish piece of knocking copy. Given the resentment that such
articles stirred up among the Cambodians, it was well to give such
men a wide berth. But the American press did include in their
number some dedicated, highly professional people whose standards
were of the highest: mostly *New York Times* and *Washington Post*,
but also some brilliant freelancers. I remember their names with
affection to this day – men like Cy Sulzberger, Seymour Topping, Joe
Kraft and Harrison Salisbury. I also gave a grateful welcome to *The
Times*, the *Observer*, the *Economist*, the *Telegraph*, the *Guardian*,
the *Mirror* and of course the (in those days, at least) wholly admirable
BBC.

When contemplating the Cambodian navel became altogether
too sterile or hypnotic a pursuit, I travelled with FO permission
outside the Khmer frontiers, the better to understand the regional
setting, and, in that setting, the better to look back and try to put the
Cambodian scene in a proper perspective.

My first zone of observation was the band of countries bounding Cambodia – Laos, South Vietnam and Thailand. Their problems were also in a sense those of Cambodia. The differences which each of them had with Cambodia were of direct concern to me. These differences were chiefly territorial – lands claimed and frontier-markers disputed – and sprang from centuries of dispute, racial suspicion and aggrandisement, and outright war. What was common to each of them was the threat of communist subversion, from the hostilities raging in Vietnam to the uneasy *de facto* division of Laos, to the first signs of revolt in North-East Thailand, to the shadow of troubles to come which lay across the frontier provinces of still-peaceful Cambodia. Sitting in Phnom Penh, it was essential to know how the other half lived and to see what was going on next door. So I went to have a look. At intervals, I popped over to Bangkok carrying the diplomatic bag, which gave me the chance to see our Embassy people there regularly and meet appropriate Thai officials. Twice, I went over to Saigon, where the Vietnamese Foreign Ministry, the British Embassy and (after their mission was withdrawn from Phnom Penh) the US Embassy were interested to receive a first-hand account of developments in Cambodia. Once I went up to Laos.

In this way, I secured a valuable professional dividend: namely, first-hand and up-to-date political knowledge, which strengthened my hand on my return. I saw far better than before how matters stood in Indo-China and I could bring back to my Cambodian clients wider horizons than those within which they operated while stuck behind their desks in Phnom Penh. After all, I had actually spoken to real-live Vietnamese, Thai and Laotians – with whom some of my Cambodian interlocutors had themselves had no recent contact of any kind.

Travel also paid another dividend: that of getting to know my British colleagues at the adjacent posts. I felt, when I first arrived in Phnom Penh, that I knew pretty well the London set-up. When telegrams and despatches and letters came out to me from the centre, I knew personally the men (and very occasionally, in those days, the women) who had penned them and how their minds worked and what their basic assumptions and objectives were, their blind spots, but also their talents and insights. But the colleagues manning the posts along my own Asian periphery turned out to be largely unknown personally. This worried me.

I suspected that my neighbours did not understand the problems at my post and the kind of handicaps under which I was operating. I

could not be sure that they had personal confidence in me as a colleague. Equally, I did not know how seriously to take them – was their observation sharp, was their judgement sound, or were they just a bunch of clever twerps? Most important was the question – were we all (they and I) capable of seeing and serving the overall strategic British, as well as the local tactical British, interest?

Our government is frequently called, in foreign affairs, to make decisions which affect not merely purely bilateral UK relations with another particular foreign country, but also our relations with several countries together. For example, it may be necessary to take some position on a frontier dispute between Laos and Cambodia. Which one do we back – or, if neither, how do we keep out? Or Cambodia may call upon the United Kingdom, as Co-Chairman of the Geneva Conference, to convene a conference to consider what should be done to help uphold Cambodian neutrality. The Laotians are in favour but the Thai and South Vietnamese are against – what do we do? In the decision-making process in London, full weight is naturally given to the views of our Embassies on the spot. Traditionally, each Ambassador reports the views of the Government to which he is accredited, assesses their likely reactions to each of the contingencies under review, and adds (with the usual preamble: 'as seen from here') his own recommendation for action by Her Majesty's Government. Very often, each Embassy favours a different course and there is a lively telegraphic debate between them and with the Foreign Office before a final option is taken up. This debate can be stimulating and extremely helpful if each Ambassador, as well as 'fighting his own corner' and making absolutely sure that the situation in his neck of the woods is clearly understood by everyone, is also willing to put his local problems in perspective and to accept gracefully and intelligently, when the occasion arises, that the Government at home should, for wider reasons, go ahead with something which will not suit – indeed, may provoke and offend – his local parishioners.

On the whole, the UK Diplomatic Service is good at ensuring that this 'creative tension' leads to collective and broadly viewed decisions. But the temptation is ever present with those in the field to peddle the easy option in the interest of a quiet life and no trouble with the natives. We accordingly occasionally have our lapses. Everyone likes to be popular with his 'customers'.

To return to my immediate pre-occupation in Phnom Penh, I had the impression, on my arrival in Cambodia, that there had been too

much pulling in different directions, each British Ambassador in South-East Asia trying to grab the blanket for himself. Reading the files, it was depressing to turn up the same tired, brass-bound objections to this or that, the same dire, old predictions of the wrath or resentment of this or that party, trotted out from adjacent Chanceries whenever some imaginative move had been contemplated. How far, I asked myself, was all this wisdom based on up-to-date information and persuasive Embassy contact with the local potentates, and how much merely dashed off from the backs of people's heads in their air-conditioned offices? Later on, I was once or twice tempted to do this very thing myself; I was to become familiar with the siren call of self-interest and expedient reporting. But, feeling a twinge of irritation when I read this sort of report and recommendation from, say, Saigon or Bangkok, I made a correspondingly greater effort at detachment and impartiality from Phnom Penh – which did not pass unnoticed in London, where it mattered.

Hence the need to get to know one's area colleagues and if possible (in my own case, as a young and inevitably inexperienced Chargé d'Affaires) to get oneself accepted by them. I worked on this, steadily. Two major opportunities to make some mark opened up for me at the Conferences of British Heads of Mission in Asia which were held in 1964 in Bangkok and 1966 in Hong Kong. Senior people came out from London and Ambassadors from the four corners of Asia closed in on the rendezvous for two or three days' discussions. Seated fluffy-cheeked at a round table of grey beards, I tried on the one hand not to talk too much, but on the other hand to contribute a solid pennyworth whenever I felt sure of my ground. Like a maiden speaker in the Houses of Parliament, I was listened to with courtesy. I made some friends and – at least overtly – no enemies.

I accordingly issued persistent invitations to my neighbouring colleagues to come over to Phnom Penh to see the local set-up for themselves. Over a two-and-a-half-year period, there came to Cambodia our Ambassador in Bangkok and his Number Two, two or three of our people from Vientiane, several men from Saigon (including the Counsellor) and finally my former boss, the Political Adviser from Singapore, and two of his Deputies. They sensibly took a few days' leave in Angkor. But for all of them I also drew up an arduous official programme – calls on Cambodian Ministers and officials, detailed briefing sessions from the Military Attaché and myself, visits up-country and out to the frontier areas. Most of them

left with greater understanding both of my own difficulties and of HMG's objectives in Cambodia.

These exchanges of people and opinions generally took place on a narrow regional basis – in my own backyard or over the garden fence. For my own amusement, but also very much for my instruction, I also took what chances were offered to wander more widely across the Asian scene. I went on business to Singapore, and returned via Kuala Lumpur, where I stayed with our High Commissioner and met some bright, young Malays from the Ministry of External Affairs. On mid-tour leave, I went back to the UK by the Eastern route via Japan and the States. The following spring, I went up from Cambodia to China, for me the greatest cultural experience of all and professionally perhaps the most profitable of my excursions. Later still, when the time came to say my final goodbye to Cambodia, I spent some of my home leave visiting Burma and Indonesia.

But I am leaping too far ahead. For the purposes of the present chapter, I am still in Phnom Penh learning the part and attempting to play it, virtually alone, with no local expertise or ongoing collective wisdom. All that oriental globe-trotting was part of the same frenzy of self-accusing ignorance that kept me compulsively reading and talking and travelling about within Cambodia. There was too much I felt I ought to know; too little chance of grasping it all. The feeling, to begin with, was unpleasant.

Over the months, to overcome it, I plotted some co-ordinates and ploddingly drew up some sort of map of knowledge. I started to write, one by one, a comprehensive clutch of reports and Despatches. I would select a subject on which I wanted to be better informed factually or more confident in my judgements. I would start to collect information about it, mull it over, consult anyone and everything likely to be helpful. Sooner or later – sometimes within a few weeks but usually much longer and sometimes after a year of patient collation – I would be able to send to the Foreign Secretary something reliable and convincing and (if possible) also readable.

Certainly, these papers found their audience in London. But what mattered to me was that each of them represented an informed opinion on something about which I had previously, and uneasily, known little or nothing. I kept them to hand and built on them until, in the end, I became enough of an expert to earn my own self-respect. Confidence grew in proportion and each Despatch gave me more pleasure to write than its predecessor. I analysed the

nature of Cambodian neutrality, the content of Cambodian foreign policy, the working of the Cambodian internal political system. I monitored the slowly growing, domestic opposition, to the left and to the right. I described the personalities and talents of the Cambodian leadership, the policies and presences of the chief foreign powers in Cambodia, the disputes then current with Cambodia's various neighbours. I weighed up the quality and impact of the mostly showy, but unsubstantive, Chinese and Soviet bloc development-assistance programmes in Cambodia. I looked at local political attitudes to communism and to Western democracy and attempted an assessment of the vulnerability of the country to Viet Cong subversion. I reported fully on major state visits, such as those paid to Cambodia by General de Gaulle, Marshal Chen Yi and President Sukarno. I estimated the development potential of Cambodian natural resources and guessed at their future adequacy. (I have, of course, drawn on most of this material in writing the present book.)

Intellectually, the greatest challenge of all was to write – without, at that point in my career, much training in economics and statistics – the required annual account of the state of the Cambodian economy and the financial and commercial trends for the coming year. These reports only just passed muster with Whitehall. (I vowed then and there to become economically literate as soon as I could – I took a correspondence course in 'A'-level economics in my spare time at my next post in Paris; I spent an entire autumn at a French Business School; and finally I went through intensive instruction for mid-career people at the Civil Service College in London. This was to come in handy later, when conducting international trade negotiations for the EU, as the Director General for External Relations at the Brussels Commission.)

Much of the above will seem – which it actually was – quite a considerable grind initially. But it was important not to let that grind show through too much, to the outside world. An insouciant, external image had to be quickly adopted. What should it look like? A more senior and experienced Head of Mission would probably have opted for a calm and collected public *persona* – bespeaking an Embassy which slid smoothly along on greased rollers – and for studied attention, in his private life, to the expansion of his collection of Ming porcelain. My choice was different, but was not ill-suited to my youth, the character of the Cambodians, and the spirit of the Beatles and the 'Swinging Sixties'.

I began to cultivate a certain *figura*. I appeared at the most formal Palace occasions in a tropical dress uniform which I had in some small part invented myself, to fit Sihanouk's Court to a 'T' – lightweight dark-blue uniform trousers with a gold oak-leaf patterned stripe down the seams, white monkey jacket – alive with gilt buttons and more oak leaves – crisp starched shirt and midnight-blue cummerbund. I liked to be seen sailing through the tree-shadowed main streets of town in my open white rag-top in a flowery sports shirt, or lounging with the girls at the edge of the blue pool at the Hotel Royal. A supposedly 'play-boy' Chargé d'Affaires, I encouraged the rumour (mostly, if not entirely, ill-founded) that after the Bar Jean had ejected the last of its late-night diners and the leading discos had finally emptied, soon after 5 am, I could usually be seen walking on the misty river bank with one last half-empty bottle of 'champers', watching, in glamorous company, the first of the sunrise over the waters of the Mekong. Nothing succeeds like excess. The medium is the message, but you have to be young.

And now, to the action.

Sunday lunch on board the Maison Flottante, *the Embassy's motor boat for water-skiing, with its captain*

A picnic for the visiting Daily Mirror *journalist, and members of the Embassy staff, at the distant jungle temple of Sambor Prei Kuk*

Taking Diplomatic Action

7

The Tribes are Restless

The British Embassy at Phnom Penh, however depleted (and, indeed, initially also demoralised), was not an idle ceremonial appendage to a minor Asiatic court. We had real responsibilities in a then extremely volatile corner of the globe. We had to watch like hawks, sharpen our diplomatic claws and be ready (in the purely metaphorical sense) to pounce.

Within a search for common ground between East and West, Britain's aim was to strengthen Cambodian neutrality. Our method was to explore how far the two sides in the Vietnam war would be prepared to agree to 'count Cambodia out'. Before the diplomatic campaign started, we did not know for certain how things would turn out. In the end it emerged that, while the Americans and their allies would so agree, the communists did not find it in their interests to do so. There was afterward little more that we could try for, but the attempt to assure neutrality was needed.

This chapter deals with the 'Indo-Chinese Peoples' Conference' (which I will refer to as 'the conference') held in Phnom Penh in March 1965. The British Government was not involved directly – my task was merely to observe proceedings as closely as I could, from without. (Which was, I admit, a hands-on operation: night and day, I had to pester Cambodian Ministers and officials, hang around the lobbies and corridors, button-hole complete strangers among the participants, grab every press bulletin and swap scraps of info with other friendly observers.) I am starting at this point, because the conference was to witness two important developments.

First, the delegates repeated the call, long uttered by the Khmer Government, for the convening of a new Geneva Conference (which I will refer to as 'the Conference') to be devoted to Cambodian issues. This renewed request was to raise the curtain on the efforts

to secure such a conference later in 1965, described in the next two chapters.

The second development was the extremely tough line taken by the Chinese and the communist Vietnamese over the war in Vietnam. They made it crystal clear that they would not hear of a negotiated settlement in South Vietnam that fell short of the immediate, total and unconditional withdrawal of the Americans. They wanted the United States out – lock, stock and barrel – and they made all progress conditional upon such an outcome. Later, they were to modify their stand in accepting, in 1968, to open talks with the Americans in Paris without such a precondition. (I was to shadow those talks then, as their observer in the British Embassy to France.) This was not the communist stance in 1965. It effectively ruled out all possibility of an East/West accommodation over Cambodia – ultimately with tragic consequences for the latter.

Now to the 'Indo-Chinese Peoples' Conference' itself. The inspiration to convene this conference came from the Cambodian Head of State, who launched the project in his Independence Day speech in Phnom Penh in November 1964. Prince Sihanouk then felt the need to take some fresh diplomatic initiative on account of what he saw as a growing danger to Cambodia's future neutrality and independence. He argued that an 'Indo-Chinese Peoples' Conference would appear in the eyes of the world as authentically representative of our three peoples' (*i.e.* the Vietnamese, Laotians and Cambodians) and would thereby constitute 'the best means of compelling the US to accept a peaceful solution in our region'.

The background to this project was as follows. As already noted in Chapter 3, Sihanouk had by 1962 concluded that the communists were winning the war in South Vietnam and might eventually win in Laos also, and that the only solution which afforded any prospect of limited success, and therefore any chance of Cambodia being left in peace, was for US disengagement and the creation of a 'buffer zone' comprising South Vietnam, Laos and Cambodia.

By the early spring of 1964, efforts to obtain positive international guarantees for Cambodia had met with failure. Britain, although in principle in favour, was in practice, because of US opposition, unwilling to join with the USSR in convening the Geneva Conference, as requested by Sihanouk.

Subsequently, and as a less satisfactory alternative, the Cambodian authorities had opened bilateral negotiations with China, North Vietnam and the National Liberation Front of South Vietnam

with a view to securing written agreements to respect Cambodia's frontiers. These also proved unsatisfactory – even though, in October 1964, Prince Sihanouk had gone in person to Beijing to seek what he wanted.

Nevertheless, both the course of events in South Vietnam, and a series of frontier incidents in which South Vietnamese forces had crossed into Cambodia in the pursuit of the Viet Cong, persuaded the Khmer leadership that they could not afford to sit still and swallow their disappointment. In the hope that, once the British and American elections were over, London and Washington would be more amenable to negotiation, the Cambodians therefore determined to raise their sights and take an initiative on Indo-China, on their own home patch. To this end, they set out to whip up, and give expression to, indigenous neutralist sentiment by the device of a popular conference.

This conference turned out to be none too completely representative of the people in whose name it met. Interest in the conference was very largely confined to the communists, who saw in it an opportunity to launch propaganda attacks against the US. Apart from the Cambodians themselves, the only genuinely neutralist representatives who attended were a handful of Vietnamese dissidents who had been flown in specially from Paris; the rest were a series of 'Front' delegations through which the communists endeavoured to dominate proceedings. The Cambodians did their best to keep down the number of these 'fronts'. In the end, they were reduced to creating front organisations of their own, with which to give the appearance of diversity to the participants.

The political attitudes struck by the communist delegations came in the event as a shock to their Cambodian hosts. Thus the Khmer Head of State had carefully prepared a forthright but statesmanlike speech with which to inaugurate the conference. This speech sweepingly advocated the neutralisation of all Indo-China except North Vietnam. The emphasis was constructive – there must be an end to pointless polemic, particularly against the Americans; an 'atmosphere of confidence' must be created; practical proposals for neutralisation must be put forward containing solid guarantees which would engage the confidence of the West in a negotiated settlement; a League of Indo-Chinese States must be set up, with its own Secretariat. But Prince Sihanouk was to be prevented in a dramatic fashion from delivering this eloquent and high-minded oration. On the eve of the conference, the National Liberation Front

of South Vietnam advanced strong objections to his proposals. Supported by a negative and unbending Chinese message addressed to the conference by Chou En-lai, calling for the immediate, unconditional and total withdrawal of the United States from South Vietnam, the National Liberation Front said that they could not accept any resolution calling for a negotiated settlement in Vietnam, or even for a new Geneva Conference on Cambodia.

After the most intense discussions (during which the Cambodians did their very best to make the National Liberation Front more amenable, and as a consequence of which the opening session had to be deferred by four days), the communists very largely won out.

President Sukarno of Indonesia, who happened to be present in Phnom Penh on a snap State Visit, was roped in to address the conference and bolster up its sagging prestige, but to no evident effect. Sihanouk deemed it prudent not to deliver his own speech to the plenary session. Instead, he followed Cicero's example and had it circulated out of court as an 'historic document' like the *Pro Milone*. Although Son Sann and Tran Van Huu, the Cambodian and (neutralist) Vietnamese representatives, argued steadily in favour of a political settlement in Vietnam, the speeches from almost all the other delegations were unconstructive and sharply anti-American in tone. Even the Cambodian delegation felt it prudent at the opening session to describe the conference as 'a fine manifestation of unity between the peoples of Indo-China, resolutely struggling against American aggression'. Norodom Sihanouk himself, in winding up the conference, did his best to minimise the difficulties and differences which it had exposed. In doing so, however, he was forced to swim with the current, heartily condemning the imperialists and reluctantly unloading the ballast of 'balance' and 'statesmanship' earlier considered essential.

Thus, the final resolutions of the conference condemned the alleged warlike and provocative acts of American imperialists. They did reluctantly in the end call for new Geneva Conferences on Laos and Cambodia; but, on South Vietnam, they solely and significantly demanded respect for the 1954 Accords. It was apparently so difficult to reach agreement on these texts that it was finally decided that each of the three major protagonists would draft the resolutions appertaining to itself, and would leave unchallenged those of the other two. The Cambodians themselves, after the conference was over, hastened to make it clear that they had associated themselves with the *desiderata* of the delegations from Vietnam and Laos solely

for diplomatic reasons, without being in any way convinced of them or feeling in the least responsible for their practicality.

A minor scheme of the Cambodians which misfired was to obtain endorsement by the conference of a resolution calling for the removal of Great Britain from the role of Geneva Co-Chairman, which should pass to France. The National Liberation Front, being opposed to any new Geneva Conference on Vietnam, was, however, also opposed to any Co-Chairmanship changes, no doubt calculating that the French would be of more embarrassment to them in this respect than the British. The final resolutions of the conference were, therefore, confined, as regards the British, to generalised criticisms.

An exotic feature of the conference was the deployment by the Cambodians of a range of weird 'Front' organisations allegedly representing various minority groupings of Cambodian origin living in South Vietnam, mainly the Khmer Krom of Southern Cochin China and the Khmer Loeu and Khmer Mon *montagnards* of Annam. These delegates, wearing a wide assortment of tribal and ethnic attire, made only a small contribution to the debates at the conference; their chief purpose was to assert a 'presence'. Prince Sihanouk had genuine concern for the destiny of the ethnic groups of Cambodian or similar stock in Vietnam who had been marginalised and all but extinguished by the Annamite southward expansion of recent history. Cambodian exigency in demanding recognition of the rights of these minorities had indeed contributed to the breakdown of some earlier talks which the Cambodian Government had conducted with representatives of the Viet Cong in Beijing in December 1964. Sihanouk's pre-occupation with these peoples was, however, evidently also of a tactical order. He no doubt calculated that his sponsorship of them could be an embarrassment to the Vietnamese communists and therefore a useful card in his poker game – which he could discard in return for concessions elsewhere. Such hopes were not realised at the conference; the Cambodian front organisations attracted the scepticism – and often hilarity – of visiting journalists and the displeasure of the National Liberation Front.

Nevertheless, certain modest advantages flowed to Cambodia from the conference. The decision, reflected in the final resolutions, to set up a permanent 'Secretariat', based in Phnom Penh, gave scope for further diplomacy by the Cambodians. The resolutions calling for a new Geneva Conference to guarantee the independence, neutrality and territorial integrity of Cambodia were most

welcome to Prince Sihanouk, who had never wavered in his demand for international assurances to which both East and West would subscribe. The 'Indo-Chinese Peoples' Conference' finally gave the Cambodians an opportunity to meet a useful range of communist leaders and, above all, to size up the nature and future intentions of the National Liberation Front of South Vietnam.

As regards the latter, my Cambodian contacts told me that they had concluded, whatever they might previously have wanted to believe, that the Front was now entirely controlled by hard-line communists. They were impressed, and were left more than a little apprehensive, by the fanaticism and rigidity of the Front's diplomacy; and they were confirmed in their impression that, if and when the Front eventually gained control of South Vietnam, the Cambodians would have acquired formidable and possibly dangerous neighbours. Prince Sihanouk himself told the press with his customary, almost child-like, frankness,

> We are not unaware that, after the departure of the
> Americans, we shall be face to face with communism,
> and worst of all with Vietnamese communism. For us,
> this is obviously the worst of all communisms.

In consequence, the Cambodian Government were now in a pessimistic frame of mind. After it was all over, their Foreign Minister told me that they saw little possibility in the immediately foreseeable future of a negotiated settlement in Vietnam to the advantage of Cambodia.

But although the Conference did not achieve Khmer aims nor afford them comfort for the future, they certainly felt no temptation to turn in their tracks and throw in their lot with the US. Prince Sihanouk personally was still convinced – and he might in 1965 still have been right – that the best hope (such as it was) for Cambodia's future peace and independence lay in adhering to a policy of neutrality calculated to give the least offence to and, if possible, to win the co-operation and friendship of the communists.

The following month, to the beating of gongs, the chanting of ancient Pali verses and all the display of Cambodian courtly panoply, Norodom Sihanouk was to supervise as in all previous years the traditional fertility rite known as 'The Ploughing of the Sacred Furrow'. Not only in priesthood, but also in politics, the Prince could not readily be persuaded to look back, once his hand had been set to the plough. I, for one, admired his resolution.

8

The Approach to Geneva – Chou En-lai's Road Block

Notwithstanding the events just described, things were at last beginning to look up, just a tiny bit, relatively speaking, for the Prince. Cambodia had one slim chance. The road through the jungle to international agreement on Cambodia appeared to be opening up a fraction. Until, that is, Mr Chou En-lai from Beijing dropped a massive tree trunk across the track – as I will now relate.

In March 1965, at the close of the 'Indo-Chinese Peoples' Conference' in Phnom Penh, the Cambodian Government once again petitioned the Co-Chairmen of the Geneva Conference. This time, they found themselves pushing on an open door, where the West was concerned. The climate of opinion had become generally more favourable. The Americans wanted to look into the possibility of an honourable settlement by negotiation in Vietnam and the British wished to open up every path for exploration. The US Government promptly declared its readiness to attend a Geneva Conference on Cambodia. The British Government informed the Soviet Government that such a Conference might now at last be convened. The two allies were inspired, in part at least, by the hope that, once the affairs of Cambodia had been satisfactorily settled, the new Geneva Conference might move on to discuss Vietnam; or at least informal contacts and discreet dialogue about Vietnam might in any case be entertained with the Chinese and North Vietnamese leadership on the margins, in the corridors and hotel bars of Geneva. These hopes were also, in the early stages, shared by the Cambodians. The prospects of success therefore seemed fair. Even if hopes as to Vietnam were eventually to be disappointed, solid gains could nevertheless be registered as to Cambodia, concern for the neutrality of which had always been a constant of British foreign policy in the area.

The Chinese were slow to react to these moves. At the 'Indo-Chinese Peoples' Conference' in Phnom Penh, as we saw in Chapter 7, they had gone along with resolutions calling for a reconvening of the 1954 Geneva Conference to consider Cambodia. On 17 March 1965 Marshal Chen Yi even publicly endorsed the Cambodian initiative. It was not until mid-April that the Chinese leadership appeared to wake up and see that, contrary to the precedents of previous years, the British had at last carried their American allies and regional friends with them. Faced with the real prospect of having to sit down at the same table with the Americans and with representatives of the Saigon Government, the Chinese took urgent evasive action to abort the whole thing. And, unknown to us all at the time, Chairman Mao Tse-tung was beginning to plan in his own mind the domestic ideological shake-up and purge which was to become the Chinese Cultural Revolution in the following year. For Mao, it seemed, this was no time for international 'statesmanship' – China must put the boot in.

In mid-April 1965, Chou En-lai and Chen Yi, and also Pham Van Dong of North Vietnam, accordingly jumped on Sihanouk at Djakarta, where they were meeting for the tenth anniversary celebrations of the Bandung Conference. It was weeks before the full story leaked out. But what happened was as follows. They told the Cambodian delegation that the Chinese and North Vietnamese had no wish to meet the American war criminals, that it was in any case the National Liberation Front and not the Saigon puppets who should represent South Vietnam at any conference, that the British and Americans had not the slightest interest in Cambodia's problems and would forget them once a conference got talking about Vietnam, that, in short, the whole idea was a put-up job by the imperialists who wanted only to trick Cambodia and escape an ugly defeat in South Vietnam. And why was a new Geneva Agreement necessary? Cambodia's only true friend was China: it was on China's assurances of friendship and support that Cambodia should rely. But friendship was a two-way matter. Cambodia would earn Chinese gratitude if she were now to re-inter the corpse of Geneva, which she had been recently so successful in raising from the dead.

After this highly effective intervention, the Chinese never let up for one moment. On almost every occasion in the following weeks on which the Cambodian Government expressed some criticism or other of the 'Anglo-Saxons', an immediate public endorsement followed within hours from Beijing. In a sneering Government

statement issued on 2 May 1965, the Chinese pointed out that the 'Johnson Administration has now suddenly changed its attitude' to a Geneva Conference 'in order to extricate itself from its difficult plight and isolation' and 'cover up its bloody aggression by a smoke-screen of "peace negotiations" so as to attain the object of perpetu-ating its occupation of South Vietnam'. A Conference on Cambodia would be used to 'open up the way to its fraud of peace talks on the Vietnam question'. When Prince Sihanouk brought a touch to the tiller in his message of 15 May to our Prime Minister, Chou En-lai intervened at once with a personal message of protest, designed to put the Royal Cambodian Government back on course. It was a slick operation, carefully orchestrated from Beijing, in which the Chinese drew effectively on the goodwill they already possessed and no doubt made full use of their 'agents of influence' within the Cambo-dian camp.

The extremely negative line taken by the Chinese was a profound disappointment for the Khmer. Out of deference to Chinese wishes, however, and perhaps still under the spell of Chou En-lai's unques-tionably mesmeric personality, Prince Sihanouk came back from Djakarta resigned to carrying out a hatchet job. In a sensational speech in Phnom Penh on 23 April 1965, he accused the 'Anglo-Saxons' of seeking to turn his honest proposal to their own dingy self-advantage in Vietnam. The situation had evolved; the Saigon regime was no longer a genuine government; neither Saigon nor Washington were therefore wanted at the Conference; nor would he grant a personal audience to Mr Patrick Gordon Walker, former Foreign Secretary and now the Special Representative of the UK Co-Chairman, who had flown out to South-East Asia from London to facilitate the convening of a Conference and whose scheduled visit to Phnom Penh was at that point in time only two days away (see the next chapter).

Subsequently (after Gordon Walker's departure), the Prince was to modify this extreme position. A development which played some part in this further policy switch was undoubtedly the very strong support for a Conference which had built up among the Cambodian 'Establishment', none of whom (including the Prime Minister) had been informed in advance of the *volte face* of 23 April. The 'Estab-lishment' had, for the most part, long entertained some degree of inner misgiving about Cambodia's apparent drift away from neutrality – and from some degree of friendship with the West – towards depend-ence on China. (The rapid deterioration of relations with the United

States, terminating in the Prince's decision to break off diplomatic relations in mid-May 1965, would in any case, even without the Conference crisis, have raised murmurs of discontent in influential quarters.) Having lectured his people for the previous three years on the theme that the main hope for Cambodia's national survival was a new Geneva Agreement, Prince Sihanouk was now in effect saying that this prospect should be forgone, and Cambodia's interests presumably thereby comprised, just to please Chou En-lai and Pham Van Dong. This went down in Cambodia like a pork chop in a synagogue. Goaded past endurance, elder statesmen, like Penn Nouth, expressed their misgiving directly to the Prince, while the Cabinet submitted on 24 April 1965 an unprecedented unanimous recommendation that Cambodia should revert to the terms of her original proposal of 15 March to the Geneva Co-Chairmen.

I must admit that I did take an active personal part in stirring up this protest, not least through a link I had established with the Cambodian Prime Minister, Prince Norodom Kantol, but also with others in the 'Establishment' (including Sihanouk's powerful cousin Prince Sisowath Sirik Matak, also the wise and patient Son Sann, Deputy Prime Minister and Governor of the Cambodian Central Bank) and with Sihanouk's own immediate entourage and advisers. Patrick Gordon Walker's visit during this time helped pile on the pressure.

Possibly for the first time in his entire political career to date, Prince Sihanouk found himself deprived of the initiative, and out of step and sympathy with most of his own elite – and indeed with popular Cambodian sentiment at large. As the memory of his traumatic encounter with Chou En-lai and the others in Djakarta grew less vivid, and his basic and sincere desire for a Conference reasserted itself, Prince Sihanouk became less and less keen on his role as whipping boy for the Chinese. It was a salutary experience for His Royal Highness.

By an all too transparent procedural manoeuvre, the Cambodian Government then attempted to put the ball back into the court of the Great Powers. Let them (Britain and the USSR, the United States and China) agree between themselves on who should attend the Conference. Cambodia would fall in with whatever they decided. By then, however, the practical prospects for a Conference had immeasurably receded. There was not the slightest chance that America and China would reach any accommodation. The Cambodians, desperate to rescue at least a few chestnuts from what had now

become a conflagration, subsequently advanced the idea of individual assurances of respect for Cambodian neutrality and territorial integrity, in which the powers would sign separate unilateral declarations, accompanied by a map of Cambodia's frontiers. But this project seemed also to raise difficulties, not least with the Vietnamese communists, who were not over-anxious to commit themselves to anything in black and white. At the end of the day, all Sihanouk's birds were deep in the Indo-Chinese bush, with none in hand in Phnom Penh. On 2 September 1965, the Prince left the country in a mood of bafflement and depression, to embark on a four-month official tour abroad.

The Russians regrettably acted with caution, even indecision, throughout the crisis. In first proposing that the two Co-Chairmen should issue invitations to a Conference, the Soviet leadership may conceivably have been bent purely on embarrassing the West, sharing the Chinese calculation that the British and American Governments would be unable to respond positively. But it seems possible that Moscow had a more positive intent. The Soviet Union still had modest influence in Cambodia. A Conference, co-chaired by the Soviet Union and leading to a binding international agreement, might both reduce the political dependence of Cambodia on China's friendship and enhance the local prestige of the Soviet Union. More than this, I had little doubt that Moscow in some measure privately shared the hopes of London and Washington that a Cambodian Conference would open up an oblique approach to the problem of Vietnam. Unfortunately, Soviet feet very quickly turned cold when it became evident that China was opposed, and that Prince Sihanouk himself had apparently in consequence modified his desiderata. The Soviets prevaricated and, despite numerous British reminders, the invitations to a Conference were never issued.

How did the major protagonists emerge from this affair? China came out on top. Anxious to avoid discussions with the West of any kind whatsoever about any part of Indo-China, she successfully torpedoed the proposed Geneva Conference on Cambodia. The Chinese did so without apparent serious damage to Sino-Cambodian relations: they could call the tune of Cambodian foreign policy on any international issue of real importance. The Soviets, on the other hand, earned the maximum of embarrassment with absolutely nothing to show for it; they were out-manoeuvred at every stage of the game. The French had long been in favour of a Conference. They said as much to the Cambodian Government. They also made this crystal clear to Mr Gromyko when he was in Paris in April 1965 and,

in effect, urged him to go ahead to convene the Conference with the UK. But there were limits to what France was able to do. Once Prince Sihanouk had made his speech on 23 April, the French position became more delicate, given the special relationship which they believed they had with him. The US took a laudable, if difficult, decision in plumping for a Conference – although far too late in the day. The UK came out quite well: Chinese intransigence and extremism had been detected and laid bare; the Co-Chairmanship telephone had been put to use (for what little it was worth); we had been able to convince most of our Asian friends that a readiness to consider giving legitimate formal assurances to Cambodia was not necessarily 'soft' or a 'sell-out to the Reds'. Anglo-Cambodian relations had been lifted above rock-bottom, and the Embassy's freshly forged links to the local 'Establishment' had stood the strain and functioned as they should.

9

Patrick Gordon Walker and the Peace Process – The Scene on the Street

Before very long, the mobs of Phnom Penh were once again mobilised by the Cambodian Government and told to go, this time, for the US Embassy. With such psyched-up and indiscriminate mobs on the loose, even a well-meaning peace envoy from the British Prime Minister was to get into difficulty on the street. He had to be led from danger by a quick change of passport and an even quicker visit to a local pub. Thereafter, everything more or less ended in tears.

If the action narrative in the previous two chapters has given the feel of an ineluctable progression to a bitter but pre-destined end, this was nevertheless not my overwhelming impression at the time, though I was conscious of the odds against success. The final outcome was not apparent to any of us, until the latter stages; and the day-to-day situation was constantly bobbing in and out of focus with the oscillation of events and the tremor of our exertions.

It was accordingly a period of stump-stirring, and abnormal adrenalin levels. For me personally, routine duties, as far as their nature permitted, were set aside. It was the time to be omnipresent and omniscient in the city, without petty distractions.

What was in last night's speech in Cambodian and this morning's official statement in French, and should it be reported to London? (Usually it had to be reported, pretty quickly, with accompanying comment – so, translate, reflect, look back, look forward, call in stenographer, take down these telegrams to the Foreign Office.) What were the press saying? Was anyone knocking or distorting the British position – or coming up with information that was new? Could we get onto them? This chore could not be delegated; only I

could judge. (So out of bed earlier, read more, get the translators scanning the Chinese- and Cambodian-language dailies full-time.)

What was the gossip? (So get on your feet, Fielding, and get out; fix that appointment; drop in at that bar; call at that Embassy, Ministry, newspaper office, cocktail party, or wherever; waylay that elusive but key player, nail him down, make him spill the beans or cough up; whatever you do, Fielding, do it gently though: keep your cool, smile, relax, enjoy it, grab that beer, and watch for the bubbly when the tray comes round.)

What were the Cambodian Government up to? Should I see the Foreign Minister *again* – I saw him only three days ago? A backstairs assignation with the Prime Minister? A few words with Sihanouk himself at the next reception? What does this mean, what does that imply, is it something else? What do I reply if they ask this, question that, seek further guarantees? Was the time ripe to put in a further Note, or send out a press bulletin? But would that risk putting backs up? How can you put the truth, but make it tactful? (They won't understand English. Put it in French – precise French. Will I impart the right nuance? Better make dead certain – get someone in who can do it really well – now, who can I trust? Get that French trans-lator in; talk it through; does this word carry the wrong political under-tone; is this finally OK? Yes. Anyway, no time and no more ideas – get out of this office, take five minutes off in the sun.)

What's going on outside Cambodia – what are the signs from Washington, Beijing, Paris and Saigon? (Read the daily flood of inward telegrams; note, correlate, comment, contest; keep things moving the right way; keep your fingers crossed too.)

What about this visa problem? (Break off to give a ruling on a complicated issue presented by the Vice Consul; quite right of him to do so; what do we do? We do this and this; and we cable to Hong Kong on that; let me know the answer; then I'll sign the necessary....)

When was Patrick Gordon Walker finally expected? In the face of Sihanouk's petulant and discourteous invisibility, whom should PGW try and see; what would be the best tactical line to take; who should come to a reception in his honour? (Write down all the names – cross out him, put her in – and then draft the speaking brief.) And so on, day and night.

Two events stand out in clear outline. The first was the circum-stances in which the Head of State delivered his bombshell on 23 April 1965.

A brand new, self-service, luxury store had been set up on one of the city's principal boulevards. There was the usual inauguration ceremony, with a large and exotically decorated stand for the dignitaries of the Kingdom and the leaders of the Diplomatic Corps. Bands played, thousands of Cambodians crowded round in fiesta mood and a great roar of applause went up when Prince Sihanouk finally arrived in his open limousine and while he walked along the red carpet in the shade of the saffron-coloured many-tiered royal parasol held over his head, mounted the tribune and took his seat on the gilded throne set there in our midst. All was well, while the Speeches of Welcome droned on.

Then it was the Prince's turn to speak. He gave instructions to his aides and a few moments later various junior notables, looking a trifle puzzled and sheepish, spread out among the Corps, descending on particular Heads of Mission, whispering that Monseigneur wished us to have translators to make quite sure that we should fully understand what he was about to say, since it was to be something of the first importance. In the event, these precautions were to be unnecessary, since the Prince, when he came to the relevant passages of his improvised discourse, was to switch from Cambodian to French, turning round to face us in order to speak with greater emphasis. No one seemed to know what was coming – certainly not my ministerial translator (Chea San, Secretary of State for Information – a man I had always got on well with, who was to be murdered by the Khmer Rouge in 1975). He shrugged and looked glum. Similar emotions could be detected, beneath the blank and respectful expressions which it was customary for the Khmer to affect on these ceremonial occasions, on the faces of some of the more senior ministers. One or two Cambodians, 'fellow-travelling' toads, were all smirks by the time the speech was over. But that was all.

After Sihanouk had spoken, and as we swarmed down the steps and across the road, to watch Monseigneur cut the ribbon stretched across the front of the store, I got in a few words with the Prime Minister and the Foreign Minister (both of them also destined for the killing fields ten years later). After the Princely entourage had departed, as we waited for our cars to come and collect us, I also spoke with the Chinese Ambassador. Things were indeed as I suspected: Sihanouk had agreed to withdraw his proposal at Beijing's behest and abjectly to toe the Chou En-lai line.

My second, equally vivid recollection is that of Mr Patrick Gordon Walker's visit from 25 to 27 April 1965, in the thick of the crisis.

The Cambodian Head of State had made it clear that he would not receive Prime Minister Harold Wilson's personal peace envoy. Indeed, to avoid all possible embarrassment (and perhaps with fore-knowledge of the riot which I describe below), the Prince had decided to take himself off to a distant hill-station, for a brief, and entirely 'diplomatic', holiday break. But the Brits were not to be put off their stroke. Gordon Walker duly arrived from Saigon tired but triumphant, fully confirmed in the support of the US Administration in our enterprise and the assent of all the Asian allies concerned. He accepted in advance the programme I had submitted to him by telegram and we proceeded to put it into execution. After the minimum of ceremony at the airport – where he was, however, cour-teously greeted by a senior Cambodian official – I whisked him and Douglas Brown (an accompanying FO official) away to the Residence.

I had never before met Patrick Gordon Walker face to face. My initial reaction was unfavourable. He seemed too 'donnish' to be true. Perhaps that was why he was no longer Foreign Secretary, having lost his parliamentary seat (Smethwick) in October 1964, and failed to secure an apparently safe seat (Leyton) at an immediately following by-election. He looked to me like a lugubrious and insecure owl, anxious to regain his perch and his dignity, like a college tutor under an unexpected challenge. At the briefing session I had set up in my drawing room, PGW launched immediately into a solemn, sombre and mistaken 'Domino Theory' analysis of the South-East Asia scene. (He was to persist with this analysis in his final report to Cabinet, on his return to London. Michael Stewart, the Foreign Secretary, who did not agree, simply sat on it. In the House of Commons, on 13 May 1965, Stewart archly said: 'Because the value to me of Mr Gordon Walker's report depended on the frankness with which he recorded his personal impressions, it is not suitable for publication'. – In those days, before 'political advisers' and 'spin doctors', Whitehall was leak proof! – Stewart then went on to praise – quite rightly – Gordon Walker's efforts for the peace.) To return to my drawing room in Phnom Penh, PGW – seeing a book on Buddhism on my book shelf – then moved on to a disquisition on the Lesser and Greater Vehicles for good, donnish measure and without drawing breath. All this, as if I was a fresher in deep ignorance.

But the poor man was stressed out and in inner turmoil. Further-more, after these initial remarks, he did, I concede, catch my body language and raised eyebrows, take a grip of himself and invite me

to open the local briefing. Thereafter, he went out of his way to be agreeable. He was complimentary about the reports we had sent him when he was still Foreign Secretary. He then asked for practical advice on the task in hand. So, we were in business. After lunch, I sent the two of them upstairs for a decent rest (PGW and Douglas Brown had covered many thousands of miles on a few days' hectic, whistle-stop tour). There followed a press conference, then a small cocktail party to meet the Diplomatic Corps (we were still technically 'in Coventry', so no Cambodians could come to the Residence), and finally a more restricted meeting in my study with the Australian Ambassador and the US and French Chargés d'Affaires, to give PGW a chance to test my own advice against that of friendly and trusted, but independent observers.

The following day, we took ourselves to the Chancery in the early morning. We looked at the newspapers, checked out the latest inward telegrams and rehearsed again the line to take with the Cambodian Foreign Minister, Koun Wick, later that morning. We also put the final touches, in the light of overnight instructions from London, to the memorandum which we were to hand over.

I had thought it essential for Gordon Walker to be able to make a written communication, so that we could be sure that our message would reach the Head of State and the rest of the Cambodian Government in an authorised, ungarbled form. I had tried my hand at a draft, duly telegraphed to London for approval two days previously. I was pleased with the final version – short and snappy, but containing all the essential points on which the Cambodian Government stood in need of reassurance, and dealing in particular with whether a Geneva Conference on Cambodia would or would not also concern itself directly with Vietnam. The text read as follows:

> 1. On 15 March 1965, the Cambodian Government invited the Co-Chairmen of the 1954 Geneva Conference to convene a new conference to be concerned with Cambodia.
>
> 2. On 3 April, the Soviet Government informed the British Government that they endorsed this request and accordingly proposed that a joint invitation should be issued to the governments which participated in the 1954 Geneva Conference.

3. The British Government support the national independence, neutrality and territorial integrity of Cambodia.

4. Mr Gordon Walker is therefore glad to inform the Cambodian Government that Her Majesty's Government agree to their request for a Conference. The British Co-Chairman is informing his Soviet colleague that he agrees to the immediate despatch of invitations.

5. Her Majesty's Government do not intend to propose the inclusion in the agenda of any questions not directly related to the independence, neutrality, and territorial integrity of Cambodia.

I had roughed out a French translation to accompany the English text. While my virtually bilingual Vice Consul and his highly educated French wife polished my French prose and my secretary got cracking with her typewriter, Patrick Gordon Walker and Douglas Brown toured the offices, relaxing for a chat with everyone.

Then off we went, the three of us, flag fluttering, bouncing along above the crowds in the aged Austin Princess. It was a good interview, in which (to the Foreign Minister's relief) PGW spoke fluent French. We went home to lunch in the certainty that the British case had been squarely put and fairly heard.

That afternoon all hell broke loose. A violent demonstration was unleashed against the American Embassy.

In theory, the demonstrators (some of them apparently delivered in bus loads from the country, but others Chinese or Vietnamese from downtown, plus the customary sprinkling of hired toughs and assorted riff-raff) were spontaneously expressing the righteous indignation of the entire Cambodian people at a derogatory article by Bernard Krisher which had appeared in *Newsweek Magazine*. This article had alleged corruption in high places in Cambodia and had even levelled wild charges (how shocking!) against the Queen Mother, some of whose income was alleged to derive from rents on real estate being used for the brothel and opium-den business (surely not!). This article was spiteful but little of it would have given offence to ordinary Cambodians and some of the charges were not far from the truth. Certainly, the US Embassy could hardly be held to blame. The purpose of the riot was, however, political – to prepare the way for a final breach with the US and to warn off Patrick Gordon

Walker (so I was told, with a leer by a senior left-wing personality) – the message being 'don't make a monkey out of us or it will be your turn next'.

When we got the news that something serious was afoot, we had a quick 'council of war' at the Residence. PGW's first quixotic reaction was to offer to go the scene, interpose himself between the US Chancery building and the mob, and try to get the rioters to disperse. In a way, this was rather to his personal credit. Men scare easily, as they grow older; yet scared, the elderly PGW certainly was not. I warmed to him further. But he was being unprofessional. I told him, bluntly, what Cambodian riots were like, and my conviction that the whole operation was officially inspired and would therefore be played through to its pre-arranged conclusion, whatever we did. Accordingly, I expressed strong objection to his proposal to intervene, arguing also that, if injury were to befall him, this might render more difficult of attainment the peace conference that we all wanted. Douglas Brown supported me.

Nevertheless, PGW had to be given something to do, by way of distraction. I therefore secured The Great Man's assent to an alternative plan of action, in two phases.

We had already been in touch with our besieged American friends by telephone and knew the scene which surrounded them – thousands of screaming rioters blocking all the streets leading to the US Chancery, a rain of missiles against the building, the flag torn down from a balcony, the windows broken, relays of people battering at the main door. Our first step should therefore be, however deaf the ears of the authorities, at least to make an attempt to get belated police protection for the Yanks. We divided forces. To keep him occupied and out of trouble, I sent Gordon Walker off on an intentionally time-consuming and otherwise pointless mission, to call on the Soviet Ambassador. The latter was then the Dean of the Diplomatic Corps and therefore the spokesman of foreign Embassies in all matters affecting their general relations with the Cambodian authorities. Predictably, the Russian – a foxy man at best, with a KGB background – shrugged the matter off, saying that he had no knowledge that a riot was in progress. At the same time, I shot off to the Ministry of Foreign Affairs (closed in the afternoons, as is frequently the custom in tropical countries), to call on the Duty Officer. He received me, suitably shifty and shame-faced, admitted that he was aware of what was afoot, and assured me that he had already notified the police. I told him in no uncertain terms that if

that were so, there was precious little result to show: on my way to the Ministry, I had been able to observe, mingling as unobtrusively as I could with the outskirts of the crowds, that the police were conspicuous by their total absence. He said he would telephone again.

Back at my house, we compared notes and concluded (as I had secretly expected) that we had got nowhere. I had already telephoned through to the US Chancery an account of what I had been able to see of how the attack was developing (they could not judge this too well from inside, as they had to keep clear of the upstairs windows and the ground-floor windows were obscured but protected by metal shutters). This completed Phase One.

Phase Two of my plan, after the tactically prudent and carefully judged elapse of wasted time, was to track the mob more closely. We went first – another privily time-wasting exercise – to our own Chancery, some distance from the American, to make sure all was well. In the anticipation that trouble might arise, I had already told everyone to go home and stay out of sight, while arranging with the Military Attaché, the Vice Consul and other male staff for regular surveillance of the Chancery premises. These were completely locked up, everything stowed away behind locks and bars, and the shutters drawn. The transport yard was empty, the official vehicles dispersed. A quick inspection showed that all was well: the streets were clear and there was hardly a sign of life to be seen anywhere. The servants' quarters were empty and locked up too: men, women and children, they had all departed with such of their possessions as they could carry, having chalked on their doors in Cambodian a plea that their houses should be spared.

Having run out of excuses not to proceed to the scene of action, I slowly drove the three of us in an unmarked car to the nearest quiet spot. There Patrick Gordon Walker, Douglas Brown and I then threaded our way along a side-street leading up to the crossroads where the Americans were located and which I had selected as more likely to bring us close up than the one I had explored earlier. The mob grew numerous and noisy and we began to attract glances that were initially merely curious but soon frankly disapproving. A solitary policeman told us that we should not be there and then turned away to talk to someone else. We sidled forward, quite close by now to the US building; but then got stuck in the press, which swayed this way and that, as the stones flew. Above the din, some people yelled at us. We avoided eye contact. It was all starting to

turn a little too 'hairy'. We started to get jostled. Being the youngest and perhaps also having been half-recognised by a local thug, I received a shove in the ribs, which I took care not to return. Accordingly I exchanged shrugs with Douglas Brown, and decided that we should pull out, discretion being the better part of valour. Pursued by catcalls, we slid back down the street and turned into a dingy, dimly lit and vaguely disreputable bar which had just decided to open its doors. So we ordered three beers (in French, so as to excite no anti-Anglo-Saxon sentiments), before starting to speak among ourselves in pseudo-Norwegian. (I had given the other two, before we came in, the cover story that we were crew from a visiting freighter in the port.) I said, as one does, *'God dag. Hoora for den Norske Fiske'* (an expression which I had picked up, naturally enough, while reading Persian as a post-graduate student at the School of Oriental and African Studies in London in the 1950s). On cue, bless him, Patrick Gordon Walker came in, slowly and with seafaring melancholy, on the broad line of: *'God dag! Ja! Ik bin enkapteinen van der "Oslo"!'*. Douglas followed in similar vein, with something like: *'Hourdan har De det? Et stort glass mørkt øl. Skål!'*. We then got going one of those brooding Scandinavian conversations, punctuated by long pauses, Nordic *'Ja-Ha'*'s and penetrating gazes into the middle distance, that Ingmar Bergman had made familiar to all. I did a running translation into French for the barman. (*'Snakker de fransk?'*) But as the gentle reader will already have realised, we none of us really spoke Norwegian. Struggling with fits of the giggles, we started eventually to lose credibility with the barman. It was time to go to the loo (*'Hvor er toalettet?'*), pay up and go outside to take another look.

This return to the charge was to carry us clear to our objective. The roar of angry voices was abating; the crowd were beginning to thin out; the police were becoming more numerous; the missiles more sporadic. We edged up to the corner of the crossroads just across from the US Chancery's front door. There we found another bar, with a telephone. I at once got on the blower to the Americans to tell them what was happening and where we were. Less than a quarter of an hour later, the roads cleared immediately to our front, the mob having broken up and gone away. The acting Head of the Political Section, Doug Perry, accompanied by a US Marine Corps NCO, came down to the ground floor, by pre-arrangement, to open the battered front doors. The latter had resisted very well but took some opening. We walked as casually as we could across the street,

as the last half bricks sailed overhead. Upstairs, the first man we met was Mr Alf Bergeson.

Alf was young to be a Chargé d'Affaires. But he was a Boston Brahmin-style diplomat, in the old tradition – courteous, conciliatory, shrewd, endowed with a saving sense for the ridiculous and with a dry sense of humour. (Almost an Englishman, in fact.) Originally First Secretary and Head of the Political Section in the US Embassy in Phnom Penh, he eventually became the Embassy's appointed chief, following the gradual removal of his seniors. The last American Chargé d'Affaires before the Embassy was finally withdrawn the following month, it was therefore he who saw out the final mob attack. We found him calmly supervising the damage control, with a lop-sided grin. In an office in which the windows had been stoved in, the furniture smashed and the floor littered with stones and rotten fruit, we heard his account of what had happened. Then he gestured, with an apologetic shrug, at the shattered air-conditioning apparatus in the corner, which was groaning and shuddering its last moments, emitting irregular blasts of noisy, hot air. Through the gaps in the window frame, the recessional roar could be heard of the retreating mob. 'Sorry about these modern machines of ours,' he said, 'don't seem to make them like we used to'.

Then Patrick Gordon Walker, Douglas Brown and I went the rounds, shaking hands with the rest of the staff and laughing – a shade too heartily it was true – at all the jokes. The Yanks were in good heart and had conducted themselves with admirable Anglo-Saxon phlegm. (Quite like those 'Norwegians'.)

I gave a dinner that night for Patrick Gordon Walker, attended by members of staff and my principal foreign diplomatic cronies. Alf Bergeson managed to make it after the soup (having had a hectic period clearing up, reporting to Washington and leaving the necessary instructions). It was a light-hearted affair, with everyone in a mood for relaxation. So there were no speeches, but I proposed one toast – 'Uncle Sam!'.

I trust that Americans reading this will note that, while the Brits have interests and form judgements of their own, they are reliably supportive in a crisis. (Greatest of all US patricians, Averell Harriman once told me, in the margins of the Vietnam Peace Negotiations in Paris, that he recognised just that.)

Late into the night and early the next morning, we cabled away our reports to the Secretary of State in London. Then my visitors flew off. As I watched their plane rise up into the grey rain clouds, I

felt I had been inwardly too critical – I had not only seen in action an experienced and (in his way) skilled politician, but also met a humane and likeable man, with his heart in the right place, who was not too proud to listen. Then I went home and fell asleep with my clothes on.

In no hurry to do so, I paid my next official call on the Cambodian Foreign Minister a few days later, after the dust had settled slightly. Choosing my words carefully and dispassionately, I politely gave him the dressing down of his life. I did so without sadism – personally I liked the man – but I did so with the determination to reserve the last word to my own Government.

In reply to the telegram I despatched to report this interview, the Secretary of State sent back one of his infrequent, laconic accolades: 'You spoke well'.

10

The Coming of the Viet Cong

As the prospects for peace receded, the Viet Cong advanced. We tried to obstruct them. Our attempt did not succeed. But it was worth trying.

Our active diplomacy in the 1966 campaigning season was devoted to attempts, at the request of the Cambodian Government, to secure international agreement that neither side in the Vietnam war should make military use of neutral Cambodian territory. What Cambodia now proposed was that the International Control Commission (ICC) in Phnom Penh be strengthened to ensure that the Kingdom's neutrality was being respected in deed as well as word. (And high time, too.)

The ICC had been set up in 1954 to supervise the execution of the provisions of the Geneva Agreements. There were separate Commissions for Vietnam, Laos and Cambodia. Each was composed of representatives of three countries without a direct stake in Indo-China, whose respective political affiliations were held to strike a collective balance in which everyone's interests were indirectly reflected. They were India, Canada and Poland. In Cambodia, the Commission's main initial task had been to supervise the withdrawal of the Viet Minh (communist Vietnamese) forces who had been fighting the French there and attempting to overthrow the newly independent Royal Government. The Viet Minh did in fact withdraw; so that, by the end of 1955, the principal duty of the ICC had been discharged. For various reasons, however, the Commission stayed on, running down its numbers as the months went by, until it eventually became a largely symbolic international presence.

On my arrival, there was a small administrative secretariat furnished by the Indian Government, headed by an Indian Commissioner who was the Chairman, plus a Canadian and a Polish Commissioner,

each with a couple of subordinates. Over the previous two or three years and at the request of the Cambodian authorities, they had been investigating frontier incidents in which South Vietnamese or American forces had attacked Cambodian villages close to the frontier in the belief that they were Viet Cong targets. Usually, such incidents were the consequence of navigational or map-reading errors; but the hard facts in burnt houses and dead Cambodian peasants remained (see Cameo IV on page xxxi), and the Government in Phnom Penh were glad to have the independent, on-the-spot testimony of the ICC on which to base their subsequent official protests.

The atmosphere within the Commission was never good. The Canadians (good people – I later on got to know their country well, while negotiating a Framework Agreement for Commercial and Economic Co-Operation between Canada and the enlarged EU at the behest of Prime Minister Trudeau in the mid-1970s) did their best to create an 'international' atmosphere and went out of their way to damp down ideological discords. But the members inevitably fell out over any politically contentious issue that was before them, the conduct of the (communist) Poles being frequently obstructive. These difficulties were compounded by the variable quality of both Indian and Polish Commissioners over the years, some of whom manifestly came from the absolute bottom drawer of their respective national diplomatic establishments. Furthermore, the Indians, who were saddled with the ungrateful task of financial administration, had to face constant budgetary problems. Contributing countries rarely paid up on the nail and China, in my day, discontinued her statutory support altogether. Nevertheless, though it was an imperfect instrument of international purpose, the Commission at least had the merit of existing. In its fashion, it worked – some of the time.

The reason why, in the first eight months of 1966, we were attempting to secure the rejuvenation of the Commission was that the Viet Cong were beginning to use neutral Cambodia as a safe haven and a source of supply in a systematic way. Accusations to this effect in the American press had begun to multiply in the second half of 1965. On 2 December that year, the State Department announced that US Commanders in South Vietnam were to have discretion to engage Viet Cong forces actually on Cambodian territory. This amounted to little more in practice than counter-battery fire and very limited 'hot pursuit'. But, naturally enough, it caused the deepest concern to the Cambodians. It also worried several allied

Governments who had no wish to see any extension to the Vietnam war and who in any case very much doubted whether the Viet Cong presence in Cambodia at that point weighed sufficiently heavily on the strategic military situation in Vietnam to make tactical excursions into Cambodia worth the political candle. We ourselves were, I think, probably less disturbed by the prospect of the odd, brief US frontier-crossing in hot pursuit, as by the possibility that matters would not be allowed to rest there by either side. Subsequent events were to confirm this apprehension.

Now for a closer look at the nature of the Viet Cong presence in Cambodia, as it developed in my day. It would be indiscreet of me to go into detail on the evidence at the disposal of the allied Governments, other than to confirm that it derived from painstaking efforts to amass and collate both overt and secret intelligence from a wide range of sources. Nor shall I elaborate on the modest but useful observational role which our own and other Western Embassies in Phnom Penh had been able to play in the matter. Suffice it to say that the business of finding out for certain what was going on was not easy; that I personally was initially sceptical of some of the wilder allegations bandied about in US military circles in Vietnam; but as the Viet Cong presence became more marked and as information concerning it became more comprehensive, my scepticism diminished.

The challenge was to keep to a balanced judgement in the face of two sins which beset American analysts, both of which were magnified by the press. The first was to think of the Viet Cong as a US-style army, burdened with all the usual Western military and logistic paraphernalia. Reading in the American press of logistic centres and supply routes and bases hidden in remote areas of Cambodia, I had the sneaking suspicion that all this was conceived in terms of metalled roads and concrete bunkers and mobile bath houses: a sort of communist Eldorado lost in the jungle or a Hollywood-style underground city ruled over by a Dr. No with a red star on his cap. Of course, it was nothing of the sort – as the more professional Americans recognised, and as visitors to these areas were able to attest (including some hard-boiled US pressmen as well as Western Military Attachés, and others). It was better to picture a shifting guerrilla population: sleeping in improvised huts or lean-tos under the trees and generally living rough, moving food and ammunition by bicycle or small carts, digging holes for their stores, hollowing out caves and tunnels to serve as command

centres, setting up training camps unobtrusively in scattered clear-ings, adept at camouflage and concealment, moving quietly, often by night, and capable of rapid redeployment. They were better understood as Asiatics, operating in an Asian environment with which they were well familiar and over which they exercised almost complete tactical mastery.

The second sin was one which I can best describe as indiscipline and partiality. As it seemed to the Western diplomatic community in Phnom Penh, several of the American agencies, special forces or other units in Vietnam which were concerned with the problem seemed to have their own idiosyncratic view of what was going on, which differed from the more detached assessments known to have been formed in Washington. At the drop of a hat, these back-woodsmen would pass on their views to journalists themselves all too avid for a new sensation in a war on which it was proving contin-ually harder to report with originality. Such briefings sometimes appeared to be based on often low-grade data, which had not been sufficiently sifted, cross-checked and related to other findings by professional intelligence experts. Aerial photographs were (at one point) in circulation allegedly showing camouflaged installations which later turned out to be fishing nets drying in the sun on a river bank. Human emotions too were liable to play their part – inter-service rivalries, frustration with the war, a desire for scape-goats. As always with Vietnam, there was a full measure of political in-fighting – with Washington wanting to minimise the problem on wider polit-ical grounds and Saigon wanting to play it up for narrowly military reasons. Perhaps there was something of all the foregoing in an incident which well illustrates what I am getting at. In 1966, a top US General from South Vietnam assured a press conference in the States that there were ten thousand North Vietnamese troops in Cambodia. The Pentagon went to the unusual extent of issuing an immediate public denial that they possessed confirmed evidence of such a presence.

Behind all this apparent confusion, the broad realities could probably be sketched as something like the following. There had been, since the Viet Minh withdrawal in 1954/55, a small hard core of communist sympathisers in Cambodia, not least among the Viet-namese minority up and down the country. There had always been, since time immemorial, a casual attitude to the frontier, across which a roaring contraband (and also a more modest village-to-village barter system) had always operated. By 1964, when I arrived, small groups

of communist soldiers were using Cambodian territory for the purposes of transit, rest and re-grouping. The Viet Cong benefited as much as the South Vietnamese from the smuggling of food, medicines and other useful commodities from Cambodia to Vietnam. But most of this was of no significance. Furthermore, the countryside in some of the frontier regions was unpopulated and difficult of access, so no one could blame the Cambodians for not keeping perfect order. But in 1965 the situation began to deteriorate. More guerrillas came and went, and in gradually increasing numbers they started to stay over and to re-supply themselves from within Cambodia. By the end of 1966, when I left, they had more or less unobtrusively set up dumps, sanctuaries, rest and re-grouping areas and supply lines in the remoter frontier areas. They had recruited helpers wherever they needed them and were on the look-out for food and medicines. Their purchases of rice (on which we were able to carry out a useful study) were even beginning to distort the national economy: the Viet Cong were taking a quarter of Cambodian production. The Government in Phnom Penh found it more and more difficult to fulfil legitimate export quotas; domestic shortages began to arise for the Cambodian consumer. (In his memoirs, Sihanouk makes no bones about admitting, for example, that, in the later 1960s, Cambodian rice, bought by Chinese intermediaries, was delivered in Cambodian army vehicles to pick-up points at the frontiers, for the National Liberation Front.) The Viet Cong also set out to acquire arms and ammunition, where they could not get these down the Ho Chi Minh Trail from North Vietnam. Rumours grew of mysterious shipments in communist vessels to the Cambodian port of Sihanoukville, whence covered lorries owned by Chinese businessmen moved up steadily by night to areas close to the frontier. All this, however, was clandestine and concealed. It was no doubt in large measure dictated by the chaos created by the American bombing of North Vietnam and parts of communist-held Laos. The diplomatic decencies were accordingly observed, at least to start with. As time went on, however, the situation was to deteriorate. Well before 1970, the concern for decency had been largely dropped, perhaps because the scale of Viet Cong operations could no longer permit good concealment, but more probably because the communists had decided that Cambodian neutrality had fully served its purpose and might thenceforth be safely compromised. Mutual restraint was no longer possible. The very serious consequences are described in Chapter 20.

But I must return to 1965, when the problem of the Viet Cong was less acute. The Cambodian Government were alarmed by what they saw as the public campaign directed against them in the US; they thought that the American press were misrepresenting the facts and conditioning both domestic and international opinion to expect punitive action against Cambodia by the allied forces in Vietnam. They therefore began by inviting a succession of reputable and fair-minded American journalists to visit – on foot, by jeep or in helicopters – the frontier regions where the Viet Cong presence was alleged to be implanted. Although these journalists had usually been carefully briefed in Saigon and elsewhere before they set out, they not unsurprisingly found nothing which specifically corroborated the accusations made. When this was seen to be ineffective as an answer to their critics, the Cambodians took a more political initiative. On 7 December 1965, the Cambodian Prime Minister formally invited the International Control Commission to supervise the port of Sihanoukville, to see whether it was true that arms were being introduced there for the Viet Cong. (This invitation was taken up in January 1966 and the port was given – slightly surprisingly – a clean bill of health by the Commission.) On 17 December 1965, the Prime Minister said that this control could be extended to cover all barracks, military headquarters and logistic centres in the country. On 18 March 1966, he was further to state that the Commission would be welcome to set up fixed control points in certain frontier areas and at Sihanoukville.

Diplomatically, this is where the Brits came back into the act. I was convinced that the Cambodians sincerely desired the strengthening of the Commission. The International Control Commission enjoyed a high reputation with them. It had, after all, effectively supervised the withdrawal of the Viet Minh and they still saw it as the physical custodian of the understanding which East and West had reached at Geneva to leave Cambodia to herself. The Phnom Penh Government had not been in a good position to keep the Viet Cong out, given the military ineffectiveness of their (tiny and ill-equipped) armed forces, the inaccessibility of much of the frontier and above all their anxiety not to fall directly foul of those whom Prince Sihanouk termed 'the future masters of Vietnam'. Perhaps the Commission could do the job for them, by acting as an international deterrent?

Prince Sihanouk's advocacy of a reinforced Control Commission was characteristically presented in an anti-Western guise, to make it

more palatable to the communists. Perhaps less wisely, although he was aware that the British Co-Chairman had proposed as early as January 1966 to the Soviet Government that the Commission should be expanded, it was not until June that year that the Prince plucked up the courage to make a direct appeal to the Russians for their assent. Sihanouk had hoped that 'The Powers' would somehow fix it up for him. In the event, this hope proved vain and the delay damaging.

The Vietnamese communists and the Chinese were opposed to Commission enlargement, because they thought it could hamper the Viet Cong fighting machine. For several months, they kept their fingers crossed in the hope that the Soviet Co-Chairman would be able to stall the British and that Sihanouk would eventually lose interest. Finally, they were forced into adducing various spurious objections, principally to the effect that an enlarged Commission would be the 'agent of American imperialism'. This shocked the Cambodians, who had hitherto assumed that they could do what they liked in their own country, provided that they kept within the letter as well as the spirit of the Geneva Agreements.

The Soviet Government found themselves in an embarrassing position. They too played it as long as they could, attempting to obscure the issue with propaganda. It is just possible that the Russians could have agreed to an enlarged Commission, if other things had been equal; they had some reason – although not as much as the West – to want to insulate Cambodia from the Vietnam war. But Soviet–Khmer relations had still not fully recovered from a row over Sihanouk's state visit in October 1965, which the Russians had abruptly cancelled at the last moment, out of pique over the Prince's servile public adulation of the Chinese leadership. For wider reasons also, Moscow could not fail to put Hanoi well before Phnom Penh when the chips were down in Indo-China, both for inherent ideological reasons and for fear of what the Chinese might say.

The chief interests involved, apart from those of Cambodia, were those of the US. A discreet and statesmanlike American offer was made to contribute to the expenses of an enlarged Commission. They did well not to mark the project too openly with the seal of their support, leaving it to the British Co-Chairman and the Cambodian Government to make most of the moves.

British diplomacy was very persistent. On a visit to Moscow, Prime Minister Harold Wilson pressed the Soviet leadership to

respond positively (only to be informed, brazenly, that they could not recall having received any such request from Sihanouk), while the Foreign Secretary sent two messages to Mr Gromyko (one of which was never even acknowledged). I myself was in constant touch with the Cambodian Government. I regularly spoke to the Cambodian Prime Minister and Foreign Minister, as well as to my Russian colleague, to influential local contacts and to the leading editors and pressmen. At the height of the affair, I asked Sihanouk personally to confirm to me in writing what he wanted. He duly did so. In the event, the exercise was not totally without reward. The proposals we put to the Russians in January 1966 for an intensification of the International Control Commission's operations in Cambodia helped to take some of the diplomatic heat out of the situation which had been engendered by the American 'hot pursuit' announcement of the month before. Advocacy of an enlarged Commission also enhanced our standing with the Cambodian Government and prepared the ground for the resumption of more cordial diplomatic relations between London and Phnom Penh (see Chapter 12).

This does not make very cheerful reading and prompts the question whether the Commission, even if it had been enlarged, would have effectively secured its objectives. It was composed, after all, not only of sturdy Canadians but also of cynical Poles, while the 'non-aligned' Indians were a vacillating and uncertain quantity. It was clear all along that our plans could be put into full effect only with the acquiescence of Poland and therefore the Soviet Union, and only provided India were prepared to show positive leadership and accept inevitably concomitant risks in a matter where its direct national self-interest was not engaged. It was equally clear that, however numerous and well-equipped the Commission might be, it could never provide watertight coverage of the entire Cambodian frontier, a task which would probably have required several thousands of observers. But every little bit would help tackle a serious and potentially dangerous situation. Even one mobile team, fully equipped with jeeps and helicopters, and making constant unheralded descents at points along the frontier, would have served some deterrent purpose, at that early stage of minimal Viet Cong deployment.

For the future, we had learned one or two grim lessons. The issue in Vietnam had assumed such proportions that it completely overshadowed not only Laos but also Cambodia. The Soviet Government were

putting into cold storage such of their Co-Chairman's responsibilities as was possible. China was rooting for the total humiliation of the US. The prospect for collective and constructive action to strengthen the neutral status of Cambodia was therefore pretty bleak.

Goodbye, Cambodian neutrality: political cartoon, showing President Ho Chi Minh destroying Prince Sihanouk's last hope

L'oncle Ho: «Vous connaissez la chaleur de mon amitié»

11

The Paper Chase

After all these set-backs and disappointments, there remained only one shot in Prince Sihanouk's locker, if he still wished to aim for some form of international guarantee. It was to try to obtain bilaterally what he had been unable to obtain multilaterally, namely a declaration of respect for Cambodia's existing frontiers from each of the other powers concerned.

This expedient inevitably offered less than a Geneva Conference proper, at which China and Russia would have accepted some degree of responsibility for the undertakings given by North Vietnam and (if it were represented) the National Liberation Front. It also offered less, in purely practical terms, than the *de facto* respect for Cambodian neutrality and territorial integrity which could have flowed from all-round agreement to strengthen the International Control Commission. But a series of individual declarations on frontiers might, so the Cambodian Government reasoned, afford at least some degree of international protection and almost anything in this direction was better than nothing at all.

I shall not describe this phase at any great length, because it was to reach its conclusion well after I had left Cambodia, and because the British Government had a less active part to play in it than in previous episodes. Essentially this was a Cambodian initiative. But the narrative which has preceded the present chapter finds its natural conclusion here.

What happened was that the Cambodian Government eventually did secure more or less the undertakings they sought – including one from the British Government – but these undertakings did not succeed in binding the communist Vietnamese to a *de facto* as well as a *de jure* respect for Cambodian neutrality. In the end, as perhaps

could have been foreseen from the beginning, the game turned out little more than a paper chase.

From the outset there was certainly no doubt as to the difficulty that a declaration of this kind presented to the communist camp. The Cambodian Government had been trying for years to extract something cut-and-dried from the Vietnamese, either directly or by means of the good offices of the Chinese. These attempts had invariably produced the same ritual dance. The Chinese would say that recognition of Cambodian frontiers was first and foremost a matter to be arranged with the Vietnamese. The North Vietnamese would point out that Hanoi and Phnom Penh had no common frontier and that the Cambodians should therefore deal first with the South Vietnamese, who did have a common frontier. The National Liberation Front (in the days before the formation of a 'Provisional Revolutionary Government of South Vietnam') would argue that they were a liberation movement, not a government, and accordingly had no legal powers to treat of such matters. All three would urge that, in any case, the first priority was to pursue the war against American imperialist aggression; it would be time enough, when peace was won, to deal with frontier questions; meanwhile the Royal Cambodian Government should be patient and show confidence in their socialist comrades and neighbours.

Nevertheless, in June 1965 the Cambodian Prime Minister informed interested Governments:

> Having taken note of the difficulties in the way of convening the [Geneva] Conference ... the Royal Government consider that it would henceforth be wiser to submit in the near future to each power concerned a draft declaration on Cambodia, accompanied by a frontier map.

The British Government replied on 25 June 1965 to the effect that we awaited this communication with interest and would give it our careful consideration. But nothing was to happen. By the end of July, Cambodian Ministers told me that 'technical difficulties' had arisen which would delay the initiative for several months. Later, they confessed that these difficulties had in fact emerged in private talks they had been having with Hanoi and the Front. By February 1966, Sihanouk was to admit to me that the Government had still not obtained any worthwhile undertaking from the Vietnamese. The Cambodians were persistent, even stubborn, negotiators, and did

not give up. Up to the end of October 1966, when I left, there was still no result to show for their effort.

It must be admitted that recognition of Cambodia's existing frontiers presented difficulties to others than the communist powers. Although the British Government were eventually to convey such recognition, the political, legal and cartographical complications were such as to impose a prudent and unhurried approach to the problem. All three frontiers of Cambodia were to some degree held in question by each of her neighbours. The actual frontier line was furthermore in some places badly traced on the maps and marked out on the ground in worse manner. (I know this because I personally checked out some of the markers on the frontiers with both Laos and Vietnam, in the course of several visits of inspection.)

Technically, the frontier with Thailand gave perhaps the least difficulty. It had been fixed by the Franco-Siamese Treaty of 1907, by which Thailand had retroceded the former Khmer Provinces of Battambang and Siem Reap. There was, however, one point on the frontier which still inflamed feeling on both sides: the temple of Preah Vihear. This ruined temple was situated in wild country on a rocky promontory of the Dangrek mountain chain and the 1907 frontier was supposed to run along its watershed. In January 1966, notwithstanding sporadic, hostile 'incoming' from small arms, I was taken to the ruins by helicopter by General Lon Nol (the head of the Cambodian armed forces and later the instigator of the *coup d'état* of 1970). The temple was relatively easily accessible from the Thai side; on the Khmer side, the mountain face fell steeply away and the approach road wound painfully up a precipice. The Thai had seized the promontory during the Japanese occupation of Indo-China in the Second World War. They were forced to withdraw under the Treaty of Washington of 1946 but returned to re-occupy the temple, after the termination of the French Protectorate in 1953. In a renowned international court action, the Cambodians successfully contested the legality of the Thai occupation: on 15 June 1962, by nine votes to three, the International Court of Justice at The Hague found that 'The Temple of Preah Vihear is situated in territory under the sovereignty of Cambodia' and that 'Thailand is under an obligation to withdraw any military or police forces, or other guards or keepers, stationed by her at the temple or its vicinity on Cambodian territory'. The Thai complained that this ruling was a miscarriage of justice, while nevertheless evacuating the temple.

A legal complication was that the Thai were entitled, under Article 61 of the Statutes of the International Court of Justice, to

apply to The Hague for revision of the judgment within a ten-year period, if they could find important new facts which had not been taken into consideration by the Court in delivering its original ruling.

A worse complication arose from the poor state of political relations between Cambodia and Thailand, and from the banditry and terrorism which prevailed in the area. Diplomatic relations had already been broken off in October 1961 between Bangkok and Phnom Penh. In early 1966, a marked increase in tension between the two countries was created by a series of sanguinary frontier incidents. In December 1965, a Cambodian frontier post was attacked, with the loss of eight Cambodians killed and nine wounded, one of the latter being the local provincial Governor. In April 1966, Preah Vihear temple itself was assaulted, the guardians murdered and the precincts occupied for a brief period. In June, a Cambodian passenger train was blown up by a mine at Poipet, near the Thai frontier. Finally, in July, the frontier was closed. It was not clear who was responsible for these outrages – Cambodian dissidents, local bandits or Thai guerrillas. The Cambodian Government inevitably saw the hand of Bangkok behind this and other episodes and began to take counter-measures, including mine-laying operations on Thai territory. Already in February 1966, they claimed to have sunk a landing-craft of the Thai armed forces which had strayed into Khmer territorial waters.

The situation had become so bad by August 1966 that the UN Secretary General, U Thant, was to send out a Special Representative in the person of a Swedish diplomat, Mr Herbert de Ribbing. This patient and discreet conciliator (with whom I naturally took care to develop a 'below-stairs' personal relationship) was to ply between Bangkok and Phnom Penh until February 1968, alas with very little to show for it at the end of the day, so deep were the antagonisms between the two Kingdoms. It was all a right royal mess, and understandably it was not one into which Her Majesty's Government in London had any urge to plunge.

The problem in regard to South Vietnam and Laos was complicated in a different way. The frontiers established by the French colonial Government within the bounds of Indo-China were essentially lines of administrative convenience, and had not received, following the granting of independence to the constituent states, the degree of binding international endorsement by a signed and duly ratified treaty which the Khmer–Thai frontier theoretically

enjoyed. The Kingdom of Laos maintained on paper, if not in active diplomacy, a claim to parts of Northern Cambodia. The Republic of South Vietnam claimed some off-shore islands under Cambodian administration in the vicinity of the land frontier. The boundary markers – as already noted – were often sparse and neglected; the maps not always accurate. On the Cambodian–Vietnamese section, the situation was the more tricky for repeated frontier incursions, as well as profound mutual suspicion at the political level.

Here too the UN had been active without much success. The Security Council sent a (rather feeble and ill-chosen) three-man Mission to Phnom Penh and Saigon, which reported back in July 1964. The mission noted, *inter alia*, that the South Vietnamese Government had submitted:

> a large body of documentation purporting to prove not only that the Cambodian–Vietnamese land frontier is not clearly marked on the ground but also that it is not properly defined on the maps which were drawn by the Geographic Service of former French Indo-China and were used in the preparation of the maps published and currently used both by the Kingdom of Cambodia and by the Republic of Vietnam. The competent authorities of the Republic of Vietnam drew attention, in particular, to discrepancies of detail in regard to the frontier line in the 1/100,000 and 1/400,000 maps prepared by the above-mentioned Service.

The UN Mission naturally recommended a resumption of diplomatic relations between Phnom Penh and Saigon (which had been broken off in August 1962), the despatch of United Nations observers to the frontier areas, the appointment of a mediator and the resumption of talks between the two Governments on matters in dispute ('particularly the delimitation and marking of the common frontier'). These recommendations were to remain a dead letter. Political mistrust was too great, chiefly on the Cambodian side. Relations stayed resolutely broken off.

Against this background, what was the British Government to do? The question was not pressing in my day, because of the communist hesitations already described, and the actual frontier maps which the Cambodians had promised on 14 June 1965 were never at any stage to put in an appearance. It was only in 1967, well after my departure, that the jam broke and the logs began

tumbling downstream, following a communist decision to give way to the Cambodians.

There was no British objection of principle to what the Cambodians wanted. The stability of the area clearly required either that the states concerned should modify their frontiers by complete mutual and freely given agreement, or that they should agree to accept the frontiers as they then stood. That the territorial erosion of the past, arrested by the French, should not resume in the twentieth century, was an understandable and legitimate Khmer concern. It was to settle this issue among others that we had seen initial merit in a Geneva Conference in 1963, and proceeded to push for one, with belated US assent, in 1965. But this all-round international endorsement was not something we could bring about by the wave of some magic wand. We were not experts on the obscure ins and outs and rights and wrongs of the existing frontier disputes; we did not possess better maps or more precise knowledge of the terrain than anyone else; we had no mandate to adjudicate or resolve the issues at stake; and we risked offending our other Asian friends and allies, whose interests were directly concerned, if we took arbitrary and isolated, unilateral action.

We solved this problem in my time in a provisional, but I thought also positive, fashion. The first step was taken in May 1966, when I delivered to Prince Sihanouk a message from Prime Minister Harold Wilson, which was mainly concerned with the Geneva Conference question and contained the following assurance:

> It is at all times the firm policy of the British Government to respect the sovereignty, the independence, the unity, and the territorial integrity of Cambodia, and to refrain from any interference in her internal affairs.

The second step followed in June 1966. Lord Walston, Parliamentary Under-Secretary of State for Foreign Affairs, who was paying an official visit to Phnom Penh, delivered a speech at a banquet given by the Cambodians in his honour which contained this carefully considered formula:

> The firm determination of the Cambodian people, under the leadership of His Royal Highness Prince Sihanouk, to maintain their neutrality and national independence, contributes in exemplary fashion to the peace and stability of the region.

> This is why Her Majesty's Government have repeat-
> edly affirmed, as I do today, that they respect the
> sovereignty, the unity and the territorial integrity of
> Cambodia.

This gave, I liked to think, some comfort to the Cambodians, without committing us to a formal act of recognition which would have been untimely and insecurely based. Later, when the timing was right, we were to do better.

On 31 May 1967, the National Liberation Front of South Vietnam finally and reluctantly steeled itself and conveyed to the Cambodian Government a declaration of recognition of the existing frontiers of the Kingdom. North Vietnam did likewise on 8 June and China on 13 June. It is idle to speculate on their motives for this move. Probably they felt in need of a gesture to Cambodia at a time when the presence of communist Vietnamese troops and supply dumps in the Cambodian frontier areas was beginning to assume major proportions, if still more or less covert. By July 1967, the list was twenty declarations long, including those of France and the Soviet Union. Germany, Australia and Japan followed, and the list grew rapidly longer still.

This suited us quite well, as there was strength in numbers. On 12 January 1968, we gave the assurance to the Cambodians that

> Her Majesty's Government in the United Kingdom
> respect without reservation the sovereignty, independ-
> ence, neutrality and territorial integrity of Cambodia
> within its present frontiers and recognise the inviola-
> bility of these frontiers.

The latter part of this formula was modified on 8 November 1968, at the request of the Royal Cambodian Government, so as to constitute a statement of recognition, not only of the inviolability of the frontiers, but also of the existing frontiers themselves.

This was the most that we could do. It was not a great deal. The assurances which the Cambodians received from the National Liberation Front and from North Vietnam were to be worth less than the paper on which they were written.

12

Bilateral Relations – The Diplomacy of Small Things

Through a mixture of 'happenstance' and hard work, Anglo-Cambodian relations came good in the end. The hard work lay, as much as anything, in the diplomacy of small things.

Throughout 1964, we stayed very much in the doldrums. The Ambassador had been withdrawn. As already noted earlier (on page 55), the reception to mark the Queen's Official Birthday, animated though it was by other thirsty foreigners, was attended by only one Cambodian – an official from the Ministry of Foreign Affairs designated for the purpose. The Mission was 'in Coventry'; the Embassy compound still full of wrecked cars and rubbish.

Three events helped, however, to draw a line under the past. The Cambodian Head of State made several *ex-gratia* payments to the British Council (for which he had a soft spot), for the damage inflicted during the riots which he had himself authorised and directed. The Conservative administration in Britain was replaced by a Labour Government without responsibility for its predecessor's mistakes and able in theory to begin again from the beginning. Finally there presented itself an opportunity for us to show – in a minor, *protocolaire*, way, but one which did not miss its mark – that we were, despite all that had happened in the streets, courteous and correct in our dealings with the Royal Cambodian Government as such. Prince Sihanouk intended to leave for China in September 1964, on a State visit; and wished to take a train to Canton from the British Crown Colony of Hong Kong. The Palace officials, who were in touch with me about the necessary visas and other administrative formalities, tactfully intimated that the Prince and his entourage would prefer to pass through Hong Kong 'incognito'. I did not see, however, how a foreign Head of State could decently be received on British territory without some degree of ceremony; nor did I think,

from what I knew of their customs, that an 'incognito' passage through the Crown Colony would be considered worthy of the god-king by the Cambodians themselves.

Accordingly I formulated my recommendations in cables to London and Hong Kong. In the event and against the advice from London, H.E. the Governor decided (quite rightly) to lay on a Guard of Honour, with band. He greeted the Prince personally, in full uniform, and not forgetting a bouquet for the Prince's Consort, Mme Monique. I was later thanked by several high-ranking Cambodians for this reception, which had pleased and slightly surprised them. A small enough thing in itself, nevertheless the gesture marked the beginning of the long haul towards a more normal and confident relationship between Cambodia and Britain.

The following year was less difficult. It began with an unexpected token of respect. Sir Winston Churchill died in January 1965. Messages of condolence were sent to the Queen and to Lady Churchill by the Cambodian Head of State. A Book of Remembrance was opened at my Residence in Phnom Penh on the day of the State Funeral in London. The Book was laid on a table covered with the national flag, and bearing a portrait of Sir Winston; flowers and a large wreath were arranged before it; the Military Attaché and myself, both in uniform, received those who had come to sign. Rather to my surprise, since we were supposed to be 'in Coventry', the Cambodian Foreign Minister, accompanied by the Head of Protocol at the Ministry of Foreign Affairs, turned up to sign on behalf of the Cambodian Government. In a short speech the Minister asked me to convey to Her Majesty's Government the sympathy of all Cambodians. More significantly, in retrospect, because he represented not only the top level of the 'Establishment' but also the moderate, pro-Western, centre of Cambodian politics, the Book was also signed by Prince Sisowath Sirik Matak, then Minister of Education, and a cousin of Sihanouk. Accompanied by the Head of Protocol at the Royal Palace, Sirik Matak delivered a personal message from the Cambodian Queen Mother. (This Prince was a romantic and ultimately a heroic figure, with whom I was to enjoy episodic but rewarding subsequent contact, which had to be handled with kid gloves and considerable discretion. I was not totally surprised, when he became the principal architect of the *coup d'état* which deposed Sihanouk in March 1970. He was murdered by the Khmer Rouge in 1975, after scorning US offers of evacuation and defiantly remaining in Phnom Penh to face Pol Pot.)

A third Minister to sign told me how he had come to respect Sir Winston Churchill through reading his famous war memoirs. This was the first occasion on which Cambodian Cabinet Ministers had visited the Embassy since the previous spring. Why? Churchill had had nothing much to do with Cambodia in his long career. Perhaps it was in part a question of a folk-myth inherited from the French, at one with respect for *La BBC* and *La Royal Navy*. Perhaps, too, there was, despite everything, the simple sense that 'a great man had passed away', as my close chum, the US Chargé d'Affaires put it, at the conclusion of his personal letter of condolence to me.

In March 1965, and ten months into my mission, I was able to sign a new Civil Aviation Agreement regulating the use which Royal Air Cambodge and Cathay Pacific could make respectively of Hong Kong and Phnom Penh airports. The value to the Cambodians of their commercial links with Hong Kong was always something worth pointing up in Phnom Penh and an arrangement guaranteeing more frequent flights between the two was therefore of both symbolical and practical advantage. In April, the British Government announced their support for the convening of a new Geneva Conference in order to endorse Cambodian neutrality. As recounted previously , the Right Honourable Patrick Gordon Walker, the former Foreign Secretary, came out to Phnom Penh as a special emissary from London to establish personal contact with the Cambodian leadership in this matter. In the event, the Geneva Conference never materialised – the Chinese and North Vietnamese were against it and the Royal Cambodian Government, with great inner reluctance, had to renounce the idea. From the point of view of Anglo-Cambodian relations, however, the score was now even: we had at last rallied to Prince Sihanouk's proposal, even if the Conference itself could not now take place.

Perhaps this was why, in May 1965, the Cambodian Government asked for *agrément* for their newly appointed Ambassador in Paris, Mr Sonn Voeunsai, to be accredited also in London. They had previously closed their Embassy in London on grounds of economy in December 1963, saying that their Ambassador in Paris would cover the United Kingdom. In practice, however, that gentleman had never showed up in London, no doubt in order to mark a coolness in relations. It was therefore a step forward that, the Cambodian Embassy in Paris having changed hands, the new man was to come to see us. Mr Sonn Voeunsai, with his appointment approved by the Queen, was to present his credentials at Buckingham Palace in November that year.

But there was more work to be done in the meantime to put things on a better footing. By the middle of the year, I was receiving hints from high quarters in Phnom Penh that a further gesture of friendship and conciliation would be well received by the Cambodian Government, if we chose to take the initiative in making one. Could some distinguished figure not come out to talk to the Prince? These hints were to result in an unorthodox British move which was to be the turning point on which the real improvement which followed was to hinge.

To the certain knowledge of the Foreign Office in London, and as my Cambodian contacts had not failed to remind me, there was really only one Englishman – or rather, Scotsman – in the world who knew Prince Sihanouk extremely well, enjoyed his genuine friendship and could speak to him frankly, man to man. Such was the Right Honourable Malcolm MacDonald. This extraordinary individual combined the gifts of politician, diplomat, writer, naturalist and statesman. A Cabinet Minister (for the Dominions and Colonies) for several years before the Second World War, he had filled with distinction, during and after the war, a succession of high-level politico-diplomatic appointments. He was a favourite among us 'Mandarin' professionals. As Commissioner General in South-East Asia from 1948–55, and as Co-Chairman of the Geneva Conference on Laos in 1961–62, he had been in regular touch with the Cambodian Head of State both before and after Cambodian independence. The two of them took to each other from the outset. Better than any other man, therefore, Malcolm MacDonald could talk over our difficulties. In 1965, he was far from South-East Asia: based in Nairobi, he was the British Government's Special Representative in Africa. But I put forward a plan of action, the telegrams flashed to and fro, and I had a slice of luck. Malcolm MacDonald would be on leave in London at the same time as Prince Sihanouk would be having a routine medical check-up in the South of France.

So, in September 1965, MacDonald called at Prince Sihanouk's holiday villa at Grasse. The two men talked for hours in a relaxed atmosphere and found common ground upon which to build for the future. At about the same time, the Prince gave a dinner at Grasse for the former British Ambassador in Phnom Penh, by now Consul General in Marseilles, and his wife, receiving them with kindness and proposing a toast to Her Majesty the Queen. The corner had been turned.

One gesture deserved another and the Cambodians responded accordingly. In November, the Deputy Prime Minister, Mr Son

Sann, paid a good-will visit to London, accompanied by a travelling exhibition depicting modern Cambodia. Son Sann was received with courtesy, and there was a well-conducted and substantive exchange of views with the Foreign Secretary and the Permanent Head of the Foreign Office. The exhibition, too, went well at the Royal Festival Hall, where it received 10,000 visitors; and there was a loyal turn-out from all corners of the Foreign Office at the associated inaugural film show. It was at this moment that the Cambodian Ambassador came over from Paris to present his credentials.

In all its phases, the operation was a success. Subsequently, Prince Sihanouk was to send a message to the Queen, published prominently in the Cambodian press, expressing the wish that the bonds of friendship between the two countries should be strengthened in a climate of 'understanding, confidence and esteem'.

The year 1965 was to end well in Phnom Penh also. There was much suspicion to overcome and it took time for the locals to size up the new Embassy team and accept that we were well-disposed toward Cambodia and her people. My own particular moment of glory, and the apotheosis of the 'play-boy' Chargé d'Affaires, was to come in the early autumn. There was a ball at the palace given to mark a wedding in the royal family. The bride, Her Royal Highness Princess Bopha Devi, was Monseigneur's favourite daughter (and, incidentally, one who was to survive the Khmer Rouge and eventually became a cabinet minister in post-war Phnom Penh). The Diplomatic Corps was naturally invited. The band started to play something (to Cambodians, at that date, totally new) by Chubby Checker and I decided I had had enough. I was bored and ill at ease. In an out-rush of pent-up complexes – as described in Cameo II (on page xxv) – I seized the bride, launched into a wild 'Twist' and was awarded by the Head of State a title and a trophy.

His was not a spontaneous gesture. The Prince had seen the chance to give an off-the-cuff signal. In December 1965, four weeks after Mr Sonn Voeunsai had presented the credentials accrediting him as the Ambassador of the Kingdom of Cambodia at the Court of St. James, I gave a dinner party at my official Residence in Phnom Penh which was attended, for the first time, by senior Cambodians. We were, at last, out of 'Coventry'. The flood gates began to open. Less-exalted, but still-important, Cambodians felt free to drop in, as did the (Twist-conscious) gilded youth of the city.

The next year, 1966, was a year of follow-through and consolidation. It was hard graft, but worth it, because we got some modest

results. What part, if any, was played in this by the Crocodile Princess (see page 215 ff.), I shall never know.

On the diplomatic front, we were able to respond favourably when the Cambodian Government appealed to the two Co-Chairmen of the Geneva Conference to strengthen the International Control Commission in Cambodia. Once again, communist opposition prevented the Cambodians from getting what they wanted. But we had tried our best and I took care that the Cambodians knew this.

Bilaterally, we were at last able to use the public media to help develop a better mutual understanding. The principal Cambodian weekly tabloid magazine, *Réalités Cambodgiennes* – at that time a high-level mouthpiece of the Government and enjoying a relatively wide circulation within the Kingdom – was running a series of supplements on foreign countries and the invitation came to the Embassy asking us to produce such a supplement on Britain. The initiative was theirs, not mine, and it came from 'The Top'. So we went to town with what was our first, large-scale, public-relations exercise since I had arrived. We knocked up a punchy presentation. I wrote a political open letter to readers of *Réalités Cambodgiennes* as the turnover piece. The rest was about 'Swinging Britain' on a theme which I thought would have resonance for a Cambodian audience – *Tradition et Modernisme*. Whatever its journalistic merits, the exercise put the British Embassy, at any rate, fully on the popular map. Nobody in Phnom Penh could thereafter be in any uncertainty that the British were back in business. With the encouragement of their editors, a series of British newsmen came through Cambodia in the spring and summer, intrigued as always by the phenomenon of a Cambodia at peace in an Indo-China at war and encouraged by the welcome which the Cambodian authorities offered them. They ran stories which helped to apprise the public at home in the UK of what was going on in that distant land. The Cambodians thought they were written up objectively and also favourably.

My own standing in Phnom Penh may also have received a further fillip from a visit I made to Beijing in March 1966. As stated earlier, the locally dominant, Asian power was China. To be on reasonable terms with China was perhaps to be in reasonable standing also in Cambodia. I felt that we British did not enjoy sufficient credit among the Khmer for having been the first Western country – in 1950 – to recognise the Chinese People's Republic. Not enough Cambodians seemed to realise, at a time when the opening of a French Embassy in Beijing in 1963 was still a novelty, that the United Kingdom had

there from the outset a Diplomatic Mission. On my arrival in Beijing, I therefore took care to send picture postcards, without delay, not only to my colleague the Chinese Ambassador in Phnom Penh, but also to all the Cambodian Ministers and senior officials I could think of. It worked.

Meanwhile, British visitors of all kinds began to be more frequent in Cambodia and I must say I was glad to see them. Tom Dalyell MP and his wife came out in June and got on famously with the Deputy Prime Minister, who gave a dinner in their honour. Later the same month, Lord Walston, Parliamentary Under-Secretary of State for Foreign Affairs, paid a carefully prepared official visit. He was received in audience by the Cambodian Head of State, who told him that he would be glad to receive a new British Ambassador in Phnom Penh and that the Royal Cambodian Embassy in London would be re-opened by end of the year. At a banquet given in his honour by the Cambodian Prime Minister that evening, Lord Walston delivered a speech supporting Cambodia's neutrality and endorsing her territorial integrity, which created a minor sensation in the city and set out British policy clearly and to everyone's satisfaction.

In October 1966, Mr H.A.N. Brown CMG, CVO arrived in Phnom Penh and presented to the Cambodian Head of State the Letters from the Queen announcing the recall of his predecessor, and accrediting him as Her Majesty's Ambassador Extraordinary and Plenipotentiary to the Royal Cambodian Court.

As his faithful lieutenant, I naturally accompanied the Ambassador on this occasion, together with the Military and Air Attachés, all of us spick and span in our white tropical uniforms. The ceremonial, which we had carefully rehearsed beforehand in the Ambassador's drawing room, went off smoothly. As we arrived, the Royal Guard presented arms and we stood to the salute as the band played first our stately National Anthem (a creditable musical performance, considering that the score had only reached the band from Hong Kong two days previously) and then (in semitones more familiar to them) the haunting National Hymn of the Khmer Kingdom, a beautiful oriental melody which always made the hairs on my neck stand on end. Cordial speeches were exchanged; a message from the British Prime Minister delivered; the precious credentials themselves, carried up the Throne Room by me on the traditional Cambodian chalice of silver filigree, safely taken up by the Ambassador and handed solemnly to H.R.H. Each in turn, we bowed (in accordance with god-king protocol, in a more extravagant manner than is

required of British subjects at Buckingham Palace), shook hands with His Royal Highness and then took our seats in that gilded hall, the sunlight pouring in through the open columns on the flank, and the glittering waters of the Mekong just visible beyond the lawns of the Palace, for an Audience of State which lasted three times the span which Protocol normally allotted. Prince Sihanouk began by saying that there were now no differences between the two countries and that he was happy that relations had been restored to normal. This was what I had waited to hear for the 28 months I had served as Chargé d'Affaires. After Prince Sihanouk had withdrawn and we stepped out of the Palace, between the lines of flashing sabres and down the red carpet to our motorcade, the event seemed quite surreal. Yet it had not been a dream. The text of the two formal speeches appeared the next morning in the newspapers, which I read slowly over a bowl of coffee. The next evening at the local flea-pit we watched ourselves enacting the scene on the newsreel.

I left Cambodia four weeks later, having seen my Ambassador well settled in the saddle and handed over my duties as Head of Chancery to a new and experienced First Secretary who had arrived after the presentation of credentials. The Foreign Office had considered that it might be unfair to me, and perhaps awkward for the new Ambassador, to leave me for too long as the Number Two in an Embassy which I had for so long run along lines of my own. I for my part, relieved though I was to see a fully-fledged British Ambassador back in Phnom Penh, had already floated the idea that an early move would be appropriate. A new team would be needed for the new political set-up, in which my own style at the post would no doubt become increasingly as irrelevant as my past experience would have become outdated. So I was offered accumulated leave and then the coveted posting (in which the Prime Minister, Harold Wilson, had taken an interest) to the British Embassy in Paris.

And so, after the customary round of farewell parties, I shook hands with friends and colleagues on 28 October 1966, and flew away, my modest mission accomplished.

*After 'In Coventry' restrictions are raised, young Cambodians relax
during a dance at the Residence*

Presentation of credentials to the Head of State, in the Throne Room, by the new British Ambassador, immediately before the author's departure from Cambodia

Other Kids on the Block

13

Cheshire Cat Chinese

In the following four chapters, I shall discuss the positions in Cambodia of certain other foreign countries. They are China, France, the United States and Australia. Why them? Because each, in their own way, carried weight – few other countries did.

I begin with the People's Republic of China, because her influence in Cambodia in my day exceeded that of any other country. It was most of the time probably a benign influence. But at times the Dragon roared and Cambodia trembled.

I had read Chinese literature in translation as a boy and volunteered (but I was sent off to learn Persian, instead) to learn Chinese when I joined the Diplomatic Service in 1956. I was delighted, eight years later, to be posted to Singapore, where I hoped to learn at least a little Cantonese. Cross-posted to Phnom Penh, I had to abandon this linguistic pretension – French and Cambodian were to be a sufficient mouthful. But in a way I came closer to China. I watched the play of Beijing's diplomacy from the viewpoint of a very interested party. I called from time to time on the Chinese Ambassador and would seek him out at cocktail parties and receptions, for a polite exchange of views. As already mentioned, I realised a long-standing ambition in visiting Beijing in early 1966. It was on these contacts and observations that a wary and qualified respect for contemporary China came to be built. My colleagues in the British Chargé d'Affaires' office in Beijing, in extensive briefings to me, left me no illusions – not least in the light of the Great Famine of 1956–61, in which 37 million Chinese had starved to death, as a result of Mao Tse-tung's foolish and criminal 'Great Leap Forward'. The Cultural Revolution which was to break out in China, shortly after my visit there, was to leave me baffled and depressed. In 1967, our office in Beijing was to be sacked by the

Red Guards and some of our diplomatic staff beaten up. But anyone who has travelled a little in China, visited some of their factories and communes, seen their patient and industrious millions and observed their spirited youth will come away with positive as well as negative reactions.

The story of China in Cambodia in my day was briefly this. In 1964, on arrival in Phnom Penh, I found Sino-Cambodian relations at their best – wisely conducted by the leadership in Beijing and gratefully sustained by the Royal Cambodian Government. In 1965, things began to go wrong. A hardening in the Chinese attitude to the Vietnam war – provoked by the reinforcement of American combat troops there and by the start of the systematic US bombing of North Vietnam – had awkward repercussions in Cambodia. As already explained, the Chinese torpedoed Prince Sihanouk's dearest diplomatic project, the convening of a Geneva Conference to be devoted to the elaboration of international guarantees for Cambodian neutrality and territorial integrity. Things were no better in 1966, when the Chinese scuppered Prince Sihanouk's further proposal for an enlarged International Control Commission. After the outbreak of the 'Cultural Revolution', things got worse and some members of the Chinese community in Phnom Penh began to behave provocatively. In the years immediately following my departure, Sino-Cambodian relations were in fact to become quite strained – although, as long as Prince Sihanouk remained in power, China was to remain what he persisted in calling 'Cambodia's Number One Friend'.

Now a look at the Sino-Cambodian scene in greater detail. Communist China had overshadowed Cambodia since the early years of independence. In a speech to the Philippine Congress in February 1956, Prince Sihanouk said:

> as long as the feelings of the Government of communist China ... are not belied by some signs of change, I cannot, as the present leader of ... a small people of only 5 million inhabitants, under any circumstances rebuff the friendship of the leader of a people of 600 million.

There were in the event no subsequent 'signs of change' in China's fairly consistent policy of friendship with Cambodia. As a result, Sihanouk's foreign policy acquired an increasingly pro-Chinese bias. But if Sihanouk was prepared to sell, would he find a buyer?

A measure of Chinese interest in Cambodia was dictated by the facts of geography and history. Geographically, Cambodia (although without a common frontier) was a close neighbour of China. For Yunnan Province, she was the second doorstep down into the South-East Asian street. Chinese cultural influence, the glory and power of the Imperial Court, even the commercial pull of her not too far distant markets, had asserted themselves in varying degrees in Cambodia for most of the Christian era. Most contemporary Cambodians – naively or otherwise – tended to interpret China's historical role as that of a sort of Indo-China policeman, a powerful but respected neighbour, concerned that order should prevail along the imperial boundaries. They kept their fingers crossed that communist China would not be too different.

However that may be, in the early 1960s, out of a population in Cambodia by then of over six million, between six and seven per cent were Chinese. This small but influential racial minority was centred in towns and major villages. In the capital city of Phnom Penh, where less than half the inhabitants were ethnic Cambodians, perhaps a quarter were of definite Chinese descent. As financiers, entrepreneurs, traders, shopkeepers and skilled workers, the Chinese controlled much of the nation's commerce. As a whole, they were respected and admired by the Cambodians. Things Chinese were auspicious and prestige laden. More Cambodians wore jewellery inscribed with lucky Chinese characters than could actually read Chinese. The ambitious and go-ahead eagerly sought Chinese partners in marriage – such interbreeding was 'good for the complexion' Sihanouk once quipped to me, with a wink.

Inter-marriage had not, however, significantly diminished the homogeneity and national consciousness of the expatriate Chinese. As so often elsewhere in Asia, they were broadly in sympathy with and compliant towards Beijing. There was an almost equally large Vietnamese minority, who were also economically influential and were also communist-infiltrated. It followed, therefore, that at least 12 per cent of the population of Cambodia, including over half that of Phnom Penh, was potentially a medium through which subversive activities could be conducted.

There was, however, no evidence to suggest Beijing was pursuing a policy directly designed to subvert the Cambodian State, fruitful though the field would no doubt then have been. In 1956, Mao Tse-tung and Chou En-lai congratulated Prince Sihanouk on his far-sighted decision to be neutral, offered economic assistance to

Cambodia (it was probably the first offer to a non-communist country made by China) and let it be understood that, if ever the Prince had trouble with the Viet Minh, he needed only appeal to Beijing to have it stopped. In a joint statement made by the Prime Ministers of Cambodia and China in August 1958, Chou En-lai specifically advised the Chinese residing in Cambodia to refrain from all political activity in their host country. Thereafter, the Chinese Government made no apparent effort to intervene on behalf of proscribed Cambodian communists, or to mitigate the damage to the commercial ascendancy of Chinese merchants inflicted by Prince Sihanouk in his various measures of economic nationalisation and so-called reform. There was a large and active Chinese Embassy in Phnom Penh. With considerable success, it put out information and propaganda of a kind calculated to consolidate the position of Big Brother, without giving offence to the Royal Cambodian Government. This began to change only in the last four months of my service, when the Cultural Revolution was approaching its height.

The Chinese programme of economic assistance to Cambodia was not anything like as generous and apt for local needs as it was cracked up to be; but it made itself felt, politically. A Sino-Cambodian trade and payments agreement of June 1956 had provided for the annual exchange of goods between the two countries, and China appeared to be ready cheerfully to accept the sort of Cambodian export which was not readily marketable elsewhere. Factories for the manufacture of plywood, textiles, paper, glass and cement were constructed, equipped and set to work in Cambodia by a floating population of up to 300 Chinese experts. Some of the projects sometimes proved uneconomic 'white elephants', but the Cambodian leadership did not seem to mind too much (albinos had always held a special place of honour in the elephant stables of the Khmer Kings). To Sihanouk what was important was that all of this aid was being given 'without strings'; impressive-looking industrial installations had been handed over free of charge to the Cambodian Government, for operation by the Cambodians themselves. The US aid programme which Prince Sihanouk terminated in November 1963 was more generous, useful and prudently administered. But somehow the Americans never got the full credit and it was the Chinese who came to lead the field, with less outlay.

China also ran a military aid programme, supplying vehicles and light weapons for 22,000 men (over two-thirds of the entire Cambodian

Army), plus a workshop for their maintenance and repair. The navy was ignored as unimportant. For the air force, the Cambodians were told to turn to the French or the Russians. No tanks or heavy artillery were provided; the Cambodian terrain was not greatly suited to tank action, nor the Cambodian soldier to the effective use of complex modern equipment. The Chinese concentrated instead on what for the Cambodians were the essentials.

It was, however, on the diplomatic front where China was most demonstrably active in supporting Cambodia, and in maintaining the closest working relationship with Prince Sihanouk personally. Sihanouk's son and designated successor, Prince Naradipo (later to be put to death under Pol Pot) had been joyfully received for education in Beijing. In May 1963, a Treaty of Friendship was signed between the two countries. In 1964 (although not the following year), the Chinese were outspoken in their support for a Geneva Conference to endorse Cambodian neutrality and territorial integrity. They vociferously took the Prince's side of the argument, throughout the series of frontier incidents in which Vietnamese and US forces attacked – accidentally or intentionally – Cambodian villages along the frontier.

At the same time, they assiduously paid court to Norodom Sihanouk personally: the latter was profoundly flattered by the lavishness of his reception in Beijing and by the individual attention invariably accorded to him by the highest personalities of the Chinese State. Later, when overthrown and in exile, he was to live as an honoured State guest of the People's Republic, in a mini-palace offering all 'mod. cons'. (Pathetically but characteristically, in his boyish glee, Sihanouk writes in his memoirs that 'China was to put at my disposal a whole complex of fine solid buildings, forming a very comfortable and bourgeois village – right in the centre of Peking, a few hundred metres from the famous Tian An Men Square. My private residence was a vast and luxurious dwelling, with numerous servants, a brigade of talented cooks, a well-equipped secretariat and all the services of a royal administration', with garden, sporting installations and a cinema.) In his declining years, after his final abdication in Phnom Penh, Sihanouk was to spend more of his time in similar conditions in Beijing and to receive medical treatment there for cancer and other maladies.

Sinologues sometimes advanced the theory that China's objective was not to subjugate South-East Asia in the sense of conquering it militarily, so much as to reduce or even exclude Western influence

and to establish control through local governments, not all of which needed to be communist in complexion. Burma was the usually cited example of where this policy had been put into effect.

I was not qualified to judge the general validity of this thesis. But it seemed to be consistent with what the Chinese were doing in Cambodia. (Incidentally, Sihanouk was to record in his memoirs that Chou En-lai continued, right up until his death in 1976, to reiterate to the Prince China's view, that 'Cambodia should remain neutral'.) No doubt the Chinese reasoned to themselves as follows: Beijing had little or no military capacity for direct intervention in this country, with which China had no common land frontier. Subversion could, for the time being at least, be ruled out as imprudent and anyway unnecessary. A neutral, but China-friendly, Cambodia would be a useful counter-balance to a reunited Vietnam. Time itself was on China's side. Events ought, therefore, to be permitted to follow their dialectically inevitable course. There should be no forcing the pace on the Chinese side nor the jogging of China's elbow by the Vietnamese or for that matter by the Cambodians either. Too much was at stake in Indo-China for local aims in Hanoi or Phnom Penh to call the tune in Beijing. But, in the longer term, the objective must be gradually to convert Cambodia, not into a formal 'satellite', but into one of a string of peripheral Asian states subservient to China.

In my early months in Phnom Penh, Chinese pragmatism appeared to have reaped ample reward. American influence in Cambodia was, at least for the time being, close to zero. China had been permitted freely to extend her foothold. Prince Sihanouk had given increasing diplomatic support to Beijing on the world stage. The People's Republic had received recognition from Cambodia in July 1958; at the Colombo Conference in December 1962, Sihanouk had declined to lend himself to schemes of conciliation between India and China which were unwelcome to the latter; in July 1963, Cambodia had refused to sign the Nuclear Test Ban Treaty, which Sihanouk denounced as a bargain of dupes and a demagogic act; in 1964, Cambodia gave full diplomatic support to Beijing over the Gulf of Tonkin incident, effusively welcomed the explosion of the first Chinese nuclear device, and undertook to lead the van at New York in calling for the admission of China to the United Nations and her admission to the Security Council as a permanent member in place of Taiwan.

What were the consequences of China's Cambodia policy for the West? Chinese patience offered us some immediate comfort. One consolation – or so it seemed to me then – lay in the fact that, at that particular critical juncture, China was, by a curious paradox, exercising a certain restraint on Prince Sihanouk's actions. Impatient of obtaining the guarantee of his neutrality which he thought a Geneva Conference could offer, Sihanouk had come round more and more to the view that he should simply recognise North Vietnam and the National Liberation Front and hang the consequences. Such consequences would almost certainly have been adverse to the West. Had the Saigon regime found it necessary to cut Cambodia's life-line of trade and supply down the Mekong River, Sihanouk might have felt compelled to retaliate by granting military facilities to the Viet Cong; South Vietnam would no doubt then have wanted to launch military reprisals in 1964 and the whole affair could have escalated much sooner than it did into a major regional crisis.

The dangers of this appeared to be better understood in Beijing than anywhere else. The Chinese had skilfully avoided formally committing themselves to military intervention in defence of Cambodia. They had declined to sign a defence treaty with Sihanouk. During his visit to Beijing in October 1964, Sihanouk was reliably reported to have been dissuaded from doing anything too radical. Chou En-lai had pointed out that Cambodia's greatest present asset was her neutrality; like virginity, it was not to be lightly discarded. This note of caution was to be repeated during Prince Sihanouk's next official visit to China, 12 months later. Thus, in a discussion with Prince Sihanouk in October 1965, subsequently reported verbatim in the Cambodian press, Chairman Mao said that, while it was sometimes necessary to react to the international situation created by the imperialists, 'Cambodia has been independent for only twelve years – if due account is not taken of this fact and if action is taken which is too precipitate, the results will not be so good'.

Trouble was already in the air. By the close of 1966, when I left, an unexpected cooling-off had taken place. This trouble began and ended with Vietnam. China's refusal, in the spring of 1965, to countenance any negotiation with the Americans, initially over Vietnam but later over anything which could conceivably impinge on Vietnam, was to cause the Cambodian Government great embarrassment and even anguish. As noted in Chapter 7, it was the Chinese attitude which greatly contributed to the failure (from Cambodia's point of view) of

the 'Indo-Chinese Peoples' Conference' held in Phnom Penh on the Cambodian initiative. Prince Sihanouk's dream of a great congress of the nations (presided over by himself), to neutralise three quarters of Indo-China, was thereby shattered. As seen in Chapter 8, the Chinese then went on to scupper Sihanouk's proposal, in March 1965, for another Geneva Conference on Cambodia. They vanished when the Cambodians had most need of them, leaving only an ironical smile, like the Cheshire Cat. Sihanouk told a prominent neutral visitor that 'these damned Chinese have put a spoke in the wheel'.

Interestingly, about this time Sihanouk placed much less emphasis than formerly in his political speeches on Chinese promises of military aid. It was true that various empty guarantees of Chinese 'full support' had been given to Cambodia. According to Sihanouk (although I myself doubted it), Chou En-lai had even given him an oral assurance in October 1964 that, if Cambodia were invaded, China would afford not merely war material but also military personnel. This was not the cast-iron guarantee that Sihanouk wanted and there had been no further subsequent improvement. Thus, in his message of 20 May 1965 to Sihanouk, Chou En-lai merely said that the Chinese people 'absolutely will not stand idly by, should Cambodia be attacked by US imperialism', and that the 650 million Chinese were comrades-in-arms of the Cambodian people. This did not afford great comfort. Given China's passive reaction to the bombing of North Vietnam, some Cambodian Ministers and senior officials were beginning (quite rightly) to wonder whether the Chinese would lift a finger if the Americans or South Vietnamese were to bomb Cambodia.

After such disappointments, some of the Chinese gilt was off the Cambodian gingerbread, and efforts were accordingly deployed by the Chinese leaders to recoup their position. They succeeded in doing so, following a great stroke of luck. As already mentioned in Chapter 10, on 8 October 1965, the Moscow leadership abruptly 'postponed' the state visit which Prince Sihanouk was to pay to the USSR four weeks later. Sihanouk was half-way through the process of paying similar visits to China and North Korea and the news was broken to him in the North Korean capital, Pyong Yang, in what was apparently an extremely tactless fashion by the Soviet Ambassador there. This miserable envoy, Sihanouk complained, crossed his legs (not what one did, in an audience with H.R.H. in Phnom Penh) and actually helped himself, unbidden, from a cigarette box on the table,

before reading out a message in Russian from a crumpled piece of paper, extracted from the pocket of no doubt an equally crumpled Moscow business suit. No convincing official reason was given for Moscow's decision. But it was clear to everyone that the Soviet leaders, at the very top, had taken strong personal exception, at a time of acute Sino-Soviet tension, to what they saw as the pro-Chinese bias of the speeches which Sihanouk had delivered in Beijing a week or so previously. However that may be, the Soviet action was an unprecedented slap in the face for the Prince; he described it as 'an unprecedented affront' and as 'an absolutely inexcusable snub, a veritable provocation to a break between our two countries'. This was where the Chinese stepped in, magnificently, to make all things whole. The Prince was due to return to China from North Korea for a second, purely private stay. But President Liu Shao-chi flew down to Harbin to meet him and a brilliant programme of entertainment was organised at short notice which rivalled in splendour the arrangements for the official part of the visit of the week before. The Prince was flattered, consoled and – above all – encouraged to see the 'Russkis' as touchy, boorish and ignorant peasants. The further economic aid which China then offered – a hospital, a medical institute, and university scientific equipment – while less than what the Cambodians had hoped for, was nevertheless worth having. The new military aid – mainly anti-tank and anti-aircraft weapons, with a half-promise of some eventual tanks and aircraft – was actually quite substantial. These consolations were followed up over the succeeding months by a series of tough Chinese statements in support of Cambodian territorial integrity – notably in December 1965, when (as previously noticed, see page 120) the American press was being comprehensively briefed about upcoming hot-pursuit operations against the Viet Cong across the Cambodian frontier.

Notwithstanding the above, signs of disappointment and even irritation with the Chinese were to multiply in Phnom Penh at all levels in the Cambodian 'Establishment'. The army (traditionally conservative) were not too happy at the prospect of having to become so dependent on Chinese equipment. An offer of Chinese financial aid to reduce the Cambodian budget deficit was declined. Pro-Chinese articles in the local press became less ecstatic and pressures on the Cambodian Government to mend their non-Chinese fences found public expression in greater press coverage of other countries, such as France and Australia, and in the efforts (described in Chapter 12) to normalise Anglo-Cambodian relations.

In the course of 1966, a growing uncertainty was also to become apparent among Cambodians as to the wisdom and effectiveness of Chinese foreign policy generally. The overthrow of President Sukarno of Indonesia and the anti-Chinese pogrom which was to follow in Djakarta and elsewhere, Fidel Castro's denunciation of the Chinese Government, and anti-Chinese manifestations in Ghana, were all carefully noted in Phnom Penh. So, too, were the excesses of the Cultural Revolution in China, involving the humiliation and overthrow of many of the Chinese leaders and such outrages (horrifying to Cambodians) as the desecration of Buddhist altars at the hands of raging mobs of 'Red Guards'. The suspicion was voiced quite widely, even in left-wing Cambodian circles, that the Chinese, not content with wrecking every effort to secure an end to the Vietnam war by negotiation, actually wished the war to continue and were happy to 'fight to the last Vietnamese'. These sentiments appeared to have communicated themselves to the Cambodian Head of State. Inaugurating a television station in Phnom Penh in early 1966, Prince Sihanouk explained to a knot of foreign Heads of Misson, including myself, that Cambodia's foreign policy was based strictly on reciprocity:

> China has always been understanding towards us and is at present – and I emphasise *at present*, gentlemen – very friendly. As long as this continues, we shall reciprocate this friendship.

More trouble was in the offing. As already recorded in Chapter 10, the Chinese told the Cambodians in June 1966 that they were opposed to any strengthening of the International Control Commission: the Cambodian Government would do well to drop their proposal, implementation of which would be giving way to the blackmail of the American aggressors in South Vietnam. This was almost Prince Sihanouk's last hope of discouraging clandestine use of Cambodian territory by the Viet Cong and thereby of upholding his neutrality and keeping his country out of the war. Later the same month, the Chinese objected to a Cambodian initiative to improve relations with Thailand, arguing that a reconciliation between Phnom Penh and the reactionary regime in Bangkok might hinder the Thai people's 'struggle for liberation'. In June 1966, Chou En-lai asked whether he could visit Cambodia the following month, but was told that it would not be convenient for him to come until September, after General de Gaulle's state visit in August. The

former then called the whole thing off, in an (untypical) Chinese huff.

The general political drift when I left Cambodia was therefore towards a stricter neutrality. This trend, stemming from the developments described above, was to gain momentum, after General de Gaulle's visit, and was indeed to find further expression in exploratory moves that autumn towards the eventual resumption of diplomatic relations with the United States. In the event, the American Embassy was not to be re-opened until August 1969, but the first overtures began in 1966. Prospects for an improvement in Sino-Cambodian relations were to be further compromised in 1967 by continued subversive excesses by the Red Guards in the Chinese Embassy and by sympathisers among youngsters in the local Chinese community (including the circulation of provocative, political tracts), which were put to an end only after Prince Sihanouk had personally intervened with Chou En-lai. Later still, in 1968 and 1969, the Chinese were to be suspected, in collaboration with the Vietnamese communists, of stirring up discontent in the provinces and of organising logistical assistance for the Viet Cong in so flagrantly open a fashion as to make Cambodian neutrality a mockery. This was a major catalyst of the tragedy recorded at the end of this book.

But I am now describing events which I did not myself witness. In my time in Cambodia, the disappointments described in this chapter were not to bring decisive change to Cambodian foreign policy; the drift towards a more balanced international posture was essentially a surface phenomenon, leaving the political depths relatively undisturbed. My first judgements were to be my last. Prince Sihanouk was never the puppet of Beijing (no more than he was anyone else's creature). He was perfectly capable of striking out on his own when he chose. There are numerous examples of his having done so – one of them being his decision (contrary to Beijing's wishes) to grant full diplomatic recognition to the newly independent state of Singapore in 1965 and another the belated resumption of diplomatic relations with the United States in 1969. But personal factors played their part. Sihanouk once boasted to me (and later recorded in his memoirs) that Mao Tse-tung (of whom he was, however, secretly in awe and afraid) had a soft spot for the Prince. The Prince's friendship with a pragmatic Chou En-lai was well known. And, in any case, the hard strategic facts remained. China was considered to be the country of the future in Asia; her long-term friendship had to be enlisted in the cause of ensuring

Cambodian national survival. Cambodian policy towards China was therefore guided by considerations not of ideology but of self-interest. There might have been an element of self-deception also, but in the main this policy was, given the basic premiss, pretty realistic in a pessimistic sort of way.

14

Feudal French

I come now to how France figured in Cambodia. But before that, I have to say a word about the French in general, because the English (and to some extent the Americans) have a hang-up about them.

It was the Duke of Wellington who famously said that England was, always had been, and he trusted always would be, the adversary of France. Some British Euro-sceptics are still of the same opinion. In my experience, even our Cabinet Ministers can find it difficult to feel as fully at home with their French colleagues and opposite numbers as they should.

I myself come out of a different corner. My father volunteered to fight in France in 1914. I myself learned French early. While still a boy, I was made to read the masterpieces of French literature. French history became almost as familiar to me as England's. My school and university plunged me into French political thought. Able to read French with ease, but unable to speak with great fluency in the vernacular, I took myself off one summer to the Sorbonne to secure some improvement. I have always thought it wrong that the beautiful and precise French language should fall into disuse before the world onslaught of Basic English. I admire French intelligence, seriousness and capacity for hard work, set off as they usually are by a redeeming lightness of touch and pleasure in being alive. I am fond of the French countryside, the most varied and beautiful in Europe and I believe Paris to be one of the most captivating cities in the world.

Of course, the French being human, there is also a less engaging side to their natures. Generalisations about national identity are suspect and should be avoided wherever possible. But a foaming-at-the-mouth British or American francophobe will tell you that he detects among some Frenchmen a peasant avarice and meanness of

spirit, a contempt for fair play, a patriotism that is all too chauvin-
istic, a franco-centrism that is akin to insularity, an impatience and
intolerance that is plain bad manners, an egocentricity and mistrust
of others that is close to being pathological, a deficiency of individual civic sense which is matched only by a chilly disregard (on the
part of the authorities) for personal liberty, an intellectual arrogance
and cultural complacency that is as unthinkingly supercilious as it is
patently unwarranted, a class-consciousness and snobbery that
would have shocked the architects of the French Revolution.

But then, who shall cast the first stone? My reply to the franco-
phobes is that the French in my day saw some of the foregoing faults,
and a good deal more besides, in the British. They observed that in
no mean number we tended to be intellectually muddled, smug,
pretentious, full of unjustified self-esteem, expecting the world to
do our bidding, cultural philistines, incompetent linguists, cynical
neo-imperialists, perfidious opportunists, hide-bound in outmoded
traditions, socially immobile and swinishly acquiescent in dull
discomfort. Also, much too close (shock horror) to *les amerloques*
(as the *Canard Enchainé* liked to call them, in my years in Paris).

There are contradictions and injustices in both these strings of
prejudice and imperfect observation. There is truth in the paradox
that, as a brilliant young French Ambassador once suggested to me,
France is England and England is France. We are in some respects
the mirror image of each other.

However that may be, what was the nature of the French
presence in Cambodia? Would it endure? What was its significance
for the West? I will begin by offering the following overview.

Among the former possessions of France in Indo-China, Cambodia
retained, in the 1960s, by far the most influential French presence.
French panache gave Phnom Penh style and distinction. Culturally,
it pleased the French, and no doubt was considered to advance what
was called the 'civilising mission of France', that Cambodia should
be francophone and francophile from the palace to the paddy-field.
Politically, France was by far the deepest rooted, and was throughout
my service the dominant, Western power. Thus, in matters of high
diplomacy and the world game, the Cambodia of Prince Norodom
Sihanouk was a useful partner for the France of President Charles de
Gaulle. Indeed, there was, at times, a feudal feel – even a proprietorial
one – to the relations of Paris with Phnom Penh.

At grass roots, the French tended to be better mixers than other
Westerners, despite the fact that they made fewer cultural or social

concessions to their expatriate environment. The inter-penetration of French experts and Cambodian officials in the government machine was remarkable to an Englishman coming from Singapore, where the local Chinese had long been accustomed to running things handsomely without our help. French advisers were at hand in most ministries, French teachers abounded in the *lycées* and universities and French military instructors trained the Cambodian armed forces (despite the fact that the latter had come to acquire quantities of Chinese equipment). A motley crew of mercenary French journalists helped the locals operate the Khmer propaganda machine.

The Cambodians reciprocated these tokens of active metropolitan interest. The Khmer élite were French-minded; they liked French food and clothes and paid at least lip-service to French culture; the best of them endeavoured to reason and debate like the products of the *hautes écoles*. The Cambodians knew that French commercial practice was often sharp and profit margins were imaginative; yet they readily did more business with their former 'protectors' than with anyone else. After a century of French rape and Cambodian concubinage, the two felt comfortable together, like that mythical old couple, Darby and Joan.

French political purpose in Cambodia was naturally Gaullist, with at times the active co-operation of the Khmer Head of State. As seen by me from Phnom Penh, a major objective in Paris was to assert at all costs an independent world status for France. Anti-Americanism came into it. The French Government wanted the Americans out of Vietnam. They were not above petty gestures, to make the point. The US Government was scouring the world for spare Skyraider fighter bombers – by then obsolete for Cold War purposes, but ideal for anti-guerrilla operations, and in short supply. They tried to buy them back from countries to whom they had sold them in the past. France, when approached, said '*Non*', but in 1965, with a flourish, the French Ambassador in Phnom Penh handed over ten Skyraiders to the Cambodian Government, as part of a military aid package. France also wanted closer relations with China. This rang all the right bells with the Prince, given his sense of grievance against the Americans and his conviction that only a friendly and placated China could bring about security in the region. So the 'Sun King' that was de Gaulle and the 'God King' that was Sihanouk joined hands with each other, paradoxically, in the conviction that they wanted very much the same things.

More specifically, the Cambodians looked to the French to give them diplomatic support and sorely needed economic aid, and also to show the world that neutral Cambodia had Western, as well as Eastern, friends. The French in their turn appeared to imagine Cambodia a potential bridgehead from which they might be able to sally forth and re-establish a healthy relationship with Indo-China after other Western influences had been ejected or diminished. More immediately, a neutral Cambodia might one day underpin a regional peace settlement of which France could conceivably even be the principal architect – thereby restoring the prestige which had been lost in the resounding French military defeat and political humiliation in Vietnam in 1954.

The French position was, however, not as strong as it looked. Much depended on personalities, and was vulnerable to leadership change in Paris or Phnom Penh. The Cambodian economy had been depressed. Business was not good. Although France enjoyed a traditional commercial primacy, for some time there had been no significant new investment by private French concerns – the expatriate French community in Phnom Penh had been slowly but steadily shrinking for years. Socially, a certain distrust of the white man as such – a formerly little known phenomenon in Cambodia – was beginning to creep into the Khmer nature, thereby eventually making life difficult for French experts, businessmen and mercenaries. Politically also, the French Government had cause for uneasiness. They had had little more success than anyone else in persuading Norodom Sihanouk to do other than his own inspiration dictated. They did not like either the extension of Chinese influence, or the growth of right-wing or left-wing opposition to Sihanouk, within the Kingdom.

How did the French in Cambodia see the British? Francis Garnier, one of the most passionate colonisers of Indo-China in the nineteenth century, was almost obsessively anglophobe. In my day, there were still one or two of his ilk left around, although we also had our share of friends and admirers. By and large, however, the general attitude was one of indifference. The French were more successful by far, and therefore surer of themselves, in Phnom Penh than in Saigon or Vientiane. Their first concern had been to stay 'in' with the Cambodian Government and otherwise to devote themselves exclusively to the French national interest. During the past few years of local difficulty for *les Anglo-Saxons* in Cambodia, the French had (understandably) held themselves aloof from us, but (unworthily and myopically) taken quiet satisfaction, some of them, in our discomfiture. There

had, however, always tended to be a conflict, as regarded dealings with ourselves, between chauvinists and internationalists, between exponents of *Action Française* and proponents of the *Entente Cordiale* – between disreputable *barbouzes* and the correct and courteous professional diplomats at the French Embassy.

The latter, to be fair, especially once the British Embassy was out of the diplomatic dog-house, were forthcoming and even co-operative. The new emphasis was probably due to the fact that the French in the field – who had to deal with stark realities to which the Paris world-view did not hold the key – were by then in doubt as to their ability to keep any sort of control over events. The French aim was to keep the Cambodian neutralist regime going, with Phnom Penh still successfully perched on the East–West tight-rope. They believed we wanted the same, and they had no illusions as to the means at our disposal and no enormous respect for our *savoir faire* in the country, but evidently they considered that every little helped.

I welcomed this evolution. It worried me more than somewhat when we did not get on together. I had a respect for French local knowledge, and made it my business to pick their brains. I called regularly at the French Embassy to talk over current events. I was careful, whenever I undertook some major diplomatic initiative, or I had useful information which could decently be imparted to others, to keep my French colleagues as closely informed as my American and Australian. I had no favourites, but I felt the French had the right to hear from my lips, and not in some subsequent garbled report from intermediaries, what I was up to, in what I freely acknowledged to be more 'their' zone of influence than 'ours'. Further, whatever the reserves I might have entertained about Gaullist foreign policy generally, I considered that, in Cambodia at least, we travelled much the same road. France under President de Gaulle might no longer represent the West, as we understood that expression; but she was undoubtedly western with a small 'w'. Cambodia was not, and never had been, strictly our affair, ever since a British general had handed it back to France in 1945, after the Japanese occupying force had surrendered to his. We had available no great resources to devote to the Khmer, even though we had chosen to make an effort to support Cambodian neutrality and slow the growth of communist influence. The French on the other hand did have such a commitment and were prepared to honour it with men, equipment and money. The influence of France in Cambodia was therefore an asset for us all.

I was to be reinforced in this view, and also to be instilled with an unwilling admiration for the man personally, when President Charles de Gaulle paid his successful state visit to Cambodia from 31 August to 2 September 1966.

International attention was mainly focussed on the significance of this visit for the Vietnamese war. The world press had speculated that a major mediatory French initiative would be launched. In practice, little of immediate practical effect was to emerge. President de Gaulle's speech in Phnom Penh on 1 September delivered a forthright attack on the American position in Vietnam, but contained no offer of French good offices. Indeed, he specifically said 'France will not attempt any mediation in this conflict'. Instead, the General simply appealed to the US to undertake to withdraw from Vietnam within an appropriate and fixed period of time.

The French President's entourage had had private talks both with the local North Vietnamese Government Representative and with members of the National Liberation Front. But they had not obtained (and possibly had not even sought) any modification of substance whatsoever in the by then entirely rigid policies of the Vietnamese communists.

This was a disappointment to me personally. My sentiments then were those expressed, at a slightly earlier stage, by the Cambridge history don, David Thomson. He wrote in *The Times*:

> President de Gaulle's finest accomplishment during his first term of the presidency was to end the war in Algeria. It would be fitting if, in his second term, he could also bring peace to Vietnam, where the United States is becoming as fully committed as ever France was. The task would need – and would receive – no less delicacy of circumspection and intricacy of manouevre than did the patient accomplishment of a cease-fire in Algeria. Nothing would more enhance the world prestige of France than for its President to accomplish it. Should hopeful opportunity arise, the President – in spite of his disavowal – would find it irresistible.

General de Gaulle's speech in Phnom Penh was, however, made for the long term and in the conviction that the Americans would eventually be compelled to withdraw from Vietnam; only then could France, if she had meanwhile won a measure of confidence from the communists as a potential honest broker, aspire to effective inter-

vention. The text of the discourse could accordingly do little more, in the months that followed, than gather dust in the archives of the Chancelleries concerned; and I coolly so reported to London. The British Ambassador in Paris (the detached and scholarly Sir Patrick Reilly – later to become my boss) agreed.

The main immediate achievement was bilateral, in the field of Franco-Cambodian relations. There was evident rapport between the two Heads of State. French policy was to support Prince Sihanouk, and Cambodia's neutrality and integrity. The state visit magnificently served both purposes. The mere magic of the General's presence usefully reinforced the Prince's domestic prestige, at a time when discontent with his conduct of affairs of state had been perceptibly on the increase among the local elite. But Monseigneur also obtained more tangible blessings from the General: a statement of respect for Cambodia's present frontiers in the final joint communiqué and agreement in principle on further French economic and military aid. France had almost (but not quite) at least temporarily displaced China as Cambodia's 'Friend Number One'. Western values generally began to look more respectable in the land than they had done for some years past.

The arrangements for the President's reception were the most lavish and spectacular ever known in Cambodia. Thus, 300,000 Cambodians turned out to greet de Gaulle on his arrival. Half the population of Phnom Penh were present for his open-air speech on 1 September. A fabulous pageant was mounted by floodlight before the brooding temples of Angkor. The French President and his wife were accommodated in the Royal Palace itself, a personal honour totally without precedent. The associated security precautions were on an equally grandiose scale. Dubious French locals were banished by the dozen to the distant seaside and almost every petrol station in Phnom Penh was drained in case someone should blow it up while the General rolled by. Armoured cars stood at the street corners and steel-helmeted troops lurked in the leafy shade of the main boulevards.

President de Gaulle himself made a remarkable figure, standing on dais and tribune with Prince Sihanouk's head coming up to his waist. The General was not comfortable in the heat and looked old and drawn. Yet he forced himself through his heavy programme with determination and dignity. Receiving the Diplomatic Corps, he had a word with each of the foreign Heads of Mission. With a handful, the General found time for a brief private chat. They

included myself (possibly because of the UK's Co-Chairmanship of the Geneva Conference, and conceivably also the prompting of Hubert Argod, the well-disposed French Ambassador). When it was my turn, I found myself exposed to a magnetic force of personality. The General spoke clearly and concisely and I listened; I spoke briefly and he nodded. I was more than flattered – I was bowled over. As for the Cambodians, he so charmed and impressed them that they could hardly keep still for excitement. Monseigneur, in particular, was constantly wriggling and bobbing his head at the General's elbow. And when the General spoke, with a rasp, of 'foreign intervention' and an 'armed expedition without benefit or justification' in Vietnam, he communicated the authority of the father of all prophets and patriarchs.

Some of the visiting metropolitan-French press found it hard to accept the evidence of their senses in witnessing certain aspects of the scene during the State Visit. They gaped at the golden palaces and glitteringly-attired, processional lictors. They grovelled before the beautiful women and guzzled at the lavish banquets. They gasped at the night spectacle of the Royal Cambodian Ballet dancing by lamp light before the massive, jungle-set silhouette of Angkor Wat. They groaned in metropolitan over-sophistication and disbelief, when, at a giant rally, an Ode of Welcome (in Alexandrine, 12-syllable iambics) was declaimed in an affected French accent by a young female 'representative of the Cambodian masses' who turned out later to be Her Royal Highness Princess Norodom Viryane.

Yet what the East hyperbolises is no less genuine than what the West understates. There was no question that the great mass of the Cambodian people welcomed Charles de Gaulle with joy, concurred (in so far as they understood it at all) in his view of the world, took comfort from his presence among them and would cherish the memory of their Wise Old Man from the West for several years to come. It was not without some justification that Monseigneur had welcomed him with the words; 'General, you find yourself here, in a sovereign country which is Francophile – and very Gaullist!'.

So much for high politics. Now for a glance at the grass roots: the day-to-day realities of the life the French led and the attitudes they held. Seen on the spot and in the flesh, what did it all look like? In what follows, I amplify the points touched upon in the overview with which I began.

There was undoubtedly a curious proprietary sense towards Cambodia. As we saw in the latter part of Chapter 2, the French

saved the country from being swallowed up by the Siamese and the Vietnamese in the nineteenth century. France had moulded Cambodia's legal, educational and political system, and given her an international language through which she could access the scientific and cultural achievements of the West. The French had also enjoyed the exclusive right to exploit the Cambodian economy and get rich quick. The French were therefore sensitive to the intrusion of foreigners from other advanced countries into 'our Cambodia'. In South Vietnam, the massive American presence was strongly resented by most Frenchmen there – and not only because they did not profit directly from it. The apparent welcome extended to the Americans by the South Vietnamese made the French feel like cuckolds. When in 1965 South Vietnam decided to break off diplomatic (although not consular) relations with France, a wave of emotion swept over my French friends in Phnom Penh, as if they had been betrayed by a loved one. In Indo-China generally, the French seemed to me to want to hang on to what they still had and if possible to make a 'come-back' where they had lost out. Politically, these sentiments found expression between the lines of a message from General de Gaulle to Ho Chi Minh in July 1966:

> You cannot be in any doubt, Mr President, of the vigilance and sympathy with which, from the beginning, and even more in recent times, France has been following the drama of Vietnam, attached as she remains to Vietnam by history, by human affinity, and by all those ties which subsist between them.

Coupled with the natural and understandable French possessive instinct, I detected traces of a complex of guilt and inferiority. The defeat of French arms at the hands of the Viet Minh had delivered a traumatic shock to the French nation which still seemed to be felt by the local Indo-China hands. As Bernard Fall put it in his book *Indochine 1946–1962*,

> Two sons of Marshals of France, twenty sons of generals, 1,300 Lieutenants, 600 other officers and 75,000 NCOs and men died in Indo-China. ... For this reason, we have no right to forget this war; whether we like it or not, it will doubtless cast its influence over our lives for several decades to come, just as the mistakes in the Crimea or in Mexico carried the seed of defeat at Sedan.

Imposed upon these defeats was the wretchedness that so many Frenchmen felt about Algeria. Underlying it were the humiliations which they had suffered in three successive major wars with the Germans, the inferiority complex engendered by economic and political weakness in the early post-war period, and their fear of cultural extinction – amounting for some Frenchmen almost to a sense of suffocation – by 'Anglo-Saxon' civilisation.

Perhaps it was this possessiveness and this guilt, combined with cultural pride and a mistaken sense of intellectual superiority, which was at the root of the bitter and condescending, anti-American feelings which were evident among many Frenchmen in Cambodia in my day. True, General Paul Ely, chief of the General Staff in Indo-China in 1953–54, had written in his memoires (*L'Indochine dans la Tourmente*):

> The power of the United States ... derives from an enormous economic boom which brought the country overnight to the rank of a world power. This explains what has sometimes been an inadequate acquaintance on their part with certain aspects of the world and consequently an often clumsy way of dealing with problems and with men. It is a weakness of youth, which will disappear with time but which sometimes is a little tainted with pride. And yet how can we not make obeisance, faced with the thirst of this great people for knowledge and understanding, faced above all with their great generosity?

Unhappily, however, not all Frenchmen in Cambodia affected such charity. Criticism of the American record in Vietnam was on the lips of many. Some of it may have constituted fair comment. But, with not a few Frenchmen, it was unfair, and a manifestation of mere *Schadenfreude*.

Local French attitudes to the British were an odd mixture: on the one hand of respect and even affection and on the other of distrust and the suspicion that we were in league with the Americans against France. Some of the more anglophobe French gave me the impression of living in the belief that the Hundred Years War was still in progress. Others, with rather more justification, treated us as idiots who knew nothing about Cambodia. Only a few were out-and-out anglophiles, who came up to shake our hands at every cocktail party. When the French were impressed

with us, it was often in unexpected and revealing ways. French visitors there tended to admire Hong Kong (its brisk efficiency and above all the remarkably pragmatic *modus vivendi* with communist China). They also spoke with respect of Singapore and Malaysia (both of them, whatever their conceivable shortcomings, enormous achievements, by French standards, in decolonisation). The numerous French serving officers in the military mission were particularly well disposed. Some of them were possibly disillusioned over Algeria or the lesser priority given to conventional arms in order to pay for the French nuclear *force de frappe*. Many of them found their professional soldiering tame and lacking the glamour and adventure which they had sought when they first took their commissions at St Cyr or Saumur. I sometimes suspected that a few of them envied their British colleagues, who could, even in an era of cut-back, aspire to command a squadron of armoured cars in the Radfan, to parachute in to quell an uprising in Africa, or to lead a company of Ghurkhas into the jungles of Borneo.

Gaullist thinking, while rejected out of hand by the few, appeared to go quite deep with the many. Whether or not the individual Frenchman agreed with this or that action or policy of President de Gaulle, the generality of the French (as the generality of the British were later to welcome Margaret Thatcher, at least in her earlier years) seemed to welcome Gaullism in so far as it had put France back on the map, restored her self-confidence and commanded the attention and respect of the foreigner. The General's aspiration to grandeur found a place in the hearts of many Frenchmen in Cambodia, however much they might have been embarrassed to admit it.

One of the more diverting political and social phenomena in Phnom Penh was that of the mercenary journalists who operated the official propaganda machine. There were seven or eight of them at the top of the tree and they churned out with considerable facility the daily flood of official protests, denials and clarifications which had become the expostulatory public vehicle of Cambodian foreign policy. They were a colourful collection of men. Most of them could write – and write well – when they chose. Some knew the country like the backs of their hands. But there were also those who, Gauloise parked in the corner of their mouth, were content with typing through the night for the morning editions such prose as:

> We Cambodians, proud of our liberty, our traditions,
> our national honour, and united as one behind our
> beloved Head of State, now issue the most serious
> warning, the most dire defiance, to all imperialists and
> neo-colonialists and lackeys of the so-called free world.
> In the name of our fatherland, our beloved Kampu-
> chea, we solemnly declare that … [bla-bla-bla] ….

But I must not be too hard here. The identification with their adopted motherland was self-interested, but also not un-tinged with idealism. The mercenaries clearly enjoyed Cambodia. There was the usual sprinkling of malcontents; and all of them grumbled from time to time about the Khmer Government. But most French expatriates seemed to me to love the life they led and to like the land in which they lived it – teachers, professional soldiers, doctors, merchants, scholars, diplomats, restaurant owners, mechanics, conscripts performing voluntary service overseas, government experts of all shapes and sizes, old Indo-China hands who expected to lay their bones in Cambodia. In human terms, they 'belonged'. They were certainly an asset to the country of their residence. A select few were worthy to be classed with the best of the nineteenth-century colonisers and explorers.

A man I admire among the latter – despite his deep-seated anglo-phobia – was the Francis Garnier already mentioned. He incarnates for me the France of my more romantic affection. He wrote in a pseudonymous pamphlet (*La Cochinchine française en 1864*):

> This generous nation … has received from Providence
> a higher mission, that of emancipation, of bringing into
> the light and into liberty the races and peoples still
> enslaved by ignorance and despotism.

When I read these words, I hear the drums of the Imperial Guard beating in the courtyard of *Les Invalides* and the march of France's legions across the centuries.

But perhaps my favourite colonial Frenchman was Auguste Pavie. In his book, *A la conquête des coeurs*, he wrote as follows of his days as a telegraph clerk in the small Cambodian town of Kampot.

> How many times have I traversed and re-traversed and
> searched them through and through, those forests, that
> plain, those swamps, those sands of Kampot? Which is
> the village in my area at whose feast I have not taken my

place; how many in the countryside have not spoken with me, if only a few words? In constant contact with the natives, I got used to the idea of living completely amongst them. And they neglected no opportunity to make my stay pleasant. It was not only to their festivities that they used to invite me. They passed me word also of their hunting trips, their fishing expeditions.

Later on in his career, as Consul General of France at Vientiane, this man was instrumental in adding Laos to French Indo-China. He succeeded in doing so, largely by the attraction of his personality and the affection in which he held the peoples who came under him, and it was in the trackless Cambodian countryside that he learned the elements of his true calling – the winning of the hearts and minds of men.

It has to be said that not all Frenchmen in Cambodia really liked the Cambodians. The light-skinned and slender Vietnamese or Laotians were usually more to the French taste – thought of by the latter as more intelligent and more receptive to French intellectual discourse, to Catholicism and to the French way of life. The darker-skinned, more stocky, Khmer were certainly less forthcoming and assimilable, socially and culturally. There was less inter-marriage, too. But Auguste Pavie was not alone in his passion for things Khmer. He left behind a tradition which was still in evidence a century later. I saw it at its best in the scholars, archaeologists, and linguistic experts of the *Ecole Française d'Extrême-Orient*: a dedicated, competent and enthusiastic band of brothers. They stood no chance of personal enrichment or (to any great degree) of personal preferment: they worked, almost literally, for love. (I address to them, in their anonymity, this respectful salute.)

My years in Cambodia were spent living in a tiny, anglophone enclave surrounded by Frenchmen more numerous, influential, knowledgeable and confident than we were. In this respect, my experience may have been similar to that of the French equivalents in, say, Kuala Lumpur or Delhi or Nairobi. This could on occasion prove a slightly daunting experience; but it was always a challenge and an enrichment. Most of my French acquaintances proved to be good companions and generous hosts. My French diplomatic colleagues were competent and 'correct' professionals, whose judgement and understanding I held in high esteem.

For me personally, the French and their works in Cambodia furnished an important part of the intellectual stimulus, friendship and amusement of the post as I knew it.

15

Ugly Americans

By contrast, the US in post-independence Cambodia did not exactly shine. In my view, US diplomacy was cack-handed and careless of what was thought in Washington to be a country of no great importance, with a vacillating and cheeky Head of State. The Americans were certainly Prince Sihanouk's *bêtes noires*. Accordingly, they had an extremely difficult time of it in my day. The US Embassy was twice the subject of serious assault by politically-directed street mobs. As things got worse, the Americans ran down the size of their mission, until only a handful of determined men remained to run the shop. On 8 May 1965, at the instance of the Royal Cambodian Government, diplomatic relations were finally broken off and the US Embassy withdrawn.

Why did this come about? I will try to answer the question by first describing American attitudes and activities in Cambodia, not as they were, but as they were viewed by the Cambodian Head of State. For the fact was that Prince Sihanouk saw the Americans through differently tinted spectacles from those of most people.

On my arrival, I found that American influence and position in the country had been, at least for the time being, reduced to near-zero. The US economic and military aid programme, worth $400 million or more over the years, had been abruptly terminated by Sihanouk in November 1963. Mr Randolph Kidder, the new US Ambassador-designate, whose appointment had already received the agreement of the Royal Cambodian Government, was refused the right to present his credentials in September 1964, and was bidden to depart almost as soon as he had arrived. In November, threats to expel the US Embassy from Phnom Penh, and thereby completely to sever diplomatic relations with Washington, reached their apogee in an ultimatum issued by the Cambodian Government.

Subsequently, they suspended this threat and accepted an American suggestion for talks on neutral ground; but the development gave the measure of the by then terminal condition of US–Cambodia relations. The Americans had been initially quite well received in Cambodia ten years before; their prestige then stood high as a result of the victory in the Second World War and by virtue of American championship of the under-developed and smaller nations. What, from the Cambodian point of view, were the causes of such a profound fall from grace?

Paradoxically, the fundamental reproach which Sihanouk extended to the United States was probably that of failure. He had no confidence in the Americans' ability to protect their friends in Indo-China. The US had attracted communist lightning a good deal too close to Cambodia for comfort. Having made (in his view) a mess of Vietnam, the US would in the end wash their hands of it and sail away to safety across the Pacific, leaving the locals to fend for themselves (which was indeed what happened). In the interest of preserving Phnom Penh from the likely fate of Saigon, Monseigneur preferred to keep the Americans at arm's length and court the friendship of the ascendant power, China.

More than as losers, however, the Prince also thought of the US government as erratic in their alliances. No Asiatics who were on the US side (he said several times to me, or in my close hearing) could be certain that they would not be 'terminated with extreme prejudice' – look at the way, he used to argue, that the Americans had thrown their former friend and ally, President Ngo Dinh Diem of South Vietnam, to the wolves in November 1963. Whatever the truth might be about Diem's downfall, this event did, I am certain, make a deep impression on Sihanouk. In his own mind, the Americans were unreliable, in a manner in which his personal friends Mao and Chou would never be.

Idiosyncratically, Sihanouk also considered that what basically inclined the United States Government to look sideways at him was the tiny size and the neutral status of his country. He once said to me that if Cambodia had a population of a hundred million, like Indonesia, the United States would soon change their tune. He felt great pride as the descendant of a long line of Kings and he was conscious of the past glories of the Khmer Empire. He was therefore all the more resentful of the fact that Cambodia was not what it had been at its imperial apogee. The Prince knew his country was small and backward; but, like a cripple with a deformity, he hated people to

notice it. He described the Washington view of Cambodia as one of 'scorn and contempt'. This frustration and annoyance was compounded by the attitude of a certain section of the American press, to which this thin-skinned and narcissistic Prince was morbidly sensitive, and which tended to ridicule him and belittle what he considered his major achievements.

The princely grudge against the Americans, however, seemed to extend further back than the mid-1960s. In April and again in September of 1954, Sihanouk had appealed to the United States for military help against the communist Viet Minh operating on Cambodian soil. Sihanouk claimed that his doubts about the value of American support had begun when, as a result of this appeal, it became clear to him that the US would (perfectly understandably, one would have thought) no more commit their armed forces in Cambodia to help make the country safe for Sihanouk, than at Dien Bien Phu to bail out the French. Cambodia's policy of neutrality was accordingly proclaimed in October 1954 (during an official visit to Phnom Penh by Pandit Nehru) and confirmed at the Bandung Conference in April 1955 (following Sihanouk's conversations with Chou En-lai). As we have already seen, Sihanouk disliked the Thai and hated and feared the Vietnamese; for him it was an article of faith that these peoples were bent on completing the destruction of Cambodia on which they had embarked centuries previously. Communism was for him only one problem among many. Accordingly, in 1956, Sihanouk began to protest against SEATO manoeuvres. Just as the Russians sometimes professed to fear that it was the Germans who ran NATO, so Sihanouk liked to claim that it was the Thai who were setting the SEATO pace. The acid test came when the South Vietnamese occupied parts of Stung Treng (later Rattanakiri) Province in 1958. On that occasion, so the Cambodians alleged, the State Department warned Cambodia not to use American weapons to oust the intruder on the grounds that these weapons had been given to Cambodia for use only against the communists. It was around that point that Sihanouk reached the conclusion that US aid gave him effective protection neither from the communist insurrectionaries on the one hand, nor Western-aligned, Asian neighbour-governments on the other.

Sihanouk found confirmation for his distrust of Washington in what he alleged was clandestine, subversive activity directed against him by the US in concert with Thailand and South Vietnam. For Sihanouk, there were three American Governments, each with its

own policy towards him; those of the President and the State Department, of the Central Intelligence Agency and of the Pentagon. Sihanouk moaned repeatedly (I really cannot say how far he inwardly believed) that the latter two organisations were implacably opposed to him and bent on securing his downfall.

In his speeches, Sihanouk repeatedly unfolded a long list of real or alleged conspiracies. In 1958, there had been the Dap Chhuon affair, in which the Governor of Siem Reap Province was said to have plotted an uprising with the approval of Thailand and South Vietnam. He was apparently caught, with two Vietnamese agents, in possession of espionage material of alleged American origin. The story ran that a diplomat on the staff of the American Embassy in Phnom Penh who may have had some contact with Dap Chhuon then left the country precipitately. In January 1959, the Americans were blamed for the flight to Vietnam of Sam Sary, a former confidant of the Prince, who risked facing charges of treason, and for a parcel bomb which nearly killed the Queen Mother in August. Above all, the Americans were held to aid and abet the activities of Sihanouk's mortal Cambodian rival, Son Ngoc Thanh, a politician then in exile in South Vietnam where he headed the anti-Sihanouk Khmer Serei ('Free Khmer') movement. The Khmer Serei beamed subversive radio broadcasts into Cambodia from mobile stations in South Vietnam and Thailand. Sihanouk maintained that this was done with US-supplied equipment. These events greatly hardened Sihanouk in his distrust and fear of the Americans. He saw their complicity in everything – including the deposition of President Diem in Vietnam already referred to – and found it frankly incredible that Washington could not put an end to the activities of his enemies if they so chose. Like the paranoid he was, he accordingly concluded that he was next on the Central Intelligence Agency's list; and he found confirmation of this fear in the growing, personal virulence of the clandestine broadcasts which he described to me as 'a nail being driven into my skull'. The dismissal of US aid in November 1963 was due in part to this atmosphere of menace, mystery and myth. He knew and admired only a tiny handful of Americans. Senator Mike Mansfield (whom I subsequently got to meet and like, when he was Ambassador in Tokyo and I was his EU opposite number) was one of them. The diplomat, Chester Bowles, another.

Finally, there had been problems in personal relations. With a few distinguished exceptions, Sihanouk did not like or understand

Americans. Although fundamentally an Oriental, Sihanouk was also in some measure a Frenchman – being French-educated, French-speaking and a respecter of French culture, manners and methods of thought. The Eastern Potentate in him was too readily offended by the back-slapping, American familiarity and informality: the Frenchman in him despised what he might have interpreted as American political immaturity and cultural impoverishment. The French themselves had usually been careful to treat Sihanouk with the deference and flattery to which an oriental monarch, nay a Cambodian god-king, might feel justly entitled. According to his own account, Sihanouk, had, however, never been treated by the Americans with proper respect. Certainly he could not forget the smallest slight, whether accidental or intended. Time and time again in his speeches, a list of familiar grievances cropped up: how he was greeted on arrival in the United States on an official visit only by an Under-Secretary of State; how in New York, where he went to address the General Assembly of the United Nations, he had been jostled aside by policemen to make way for Mr Khruschev. 'Questions of honour', Sihanouk once wrote, 'are much more important for a well-born Asiatic than money'.

The early diplomatic representatives of the United States in Cambodia did little to redress the balance. Sir Christopher Meyer, an acute observer of official America while our Ambassador in Washington, quite rightly insists (*DC Confidential*, page 84), 'The very best American diplomats are pound for pound as good as any you will find anywhere, and often better'. But virtually none of their calibre ever got anywhere near the US Embassy in Phnom Penh in the years that were formative and crucial. Since Cambodian independence, a succession of American Ambassadors had failed to establish effective, human rapport with Sihanouk. Most of them were ill-fitted for their job with this particular Oriental Prince and probably of poor quality generally. About their idiosyncrasies, there was still current in Phnom Penh in my day a series of remarkable legends, some far-fetched, but all eloquent of a certain insensitivity. Robert McLintock, the first Ambassador of the United States to the Cambodian Royal Court, so the wags had it, had appeared at the Palace to present his credentials appropriately dressed in silk hat and trimmings, but accompanied by two large dogs – animals for which Asians do not share the regard of the Anglo-Saxons. On another occasion, according to legend, the same Ambassador had appeared at the airport to greet (or bid farewell to) the Head of State

clad only in sports shirt and shorts. On a third occasion, he was said to have been clumsy and insulting. Opening a US-supplied maternity clinic, the Ambassador had said to the Prince: 'This should particularly interest you, as a great one-man manufacturer of babies!'. The next US Ambassador was said to have carried everywhere with him an ornamental stick: but a stick (so professional anti-Americans were quick to point out) was associated in the Cambodian mind with arrogance and aggression. A third US Ambassador was reported to have had an unfortunate manner which got on Prince Sihanouk's nerves. Towards the end of his service in Phnom Penh, this particular diplomat was rumoured to be in the habit of closing his eyes and muttering the phrase 'How I hate that man'. Even the sharpest of Phnom Penh critics could find nothing to say personally against the fourth Ambassador, whom the Prince accepted. But I was gloatingly assured that, on that Emissary's watch, it had come to Sihanouk's attention that the Princely voice, shrill and staccato, had been imitated by junior staff down the corridors of the American Chancery, and the Princely person likened by them to 'a little monkey'. All without impediment and correction from their boss.

From the outset of my service in Phnom Penh, the outlook for Cambodian–American relations was therefore discouraging. In early 1964, the South Vietnamese and the Thai had come in for swingeing attacks. Now it was the Americans who were held responsible for their policies. The Prince apparently came so to suspect and fear the Americans that an evil construction was placed on almost everything they did or said. The temptation to sever all relations with the US increased with the news of every successful engagement fought by the Viet Cong – and with every fresh attack on Cambodian frontier posts and villages by the armed forces of South Vietnam. Sihanouk had been criticising the US with increasing bitterness and intensity. By Christmas 1965, he was doing so almost to the exclusion of all else.

In what is written above, I have tried to put myself into Sihanouk's shoes and to express his own peculiar viewpoint. But the question remains, were Sihanouk's complaints justified and, if so, what could have been done to put matters right?

Much of Sihanouk's thinking about the US seemed to me out of date or mis-conceived. Like many others round the world, Sihanouk had exaggerated American characteristics and created for himself a caricature which bore little relation to reality. Whatever might have

been the explanation of the Dap Chhuon affair, there was no reason to suppose that the Americans had ever attempted to interfere in any grossly inadmissible manner in Cambodian politics, much less actually to overthrow Sihanouk – even if, unwisely, some US agencies were tacitly supporting, as were the Thai and South Vietnamese authorities, the exiled Son Ngoc Thanh and the overseas Khmer Serei movement. The State Department may have been slow to move out of the bi-polar, black-and-white world of the middle 1950s. But ten years later, to my certain knowledge, there was no real quarrel with Cambodian neutrality; indeed, the Americans had been doing their best to support it, until Sihanouk put an end to their more active endeavours. The mannerisms and possible idiosyncrasies of US emissaries at the Cambodian Court might or might not have been irritating, but were of no enduring importance for foreign policy. In a sense, the boot was on the other foot: what more should Sihanouk have said and what else should he have done, to be taken by Washington as a serious and responsible leader? Certainly, Sihanouk had done himself no favours at the White House with his cowardly mob attack on the Phnom Penh Embassy. (Even in London, where post-imperial *sang froid* in these matters was still the vogue in the 1960s, Prime Minister Harold Wilson could never fully dismiss from his mind the notion that Sihanouk was merely a pathetic little 'Embassy sacker'.)

Could US–Cambodian relations eventually be improved? The prospects were not good. Cambodian neutrality did not seem to me to be able to survive the stresses and strains in Indo-China much longer. Moreover, the American political establishment would have had to devote much more time and trouble than theretofore to the one man who then mattered in Cambodia, namely Sihanouk himself. This would have required psychological insight as well as political and diplomatic adroitness. The Americans might or might not have possessed these capabilities. Frankly, I doubted it; but even if they did, they could not have deployed them to any effect in Phnom Penh as long as wider considerations obliged them to do nothing which could cause offence in Bangkok or Saigon.

Nevertheless, the elements for a deal still conceivably existed. Emotionally, the Prince was probably pretty well through with the Americans. But he was nevertheless a political animal whose heart did not always rule his head. He professed readiness to preserve 'correct' relations with the US. Although he believed that the Americans should withdraw from Indo-China with whatever dignity they

could muster before they were kicked out, he made it repeatedly clear that he wanted them to remain in the region, in order to keep the balance of power with China. If the clandestine radios could have been silenced (which they should have been, in my view, and would have been, if it had been our show), Cambodian dissidents such as Son Ngoc Thanh packed off quietly to the South of France, and (*per impossibile*) a major military set-back be inflicted on the Viet Cong, the major causes of friction between Cambodia and the United States would have been removed.

In the event, none of these things came about and the Americans withdrew their diplomatic presence from Phnom Penh in May 1965. I was to miss them – but that, of course, was the least of it. The fact was that, much more than London, Washington had, in a sense, 'screwed up'. Above all, they had missed their chance, in 1963, to give Cambodian neutrality a boost and thereby to make life more difficult for the Viet Cong. It might not have made much difference to the final outcome in Indo-China. But Pol Pot would almost certainly never have been given his evil opportunity.

16

Bonzer Australians

For Australians generally, I have always shown respect, felt an affinity and in fact nurtured a soft spot, despite being resigned to my occasional dismissal as a 'typical, bloody "Pom"'. They may come from a small country, but they are big people. I have never much detected what, in their self-disparagement, they sometimes term their 'cultural cringe'. Diplomatically, they can, when they choose to, punch above their weight. And in the 1960s, Australia came to be seen by Cambodia as a Western friend and advocate – even if inevitably falling some way behind France.

Others were burdened with diplomatic disadvantages. Japan had her sanguinary Asian war record, and her consequent post-war 'low profile'. In the Cold War, West Germany was at loggerheads with East Germany, which was forever (in those days, before the collapse of the Berlin Wall) clamouring for parallel recognition by Cambodia. Britain, for her part, was believed to be too readily swayed by the whims of Washington.

Yet the stronger Australian position was not just a function of the handicaps and misfortunes of others. Australian policy towards Cambodia looked to me, on the ground, something like this: for some years past, influential Australians had accepted that living in Asia gave them Asian responsibilities. The view was beginning to take shape that Australians ought to be comprehensible not only to their American friends and European ancestors but also to their regional Asiatic neighbours. In a lecture to the Australian Institute of Political Science in 1964, Sir Garfield Barwick rejected the idea that Australia should constitute a bridge between South-East Asia and the former colonial powers, but nevertheless laid claim to a 'special status' for a nation which was 'neither European nor Asian'. Much of this may have been mere talk. To an outsider in the

mid-1960s, Australia still looked militarily too weak, politically and socially too inward-looking and in almost all respects manifestly too dependent on the US, to be capable of developing greatly independent policies of her own. Yet the Australians were devoting an increasing effort to ensuring good relations with their Asiatic and Far Eastern neighbours. In Cambodia, it was not without some success.

Cambodia was, for many Australians, a small and intrinsically unimportant country of no trading interest. There was certainly no permanent Australian community in Cambodia, only a shifting population of diplomats and technical advisers. Nor was there any traditional political link or cultural common ground between the two countries. But Cambodia is not that far from Australia's garden gate. Already back in the 1960s, Canberra therefore decided that, within the modest limits of Australia's capability, Cambodian neutrality and independence should be underpinned and Cambodia's economic development assisted. The awkward fact that Cambodia was at daggers drawn with South Vietnam and Thailand, both close friends of Australia, did not seem to have presented an insurmountable difficulty. (The Australian Government always avoided 'choosing' between neighbours – they took their time before deciding to support Malaysia against Indonesia during President Sukarno's 'confrontation' campaign.)

The Australian Government set up a Diplomatic Mission in Phnom Penh in 1956. From a tentative, novice Legation it grew to be a confident and effective, small-sized Embassy. In my day, it directed a practical and down-to-earth aid programme. After Sihanouk's decision to break off diplomatic relations with the United States in May 1965, the Australians agreed to represent American interests in Cambodia. This dubious chore unexpectedly turned out to be a blessing. Australia handled US–Cambodian relations with tact and courtesy. This in turn conferred status and prestige locally. The value of having a fair-minded and influential friend at court in Washington was, furthermore, not entirely lost on the Cambodian Head of State. In August 1965, the Australians were paid the further (in Sihanouk's eyes, high) compliment of being invited to represent Cambodian interests in South Vietnam. The Cambodian press, bitterly hostile towards the US and South Vietnam and none too gentle with the UK, gave infrequent, but always friendly, coverage to Australia.

What were the ingredients of Australian success? A combination of the unearned and the deserving. The former was clear to see:

Australia was a minor power unencumbered with either the substance or the shadow of worldwide influence. Britain's stronger position at the time had paradoxically proved an obstacle to good bilateral relations with Cambodia. Although aware that our status as a world power was then on the decline, the Cambodians nevertheless always believed us to wield more influence than we in fact did; and expected us to exercise this influence in their own interests, beyond our own capacity and reasonable inclination. If they ever doubted whether British authority and strength was for real, these doubts would have been assuaged by external appearances – by our influential position in the Commonwealth, by our standing as the principal ally of the United States, and by our traditional and prestigious imperial-military presence in the area (still then apparent to the naked Cambodian eye in Hong Kong and Singapore).

The Australians suffered from none of these disadvantages. They were therefore able to develop their bilateral relations with Cambodia in a watertight compartment, more or less sealed off from what Australia might be doing in neighbouring countries. For example in striking contrast to his more discreet colleague in Phnom Penh, one Aussie Ambassador in Bangkok was very publicly pro-US, pro-war, anti-Brit and sceptical of Sihanouk; but no one cared too much – Australians are rugged individualists anyway! Australia had even had some limited success in presenting herself as an 'Asian nation' – Cambodians knew little and cared less about the former 'white Australia policy'. Perhaps more significantly, Australians were able to exploit what one might ungenerously term their 'stooge status'. When Canberra put troops into South Vietnam or Malaysia or performed any other imperialist act, the Cambodians tended to say, 'Ah well, Australia is such a small, dependent and exposed country that she has to seek powerful friends and do as they tell her. It is not really Australia's fault'. Whenever the British performed comparable manoeuvres, or gave overt diplomatic backing to this and that American move, we received the full weight of Cambodian censure, because we were seen as a major player, free to act as we chose and capable of doing better.

There was also, however, a brighter side to the coin of Australian achievement. That Australian interest in Cambodia had been translated so successfully into action was in part due, as I saw it, to inherent and admirable national virtues. They have an unpretentious and indeed unself-conscious gift for falling readily in with strangers. Their egalitarianism is a well-attested, sociological phenomenon.

Australians who worked in Cambodia seemed to like the place and people and sided instinctively with Cambodia as the underdog. They gave me, at least, the impression of wanting to do their level best to get things moving in the right direction.

Australian–Cambodian relations were also informed by what one can only term the *curiosa felicitas* of Australian personal diplomacy. The then Australian Ambassador was the late Noel Deschamps. I saw a lot of him, socially, during my time in Phnom Penh, and learned a great deal from him. Subsequently I kept in touch, virtually until his death in 2005. I teased him, sometimes, for his over-enthusiastic and uncritical advocacy of anything to do with Norodom Sihanouk. Of course, he was never given anything too tricky to handle. (Deschamps wrote to me, in his retirement, that 'during the whole of my tour in Cambodia, I received minimal instructions of any kind'.) The fact remains that Noel St Clair Deschamps was a highly effective Ambassador for his country. An outwardly unassuming man, who spoke good Cambodian and bilingual French, he built up a remarkable local position for himself during his service in the country from 1962 to 1969. Deschamps avoided the natural (but, in Cambodia, potentially disastrous) temptation to head for the big-time. He had never pestered the Head of State for private audiences and did not make it his practice (as an Ambassador might legitimately do in most other countries) to busy himself lobbying Cambodians on other than purely Australian, bilateral business. Deschamps did not make lofty public speeches on international issues. He wisely chose to build his house to a simpler plan, with smaller bricks.

The foundation was laid with cleverly conceived economic aid. There were no loans or grants-in-aid (which might find their way into the wrong pockets). Australian experts and advisers were kept to a minimum and expected to do a solid day's hard work of practical example, sweating it out in machine shops and on dam sites (unlike the pampered but feeble prima donnas that other Western countries sometimes extruded to the Third World). Most of the aid was solid hardware of direct service to the man in the street: hydraulic pumps, railway rolling stock, road-making equipment. Good public relations were cultivated bit by bit with sporting encounters, balanced but friendly Aussie television and newspaper coverage of Cambodia, and the exchange of good-will visits.

This patient effort chimed harmoniously with certain themes in the flexible foreign policy of the Cambodian Government. Sihanouk, who still clung to some sort of neutral status for his country, needed

friends in the West. This need became particularly acute, following the eclipse of the British in 1964 and the dismissal of the Americans in 1965. France alone was not enough; Australia made a desirable additional makeweight. When rejecting the charge that Cambodia had become a Chinese satellite, Sihanouk found it convenient to point to his friendship with Australia. The token Australian military contingent in South Vietnam did not spoil things. In a speech of welcome to the Australian Foreign Minister, Mr Hasluck, in December 1965, Prince Sihanouk insisted

> the harmonious evolution of our relations therefore shows that a divergence, and even an opposition of points of view, on certain international problems do not necessarily constitute an obstacle to friendship.

Did this Australian success seem likely to last or was it a mere flash in the pan? No Government, not even perhaps the Chinese, could be confident of enjoying the Cambodian Government's perpetual favour. If Australian troops had ever crossed into Cambodian territory in pursuit of the Viet Cong, the work of years would have been undone in a trice – or, for that matter, an article in the *Sydney Times* exposing some alleged scandal surrounding the Khmer throne. Some brash new Aussie Ambassador might quickly have put his foot in it. Mercifully, none of these things came to pass. My Australian friends occasionally gave the irritating and indeed ludicrous impression of thumping themselves on the back for being the only people really to understand Cambodia. But most of them realised that they were still on thinnish ice and no doubt took comfort in the 'Strine' dictum: *'Zarf trawl Leica nony doomy Bess'*. ('After all I can only do my best'.)

What were the practical consequences for the British on the spot, of Australia's coming of age in Cambodia? In some ways, they were slightly trying. When I first arrived at the post, Australians in the bars about town were free – in a loud-mouthed, 'Pom'-bashing fashion – with their criticism of HMG's policy. Our inability to secure a Geneva Conference at the right psychological moment in the spring of 1964 was alleged to have increased Cambodia's dependence on Beijing, to Australia's disadvantage. This was the street where they lived; short of being able to tow Australia to a point off Land's End, or Key West, they were there to stay. They believed that we Brits were lodgers who would one day move on, so they expected us not to make trouble for them with the neighbours. Donald Horne

illustrated the underlying sense of vulnerability of some Australians when he wrote in *The Lucky Country*: 'Chinese communist victories in South-East Asia could mean a threat to Australian sovereignty or its collapse. But the rest of the world could survive'. Or, as the Australian Prime Minister, the late Mr H.E. Holt, put it in September 1967, 'Australia cannot be completely independent in defence for at least several decades. Australia eventually will be self-reliant; but not in my lifetime and not in the lifetime of many others.' I quickly warmed to the responsible and innovatory, Australian official diplomatic presence in Cambodia. Indo-China was not the long-term interest for Britain that it was for Australia and it seemed fitting that Australia should come forward to uphold responsibilities which would be less and less our own during the years to come. While we still had a role to play, the Australians (who shared most of our immediate aims) could help us influence the Americans (who in some – albeit very limited – respects were more inclined to lend an ear to Canberra than to London). Finally, I resolved to learn from Australia's local achievements, as I set about rebuilding the British position in Cambodia. On assuming charge of our mission, it was a pleasure for me to be able to do business with the Australians to our mutual profit. Their small Embassy in Phnom Penh was staffed to a man with robust and able officers, to whom I came to owe, in the end, a debt of gratitude which was both personal and professional.

I discharged some of this debt, on leaving Cambodia for good, by making my pilgrimage to 'God's own Country'. Not unexpectedly, I felt relaxed and instantly at home. I have since been back, repeatedly. For ten years, in the European Commission in Brussels, I was responsible for the EU's relations with Australia. The place was for me – with France – one of the only two countries outside the UK in which, if I had had to settle down permanently, I should have been happy to live out the remainder of my days. Indeed, in the early 1980s in Japan, where I headed the EU Delegation, my wife and I were at one time on the brink of a change of career which would then have enabled us to settle in Australia for good. But Brussels intervened, to make me an offer I couldn't refuse, as the grand Panjandrum with the little button on top, in charge of the EU's relations with the entire world. We still doubt whether I made the correct decision.

Goodbye to All That

17

Feelings in Retrospect

My feelings on departure from Phnom Penh had been mixed. It was an unexpected wrench to leave the people and the place. But it was also a relief, once the new Ambassador had come, to descend from my isolated pinnacle and to reintegrate myself into a machine in which I was once more a subordinate, and no more the master. From being endlessly in the spotlight, observed minutely not only by staff and servants but by the Cambodian press corps, the political 'Establishment' and the Head of State himself, I passed gratefully into the shadows.

There followed a month or so of escapist leave, in South-East Asia and the South Pacific, followed by a complete change of scene on posting to Paris. Landing at Orly after 17 hours virtually non-stop flying from the beaches of Tahiti, I heard Christmas carols on the public address system and saw for the first time in three years the wonder of snowfall. Yet as I walked slowly out into the cold and felt the flakes whirl down through the arc lights to settle on my hair and sleeves and shoulders, I experienced a sense of loss.

As I look back, I see four unusual features to my assignment to Phnom Penh, which made it exceptionally hard work.

The first was the necessity for the Head of Chancery and the Head of Mission to be one and the same person.

It is an uneasy experience to find oneself both factory manager and company chairman. The former serves as a buffer between the latter and the raw realities of life on the shop floor; while the latter affords the former a necessary nebulous support from on high, standing ready as he does to intervene on all major issues and assert overriding leadership. To have to discharge both functions simultaneously was awkward. The solution which I devised was pragmatic and effective, in a bizarre sort of way: I developed a spuriously

avuncular personality. In my early thirties, I was too young to play a paternalistic role. So I became an 'Uncle' to my staff, to the anglophone community and even to the French ('*Ton-ton Lesslee*', they came to call me). I adopted middle-aged attitudes and addressed even my manifest elders as if they were younger brothers; while everyone else was naturally enough a 'niece' or a 'nephew', 'my son' or even 'my child'. I spoke of myself in the third person. Adulatory jingles and loyal catch-phrases went the rounds – most of them, I must admit, put into circulation, out of self-mockery, by myself. But the prize went to the Australian scholar and ex-diplomat, Milton Osborne (see Select Bibliography), then in Phnom Penh for extended research, for cooking up: 'Uncle Leslie, he's True Blue; Uncle Leslie cares for you; Uncle Leslie sees you through'. This was all quite absurd, even at the time, and hugely embarrassing today. But it caught on and acquired strength. It was a desperate device that nevertheless worked.

A second difficulty was the obligation to start everything from scratch (see Chapter 4). No archives, no staffing continuity, no institutional memory nor accumulated wisdom nor local expertise. This, too, could not be helped; given the exceptional nature of the situation, it could be overcome only by exceptionally hard work and the exercise of a certain humility. To begin with I leaned heavily on scholars, journalists and diplomatic colleagues for explanation and advice. Until I had got some serious reading done and gained practical experience of my own, for the most part I had to rely on my intuition about their characters so as to get the measure of the value of what they had to say. A principal 'Guru' turned out to be the Australian Ambassador, the only Head of Mission in Phnom Penh who could read and write Cambodian.

The third difficulty was, of course, the very bad political situation. Here I was to be undeservedly fortunate. I got off on a friendly basis with Cambodians from the start. It used to be said by Westerners who knew them well, that the Cambodians made up their minds very quickly about a newly arrived foreigner; that an important factor was whether or not they thought that the foreigner in question liked or despised Cambodia and Cambodians; once they had so formed that instinctive opinion they rarely, if ever, changed it.

I, for my part, was far from delighted, at the outset of my mission, to find myself in Cambodia at all; and I found the country's inhabitants, while agreeable enough, both maddening and mysterious. But arrogant and aloof I was not. This was where I was lucky; the

Cambodians probably guessed my initial attitude, but did not judge me too strictly upon it – I was tacitly accepted by them, from near the outset. The *persona* of the 'play-boy' Chargé d'Affaires also appealed to one side of the Khmer character. Then too, I had acquired from my reading in Singapore, and perhaps communicated upon my arrival in Phnom Penh, at least a glimmer of understanding of and indeed sympathy for the Khmer point of view in international affairs.

But, as I look back, I think that probably what helped most was the habit I soon acquired of speaking in a calm, quiet voice, and of adopting a publicly detached and unemotional approach to all difficulties. There seemed to me no point in raking over past feuds. To be sure, on two or three occasions I was to tell my interlocutors some unpleasant home truths, but got away with it because they knew me well, because I smiled and because such occasions were rare. Normally I interpreted my mission, for good or for ill, as a search for common ground by the use of sympathy and gentle persuasion; it was, in any case, the only role permitted in Cambodia by that art of the possible which is called politics. Also, I told the strict truth whenever I could; and when I couldn't tell it, because to do so would cause damage or offence, I kept my silence. I never took anyone for a ride: people will be led once, but once only, up the garden path.

The fourth difficulty was one simply of moral and physical isolation. I was alone, at the top of my tiny Embassy tree; far distant from the London base, without frequent contact with colleagues in the Service at adjacent posts; immersed in an alien and initially by no means amicable environment. In these conditions, diplomatic emissaries of all nationalities are sometimes menaced by neuroses and mad moments of disequilibrium. They call it 'culture shock': my situation was no exception. Phnom Penh could be claustrophobic and unsettling. It was a struggle to keep matters in the serene proportion in which the Foreign Office in London saw them, and expected me to see them also. It was not always easy, not to lose patience with the Cambodian Government and not to focus too much on the ludicrous aspects of the local scene. Yet, at the same time, it was hard to resist complicity with Cambodia. The land and the people were so obviously misunderstood, so much the underdog, yet so justified in their fundamental aspirations, that it required a continual effort to retain some detachment and not to see the world too much through Cambodian spectacles.

One had to be careful not to be too impatient with one's own side, by surrendering to the temptation to divide the Service into 'us' in our Embassy and 'them' in London, or 'those buggers' in Saigon. Little things could prove quite unnecessarily irritating, down to minutiae like the delivery of new air-conditioners of slightly the wrong power rating. A good many explosive telegrams on various issues were dashed off in a white heat and then (most of them) quietly torn up and thrown into the confidential waste-bin as passion ebbed away. Everyone was working under tensions which were not always apparent on the surface of things. I found that a good antidote was to go home, pour a long gin and tonic, turn the gramophone up full blast and listen to a Bach organ cantata or sing with Verdi, or pace up and down to the bagpipes of the Highland Regiments and the massed bands of Her Majesty's Foot Guards.

The main problems in Phnom Penh were, naturally, never completely resolved. Minor mistakes, in the early stages, were easy to make. But somehow the mission went forward, with a loose and sympathetic rein from London, and propelled by our own, all too human, endeavours in the field.

Thinking it all over, from a new millennium, I am impressed by the fair-minded and even courteous concern which the Government in London displayed in all their dealings with Cambodia during my time in Phnom Penh. The British position in Cambodia was different from that of each of the four foreign countries which I have described in the preceding chapters. We had no traditional stake to defend, no compelling, purely national, interest to serve, no elaborate future ambition to advance. We had no ancient suzerainty or modern over-sight to exercise, like that of the Chinese over the periphery of the Middle Kingdom. We had no material and cultural investment, no sense of intimate affiliation, as did the ex-colonial French. We were not committed to the war in South Vietnam, nor called upon to exercise the responsibilities of a superpower along the *glacis* of the mainland of Asia, of the kind shouldered by the United States. We did not inhabit the Southern Hemisphere, like the Australians; our military and colonial and other commitments in the area were running down, while Australia's responsibilities were, if anything, on the increase.

Our presence in Cambodia was organised on a modest scale, to achieve modest objectives. I recall Lord Moran's diary, recording Sir Winston Churchill's muttered aside, to the effect that he had not

once again become Prime Minister of Great Britain to worry about 'bloody places like Cambodia'. In the darker days of my mission in Phnom Penh, I used sometimes to ask myself why we were there at all. (I confess that at one point I submitted to London the recommendation that the British Embassy should be closed and diplomatic relations entertained by accrediting the resident British Ambassador in Vientiane as non-resident Ambassador in Phnom Penh, in the same way as the Cambodians were accredited to the Court of St James through the person of their Ambassador in Paris.)

Yet, in continuing to maintain a diplomatic toe-hold in Phnom Penh, we were probably sensible. The Government in London still clung to the role they played with the USSR as Co-Chairmen of the Geneva Conference on Indo-China. Of course, it gave them additional international status in a world in which the UK was less influential than it had been. But also, British Governments had consistently attached importance to Cambodian neutrality. The British rejected the US so-called 'Domino Theory' (see the Epilogue, below), and thought that an independent and more or less neutral Cambodia could and would be good for the stability of the area – for SEATO generally and for the security of Thailand and ex-British Malaysia in particular. There would be one less source of international friction, in a region already showing signs of over-heating. Undertakings of respect for Cambodian sovereignty, independence and unity were written into the agreement reached in 1954 at the international Conference in Geneva, crafted by Sir Anthony Eden, which had finalised the liquidation of the French colonial empire in Indo-China. It was natural that, thereafter, we should have followed the fortunes of Cambodia with solicitude. Cambodia was independent, thanks to France; Cambodia was neutral, thanks to us and the then consensus of all the other interested powers.

Setting the seal of full international recognition upon the new deal called for flags to be flown in an otherwise marginal and insignificant Phnom Penh – the arrival of Embassies, the inauguration of economic aid programmes, the opening up of trade with the outside world, the incorporation of the new state into the international community at large. In this process, as at the Geneva Conference which preceded it, we played our part, not as lords of the earth and sole disposers of the fortune of nations, but as one well-wisher among many. Our technical assistance programme, cultural co-operation and trading partnership with Cambodia were symbolical rather than substantial. Like our tiny Embassy, these were tokens;

but they were nevertheless the modest diplomatic means to a constructive political end.

It was against this background that I saw my own duties in Phnom Penh. The basic task was to set about the patient and unapologetic restoration of the happier relations which had existed between Cambodia and Britain in the past. Whether I failed or succeeded would scarcely make much difference to South-East Asian politics. But I had my instructions. As time went by, and I grew in understanding of the country and its leaders, London's mandate gave me professional satisfaction – just as the progressive improvement in Anglo-Cambodian relations gave me personal pleasure.

With the benefit of hindsight, I personally think it was a pity that the Government did not over-ride the objections of some of their allies and really insist on convening a Geneva Conference in 1963 or 1964, when the moment was ripe: the 'Geneva Spirit' had not yet completely evaporated, and the West stood so much to gain from an international understanding on Cambodia. But the political arguments at the time were finely balanced and I concede that the final decision was honestly arrived at and well-intended. After the reaction in Phnom Penh on 11 March 1964, of which a description has been given in the introductory Cameo I (page xvii), and in view of the flow of appalling official Khmer invective which followed it, the British Government might have been pardoned for closing down the British Embassy altogether, and washing their hands of all further responsibility towards Cambodia. But this contingency was never entertained by anyone in London. On the contrary, our diplomacy was, after a brief period of decent disengagement, to be committed as actively as ever. At the time, I found it hard to imagine many, if any, other Governments prepared to work as persistently and actively as we did, despite both provocations and set-backs, for the peace and welfare of a country so absent from our traditions and so remote from our national interests in the narrower sense.

The foregoing naturally made me all the more determined to see the job through. So did the backing which I personally received from London and adjacent posts. Unstinting and alert teamwork made the 'FO' the second best 'club' in the world (after – for different reasons – the House of Lords, that is), and ours the best Diplomatic Service of its size in the world. I mention 'The Lords', because 'The Office' shared one of its more generous traditions: that of hearing a maiden speech with tolerance as well as ritual courtesy. As a youthful and inexperienced Head of Mission, I could not have

had a fairer hearing – with one individual exception (a desk officer who found me irritating and who later left the service for a more soothing life in industry) – from the South-East Asia Department or received the clearer impression that I was treated on very nearly the same footing as Ambassadors of nearly twice my age. Under-Secretaries of State sent me personal letters of encouragement and much more importantly (as I see from the archives now open in the Public Record Office at Kew) supported me, in confidence and without telling me so, within the Office. Foreign Secretaries dropped me a line to thank me for this or that Despatch, or cabled, like that terse yet powerful 'You spoke well' previously mentioned. The Service was not rank-conscious nor hide-bound in that sort of way. When there was the nation's business to be about and a diplomatic crisis blowing up, it was second nature for my colleagues to refrain from the sorts of question which engendered rancour (who that Chargé in Phnom Penh was and how recently had he scrambled up in grade from Second to First Secretary to acting Counsellor). I was made to feel at home and accepted, even on routine occasions. I have already mentioned the two meetings of Far East Heads of Mission which I attended in the field – one in Bangkok and the other in Hong Kong. I found myself in the presence of intellect, distinction and richness of professional experience. Yet there was a place for me at high table and I was given my fair share of time to talk. Likewise, from adjacent posts, in Bangkok, Vietnam and Saigon, Tony Rumbold, Fred Warner and Gordon Etherington-Smith – all much my seniors – must often enough have found me (so comparatively young and innocent) an inconvenient colleague, yet they spared me the brash pugnacity I sometimes directed at them and invariably tried to meet me more than halfway.

In a word, therefore, the FO circus went on, even with only a junior acrobat perched in Phnom Penh, and it was a smooth-running and quietly professional circus. In routine operation, it was already impressive – the Queen's Messengers and the telegrams, the intelligent ordering of all business great and small, the bustle of activity and the sense of purposeful dialogue throughout the world. In emergency operation, however, it was quite at its best. It is exhilarating to play some role when the Diplomatic Service is handling a crisis. The pulse quickens and reserves of energy are summoned. The action speedily unfolds night and day at different posts around the globe, co-ordinated by 'The Office' in London. Teamwork, ingenuity, local knowledge and professional skills all come into their

own. Such excitements as these were certainly mine to experience in Cambodia.

So much for the Service as it then was. How does the author himself emerge now in retrospect? What was it that made me tick? Did I become a changed man, afterwards?

I arrived outwardly a creature of the 'Swinging Sixties'– disco-going, a Beatlesmaniac, outwardly irreligious, politically slightly cynical (gloating over *Beyond The Fringe* and *That Was The Week That Was*), permissive and hedonistic (if in a slightly haunted way, as might have been expected of a former aspirant Anglican Ordinand – I was still 'doing a runner' from the Faith or at any rate the Estab-lished Church). I was still, even if not normally given to annoying elders and betters, on occasion tempted to *épater les bourgeois* ('shock the bourgeoisie').

However, I discovered when it came to the crunch, that I fell back naturally on the more traditional elements in my background. One was the British Army. I had been far from an outstanding soldier during my uneventful two years of National Service, spent mostly in Wales. I longed to get it over with, so that I could go up to Cambridge. But I did learn something of the ways of the world after a sheltered boyhood. Also, I learned about people. I was offered David Niven (in *The Way Ahead*) as role model; I was taught the basic elements of man-management; and I was sent to practise them as a young subaltern in charge of my own little semi-independent unit on a live-firing range. To my surprise, I not only quite enjoyed it, but was considered not to have been too hopeless a dunce. (An immediate Short Service Commission, perhaps ultimately a Regular one, was floated by my Colonel and anyway an extra 'pip'.) The psychological upheaval of it all proved such that it took me a full year afterwards to settle down properly as an undergraduate.

Another traditional asset was what I had picked up in reading for the Historical Tripos at Cambridge (particularly in the medieval part) and later, when reading Persian literature at the School of Oriental and African Studies in London. This was a limited ability to suspend my usual, then-twentieth-century, West-European outlook and temporarily to construct for myself – as it were from the inside – the psychology and outlook of other eras and peoples.

Further insights and tricks of the trade came during my appren-ticeship with the Diplomatic Service, as a Third Secretary in the Chancery at Tehran; then as a desk officer in the Western Organisa-tions Department of the Foreign Office and as Resident Clerk.

Although scarcely realising it at the time, I was throughout those busy and sometimes frustrating earliest years acquiring skills and absorbing practical experience on the job which – however hesitantly and crudely I employed them – I was to need to the utmost in Phnom Penh.

All in all, I discovered that I had inherited unawares that 'stiff upper lip', that slightly stubborn notion of public service which bore me up when purpose faltered and easy options seemed the better way out. Like it or not, I had, after all, been groomed by a school and a college that had educated clerics and functionaries of Church and State for centuries. I was the product of a nation and of a diplomacy that was deeply rooted. I found that people are often sustained in tight corners by tribal instincts and traditions which are hard-wired within them.

Additional to the foregoing was a new personal idiosyncrasy, which surprised and puzzled me, and about which I said nothing to anyone, at the time. When approaching difficult decisions, I would find that a separate process was under way – in parallel to the normal process of calculation and execution. At this separate level of consciousness, there would assert itself a growing inner confidence, in relation to the way ahead. In its rarest form, I would have the sensation of being under observation by people I did not know. Although they gave a vague encouragement, they did not tell me what to do, nor promise to protect me from the consequences of my actions. They were witnesses of conscience, before whom I was acting through my obligations. There may one day be a completely natural, so-called 'scientific' explanation – after all the experience is not uncommon. Nevertheless, in Cambodia, I found the spiritual imperative – rejected in my early twenties – began very slowly to reassert itself. And once more there stirred the vocation to some form of priesthood. (William Shawcross, in touch with me, when writing his *Sideshow* – see the Select Bibliography – commented wryly that Cambodia could do odd things to one: meaning, I suppose, that it could get under the skin and provoke moral reactions.)

But none of all that cut too much mustard, in the day-to-day. The best tonic was to get up and do something. For too long I had been too much of a plastic hippy; then I had been living without full commitment and merely on the fringes of the society of which I formed a part. Now in Cambodia, I had serious and solitary responsibility thrust upon me; the chance to enlist in a deserving cause, in which I became convinced it was good that the British voice should be clearly heard.

Certainly, we had all missed the high tide in 1963. By 1965, the waters were far on the ebb; while in the following year they were becoming virtually unnavigable. A certain fatalism began to settle on the Cambodian administration as the full nature of the national predicament sank home and as both sides in Vietnam prepared to fight that senseless and cruel war on an ever-mounting scale of military commitment. There was progressively less and less scope for action by Britain in Cambodia; there was less and less prospect that any steps we might take would prove effective.

In my submission at the time, however, this did not mean that we should allow ourselves to be too disheartened. Having once arrived at a sound Cambodia policy, we could not (to draw upon a phrase of Chairman Mao Tse-tung) merely have contented ourselves with talking about it: we had to translate that policy into action. Inherently 'European' in outlook and more at home across the Channel than in much of the Commonwealth, I cannot decently be accused of still living in those jingoistic days, now long forgotten, of seeking to prolong East of Suez an Empire that is now gone forever. There was no place in my concept of British diplomacy for pretensions of any sort, especially those which tended to busy-bodying, because I found they were inappropriate to the age and unwarranted by the realities of power and influence. But the effectiveness of that diplomacy, where we decided to exercise it, and (dare I add?) the honour of England, remained a legitimate and consuming care.

Such were my feelings and impressions – those were the colours I nailed to the mast when I was in post in Phnom Penh.

18

The Prince in Perspective

Norodom Sihanouk was an odd character. Not everyone adored him. Some found him exasperating.

Yet the Prince mattered to me in my years as the British Head of Mission more than anyone or anything else in Cambodia. He was not by any means easy for a foreign emissary to keep up with, let alone actually deal with. I had no option but to engage with the Prince respectfully and prudently. (The wise and experienced Australian Ambassador once said to me, sadly, that Phnom Penh was the graveyard of many an Ambassadorial reputation.)

Diplomatists quite often have warm hearts; but they must also have cool, unemotional heads. They must be capable of reaching detached and objective conclusions. They are not supposed to be easily misled. (I recall, after President de Gaulle's state visit to Cambodia already referred to in Chapter 14, a friend at the top of the French Embassy telling me that 'the General has not been taken in'.) As I shall confess in what follows, I myself had to struggle to achieve a balanced and independent view of Sihanouk, warts and all: to be both crocodile and warm heart. Much of the time, I probably succeeded. But with a slight sense of being, ever so discreetly, somewhat two-faced. This, because, fundamentally, I both warmed to the man personally, and had my doubts about him professionally.

In a very small way – a mere Chargé d'Affaires did not count much, if at all, with him – the Prince also possibly quite liked me. When he nominated me the 'Number One Twister of Cambodia' (see Cameo II, on page xxv), it was to find a face-saving way of conveying to his people, without any suggestion of blame on his part, that the Brits were out of the dog-house and that Cambodians were no longer forbidden to talk to us. Perhaps it was also because I

amused him – and his favourite daughter, likewise. After I had persuaded the Governor of Hong Kong (see Chapter 12) to lay a red carpet across the runway at Kaitak, for his transit of the Crown Colony, at a time when the British Embassy at Phnom Penh still bore the scars of mob attack, the Prince, who was ever sensitive to personal slights and also gripped by apprehensions of being seen to be 'put down', felt unexpectedly relieved. He remembered the gesture (like one of the royal elephants in his stables) and put it down to my credit. Later on, the Prince knew that I was actively lobbying (on his behalf as well as HMG's) the Soviet, Chinese and French Ambassadors and all others who mattered for international guarantees for Cambodian independence, neutrality and territorial integrity, and for a more pro-active role by the International Control Commission, to the same purposes. When the British Government sent Malcolm MacDonald to talk through with Sihanouk, at the latter's holiday villa in the South of France, the reasons for the breakdown in Anglo-Cambodian relations, and the prospects for their restoration to a more normal state, MacDonald recorded that the Prince had made a point of saying that he had found me, as the British Chargé d'Affaires, 'both wise and helpful'. Later still, when a Foreign Office Minister, Lord Walston, came to see Sihanouk in Phnom Penh, in the final stages of restoration of normal diplomatic relations, Sihanouk (jokingly but pleasantly) waved in my direction and suggested to Walston that the Queen should appoint me, the man on the spot, the next British Ambassador. Just before leaving the country, on posting to the British Embassy in Paris, I wrote the Prince a short personal letter of farewell in my very best French, to which he replied magnanimously and by return, thanking me for my efforts to improve Anglo-Cambodian relations, assuring me that I had succeeded in clearing up 'numerous misunderstandings' and expressing the hope that he would see me in Paris. (I was later told that, in bed with a cold, he had dictated it himself to a stenographer and had not had to resort to an adviser.) Sadly, it proved inexpedient for the British Government that I should take up this invitation. I was, in fact, never to see the Prince again except once – unintroduced across a crowded room in the Palace of the People in Beijing, when I was in China with a visiting EU delegation and the Prince was the banquet guest of the Chinese Head of State, at 'High Table'.

I had initially spent much time and energy in Phnom Penh picking up everything I could glean about the People's Prince. I subsequently saw the genuine mutual affection when he mingled

with ordinary Cambodians in the countryside. I followed carefully his frequent political speeches. I participated in diplomatic and public audiences with the Prince. I endeavoured to put myself into his shoes. I observed him at close quarters: short, plump, full of nervous energy, a non-stop talker with a constant nervous laugh, his face full of the emotion of the moment, his gestures large and expressive. I drew his confidences – once, about General Lon Nol, his army chief (absurdly gung-ho, ready to invade Vietnam any day, no political commonsense), once, even about Mao's Cultural Revolution (explicitly critical – but with an abrupt change of subject on the approach of the Chinese Ambassador, the latter's city-slicker suit recently discarded in favour of baggy denims, 'Red Guard'-style). I often cast a fly over Cambodian and foreign friends and acquaintances, as a cross-check on what I had discovered and understood. I constantly talked to the more sensible people in other Embassies.

But, at the end of the day, I had to form my own best judgement. It was not in all respects overwhelmingly flattering. Thus, within my first few months *en poste* in 1964 I became aware of, and duly reported to London –

> indications of a vaguely felt loss of confidence in the
> Prince personally and of resentment against what is
> considered as the increasing arbitrariness of his actions
> and his growing disinclination to accept advice.

Things began to look worse as time moved on. By 1965 I was reporting that Sihanouk's character might be undergoing a subtle deterioration, and that, within five years, an indigenous opposition might overthrow him (something which in the event took place, on schedule, in 1970). I am on record, in October 1965, as advising the Foreign Office that the Prince was 'past his peak of popularity and performance' and that his actions might, 'with increasing age, become increasingly eccentric and ill-judged'. In January 1966 (see below), I reported that he was 'likely to decline and eventually be ushered off the Cambodian scene' – something, I hasten to add, which I argued was not in the least anything which the British Government should welcome.

Certainly, Norodom Sihanouk, as Head of State in the mid-1960s, made political and economic mistakes. The Prince was also eccentric and superstitious, and suffered from serious weaknesses of character. As he has since explained with disarming frankness in his own memoirs (*Souvenirs doux et amers*, 1981, pages 25ff.) he was,

the offspring of a cross between a half-brother and
sister, between an uncle and niece, between cousins,
all of whom had as grandfather or father the great …
King Ang Duong.

So Sihanouk's genetic make-up was conditioned by a degree of royal
in-breeding. This produced in him megalomania, bouts of paranoid
schizophrenia, and occasional moments of near-madness. He could
not delegate, would never accept criticism, only rarely listened to
advice, invariably played policy and tactics off-the-cuff. He could not
live with the idea of a legal political opposition. And he believed
himself personally, in any case, totally indispensable to his country.
While undoubtedly nimble-witted, he was seriously under-educated
– a few idle and undistinguished years at a French *lycée* in Saigon and
a brief spell at the Cavalry School at Saumur – and has admitted
freely in his memoirs to being a complete dunce at science and
mathematics. (To this, I would add that he was said never to read
books – his only systematic reading was articles in the international
press about his country or his own person.) He was given over,
more than most of us would be in his shoes, to constant comfort and
lavish luxury: the best French food and wine, sumptuous palaces,
the finest tailoring, the most compliant women, the most flattering
of toadies in his immediate entourage, 'Yes Men' in his Cabinet, *etc.*,
etc., *etc*.

I also knew that Norodom Sihanouk had an even darker side.
Back in Singapore, reading myself in, I had noted Embassy reports
of a revealing incident. In the autumn of 1963, an emissary of the
Cambodian opposition in exile, Preap Inn, had entered Cambodia
to parley with the Government. He was given a safe conduct by the
Governor of Takeo Province. For political reasons connected with
the tension then obtaining between Cambodia and Vietnam, Sihanouk
decided to arrest him. The man, with his companion, was arraigned
before a National Congress and mercilessly bullied. The companion,
who caved in and gave the right answers, was set free. Preap Inn
(who defended himself with dignity) was screamed down by the
Prince, who then disallowed the safe conduct and had the man shot.
The proceedings had been broadcast. The bearing of Preap Inn, and
the arbitrary cruelty of the Prince, were not lost on the Cambodians
at large, who murmured against the sentence.

It was at this time also that, following a series of screeching and
hysterical speeches in which he seemed to be close to losing his

sanity, Sihanouk abruptly announced the rejection of United States aid and launched, without the slightest advance consultation with his Cabinet, a range of inept measures of state control over the economy. There were objective and provocative political factors which precipitated the crisis, but Monseigneur's state of mind was his own.

Other bizarre developments followed. In March 1964, at a work session with his underlings late in the night, Sihanouk decided that mobs should be sent out to sack the British and American Embassies. He thought he would model himself on President Sukarno, who had made attacks on foreign Embassies the fashionable thing for a Third World leader to institute – even China was subsequently to follow this example, before the end of the Cultural Revolution, in sacking the office of the British Chargé d'Affaires. And worse has since happened in Beirut, Istanbul, Tehran and elsewhere. But in 1964 the phenomenon was more or less new – and entirely without precedent in Cambodia itself. The operation was mounted the following morning, mercifully without injury or loss of life. (Cameo I, page xvii.)

The decision was a foolish one. In a more balanced frame of mind, Sihanouk would have realised that a mob attack could not possibly modify the policies of the British and American Governments; such an attack would only alienate the sympathies of those in these countries who wished Cambodia well (which it largely did, in Washington if not London); and it might give the mobs a taste for action which they could one day wish to satisfy at the expense of the Cambodian Government and Sihanouk himself. Then, the following month came the Prince's instruction to his subjects not to mix with US or UK diplomats nor accept invitations to their Embassies.

I noticed in the period immediately following my arrival in Phnom Penh in May 1964, that Monseigneur's appetite for luxury and comfort, formerly under some sort of loose self-control, was showing signs of quickening. In order to meet Cambodia's acute budgetary difficulties, Sihanouk had proclaimed a regime of austerity. Redundant officials were being sacked; luxury imports were slashed; air-conditioners and even fans were being switched off in Government offices. For a month or two, Sihanouk conformed, after his own fashion, to the austerity pattern. But he soon slipped back into busily planning more luxury villas for himself, purchasing new motor cars, and generally throwing the state revenues around. Finally, notwithstanding the financial straits of the nation, there

seemed to have been no lasting retrenchment in Sihanouk's ambitions for the expansion and embellishment of the Kingdom. Anything other Heads of State could achieve, he would do at least as well. Fresh instructions for schools, hospitals, factories and roads, far beyond the resources of his compatriots to realise without halting other work already in hand, continued to flow from the Princely Palace.

Sihanouk's personality – which I felt, in the end, that I myself had finally understood – did indeed prove far from easy for British Ministers and for my senior official colleagues to wrap their minds around. Unsurprisingly, Sihanouk was unique in their experience. As soon as I felt sure of my ground, I attempted an in-depth study of his personality, in what I tried to make the 'definitive Despatch' to the Foreign Secretary, in March 1965. The scholarly Research Department found it illuminating and original; but the desk man in the South-East Asia Department (a critic of mine) disliked it, and recommended that the report should not be printed and circulated, (as previous and future Despatches had been and would continue to be). In the end, after raised eyebrows from senior people who had seen copies and thought it worthwhile, it was printed for record, but not widely circulated. The document has, moreover, subsequently been withheld from release to the Public Records Office in Kew, despite the 30-year rule, until the year 'X'.

Happily, a subsequent report of mine, dated 23 January 1966, is already open to the public. It took the form of a letter addressed to James Cable, the Head of South East Asia Department in the FO (the key figure mentioned on page 68). It was not intended for the eyes of Ministers or top officials. It said it all, as far as I was concerned:

> We must not romanticise Sihanouk or invest in him excessive hopes for the advancement of British policy and interests in his region. The man is a god-king and one with whom it is extremely difficult for diplomatists to deal. It is doubtful if anything we can do is likely to have a decisive effect on Sihanouk's policies. Our Englishness and our wider interests and commitments will always hamper us in our dealings with him. Moreover, he is past his peak in performance and seems likely to decline and eventually be ushered off the Cambodian scene.
>
> While he is still on stage, however, we should not regard Sihanouk as an entirely inexplicable phenomenon. In

some sections of the world press (which are invincibly ignorant about Cambodia) and sometimes among baffled diplomatists (especially if they are not resident in Cambodia), one sees spuriously attributed to Sihanouk this or that sinister motive or erratic and even insane characteristic. Yet Monseigneur cannot easily disguise his feelings and is constantly moreover explaining himself and his policies to the general public. To those who have the time to watch and listen carefully to him, he does not at all appear the traditional inscrutable Oriental. It is, of course, necessary to practise some degree of 'suspension of disbelief'; one must be ready to step outside Western dimensions in an effort at understanding. But such effort is no doubt necessary throughout the Asian context; as Lord McCartney wrote in 1794: 'Nothing could be more fallacious than to judge China by any European standard.'

Western policy towards Sihanouk therefore needs to take account of him as he is really is: above all in essence a most zealous patriot, madly independent-minded. He has no loyalties to foreigners nor any absolute respect for the values of other civilisations. He will no doubt pay lip service in some particulars to China and in others to Peru. But for him there is only one major issue: the survival of the Khmer nation by fair means or foul. All other things are ultimately subordinated to this end.

Of course, we should continue to take Cambodia and its Prince with a grain of salt. There was nothing strictly inevitable about our eclipse in 1964; moreover, the Australians have since demonstrated how much can be achieved by cultivating Cambodia painstakingly on a purely bilateral basis. But if we do not succeed in re-establishing a useful and cordial relationship with Sihanouk's Cambodia, we should take it philosophically. If diplomatic relations between London and Phnom Penh are one day severed, the yellow hordes are not going to pour in immediately through the breach; nor will the body politic of Cambodia disintegrate and crash to the ground when it is no longer supported by the broad shoulders of a resident Representative of Her Britannic Majesty.

My conclusions for the future are these. Sihanouk is still in control of Cambodia, which is still an oasis of peace. Sihanouk still wants (purely in the interests of national survival) to straddle East and West; he is certainly still not communist. What Monseigneur screeches at us is not always what matters (words do not break bones like sticks and stones); it is what he *is*, that should determine our attitude towards him.

Because the future after Sihanouk is so uncertain, and the prospect that Cambodia might one day become another Laos or even Vietnam is so appalling, we ought to make the best of things as they are, by helping Sihanouk to help himself. This means resigning the hope of influencing Sihanouk against his own wishes or instincts, but being prepared to allow him to make use of us for his own ends where we judge these to be good (*i.e.* to be in the interest of an independent Cambodia). We must not run after Sihanouk or cheapen ourselves in his eyes; but we ought to treat him with courtesy and even a fair amount of flattery. Where we think that he is liable to drag us into deep water, we should keep our distance and take no notice. But I believe that we should not hesitate to take initiatives on major issues where we are confident of success or where we identify so strong a British interest that we are prepared to knock some heads together in order to satisfy Cambodian requirements.

I have deliberately set out above not to whitewash Prince Sihanouk. Indeed, in some respects he is an Emperor who has no clothes, to whose nakedness we are too polite to draw attention. Thus I have had, in writing this letter, to suppress the following fundamental, if not particularly original, instincts:

> that the British presence and effort in Indo-China is in the long-term a nonsense (because we cannot be everywhere and do everything and the area is too remote from our vital economic and strategic interests);

that Sihanouk, for all his charm and achievement, is basically alien and unbalanced (there is more than a touch of madness in him and his ruthlessness and megalomania can be repulsive).

But these considerations are not likely to be relevant to our day-to-day diplomacy during the coming year. We all find Sihanouk absurd and infuriating from time to time; but he will not be with us forever and we must continue to make the best of him, at least as long as Anglo-Cambodian relations still have some minimal reality and importance.

That was the view I took, in my final year in charge. For my successor as Head of Mission in Phnom Penh, I went for something less pompous, and more jokey. This took the form of some earthy and practical rules of thumb, set down in postcard – or, rather, 'promptcard' – format. I came across them, in a yellowing notebook, recently. They went as follows:

Rules of Engagement

Do
- look as if you are enjoying every moment of your time in Cambodia. (Sihanouk will quickly learn if you are fed up or critical.)
- carry on looking that way even at three in the morning at a dance at the Palace, or when HMG are under attack by radio, press or *allocution improvisée*. (People will be watching closely for signs of weariness, irritation or impatience.)
- keep Phnom Penh in proportion. There is no narrow British interest at stake. (You can only do your best.)
- remember that, in Sihanouk's eyes, an Ambassador is a lowish life-form (*i.e.* enjoys the same status as the Cambodian Foreign Minister).

Don't
- expect to develop a 'personal relationship' with Sihanouk (it could well all end up in tears) or try to say very much at an

audience with him (which will be a monologue and not an exchange of views).

- look to Sihanouk to keep a confidence. (He may pass it all on to the nation by radio before the day is up.)
- take anything which Sihanouk may say in his speeches as official unless it is printed in the *Agence Khmère de Presse*. (What the Prince says in Cambodian to his own people is not intended by him for your ears.)
- discuss Sihanouk pejoratively, even with the *chers collègues*, because it will get back.
- be too precipitate in making protests, which are invariably counter-productive. The most effective response is a detached silence; avoid a gubernatorial frown.

Desirable Extra Official Accomplishments
- learn to perform the following dances:
  The Twist,
  The Madison,
  The Let's Kiss,
  The Surf
- cultivate a Boddhisatva-type expression (when in repose, the face should be serene, unemotional, with a slight smile). If you have a mouth which tends to turn down rather than up at the edges, change it by plastic surgery.
- take up a soothing hobby like roses, book-binding or goldfish. (Everything passes; very little matters; most things don't matter at all.)

I had suggested, tongue-in-cheek, that the next British Ambassador to Cambodia needed to have a 'soothing hobby'. I did so, out of sympathy for the Ambassador from whom I had taken over in 1964, the late Mr Peter Murray, then 48. A slightly dour introvert, he had been brought into the Diplomatic Service from the former colonial service in Burma. He spoke fluent Burmese and well understood the Asian mind. But he was not Viceroy of India, and Sihanouk was no recalcitrant Maharajah. It was the talk of the town, towards the end of the Peter Murray period, that the British Ambassador could not conceal his exasperation, even in the presence of the Prince, with the latter's egregious and confusing foreign policy somersaults. This was perfectly understandable, but not in all respects helpful. The more so, because Sihanouk respected Murray, and (as

already noted) later gave a private dinner for him in France, after he had been installed at the British Consulate General in Marseilles. Sadly, each at the crucial stage succeeded in getting under the skin of the other badly and subsequently Murray was to finish his career on a smallish job in Africa.

The incoming new Ambassador in 1966, the late Mr Harold Brown, then 51, was mercifully much more relaxed. He was a kindly man who got on with everybody. His previous job in the Foreign Office, before being appointed to Phnom Penh, had been in the Inspectorate; and he had by happy coincidence indeed inspected me and my mission back in 1964, a month after I had taken over, and told us that he had been delighted with what he found – including high staff morale. He added that he would mention in his report to London, with approval, that I was the first Head of Mission whom he had inspected who had played Beatles music at an official Embassy reception. Brown was then, and remained thereafter, genuinely avuncular and supportive. I was pleased with this appointment to Phnom Penh, and more than content to leave the Embassy in his care. A few months after he had taken over, Brown was called back to London, for consultations. When these were over, on his way back to Phnom Penh, he passed through Paris in order to tell me, in confidence, that I had been put up for an Honour in recognition of services supposedly beyond the normal call of duty, and that he expected me to get it. I was deeply touched. (Alas, the Rt Hon. Harold Wilson, PC, OBE, was then to change the rules; any civil servant likely to receive a higher award later, was in principle not to be given a lower award earlier. Wilson had – quite rightly – a horror of a Sir Frederick Fishface KCB, CMG, OBE, MVO.)

Ambassador Brown, in his reports to London, was to adopt the opposite position from that of Ambassador Murray: H.R.H. Prince Norodom Sihanouk was saner than he seemed; there was no real problem; all would be well. Such judgements were, sadly, not borne out by events. He went on to be Consul General in Johannesburg and retired as Minister (*i.e.* the Number Two in the Embassy) in Pretoria.

To be fair, by that point the British Government had largely washed their hands of Sihanouk personally, if not of Cambodia politically. We had done our best. The pressure of events had moved elsewhere. And the Personnel Department in London always had to try to offer most people some sort of phased career, and find posts for diplomats whose turn it was to be Head of Mission. I neverthe-

less cannot fully put out of mind what Lord Curzon once so wasp-ishly wrote (*Problems of the Far East*, 1896), to the effect that:

> The Foreign Office has sometimes appeared to regard
> certain of these posts as of only secondary importance,
> and as refuges for failures elsewhere, or at least for
> persons possessing no peculiar qualifications. ... It
> has in times past occurred that gentlemen have been
> appointed to these posts who have no personal
> acquaintance with the East or knowledge of the
> problems with which they may require to deal.

Curzon apart, however, Phnom Penh was not exactly at that time the most senior post in the Service. At Grade 4 (the equivalent of 'Coun-sellor' in our Service, or 'Assistant Secretary' in Whitehall), it came below Vientiane, Saigon (both Grade 3 or Under-Secretary) and Bangkok (Grade 2 or Deputy Secretary). Gordon Etherington-Smith in Saigon was a competent, energetic and optimistic diplomatist, who honourably and perhaps rightly resisted rushing to the conclusion that the US would eventually lose the war. A devout (but slightly 'chip-on-the-shoulder') Roman Catholic, he furthermore tended to see that war as a vital anti-communist crusade. None of the rest of us in the field, or back in London, believed this: but it was good to hear the other side of the argument. Etherington-Smith was to finish his career as Ambassador in Khartoum. In Thailand and Laos, our men were of the first quality – the youngish Fred Warner in Vientiane (later Ambassador in Tokyo and, after retirement from the Diplomatic Service, a leading MEP) and the more senior Anthony Rumbold in Bangkok (a baronet and landowner, but also a devoted public official and as shrewd and independent-minded a diplomat as they come).

I left Cambodia in November 1966. Before that, instinctively liking Prince Sihanouk as I did, and believing that the British Govern-ment should not write him off completely, in whatever residual political designs they still had in South-East Asia, I composed, with care, my final, farewell despatch to Her Majesty's Principal Secretary of State for Foreign Affairs and sent it off during my last week still in charge. Not trusting a Cabinet-level audience with the working-level, cold-like-a-crocodile reports quoted above, I laid out, instead, the following less gloomy basic thesis:

As long as he remains Head of State, the Kingdom of Cambodia is Prince Norodom Sihanouk. He is at once the most attractive and most infuriating of Asian leaders. Attractive, because his profound concern for his people, his dynamism and sheer native wit make him a national leader of international standing. Infuriating, because of his extreme sensitivity to criticism, his resistance to well-meaning advice, the unpredictability of his day-to-day conduct of affairs and the urchin-like quality which prompts him to hand out mockery and abuse on all sides.

Fortunately, the Prince has visibly slowed down over the past two years. The intractable problems with which he is faced, the various reverses with which (perhaps for the first time in his life) he has been confronted, and the growth of criticism at home, all have left him a quieter and (hopefully) a wiser man. Some say he is becoming a burnt-out case. But my astrological faculties assure me that the Mandate of Heaven has not yet been withdrawn from the God-King. Norodom Sihanouk is likely to control the destiny of the Kingdom for as far ahead as we can see; our diplomacy must take the fullest possible account of him. For all his foibles, he is a good thing and there ought to be more like him in these parts.

Was I right to do this? I may have lulled Ambassador Brown into a false state of inobservance. The rot was to set in, progressively, from the following year. Nevertheless, despite everything, I still think that His Royal Highness, Prince Norodom Sihanouk, the Former (and, as it was to work out, the Future) King, deserved this valedictory encomium.

19

The 'Crocodile Princess' in Remembrance

At the end of Book IV of *Georgics*, Virgil recounts the legend of Orpheus and Eurydice. The story ends badly. And as a sensitive sixth former, my eyes pricked, when I read:

> She spoke and immediately vanished from his sight,
> like smoke in thin air; nor did she see him again,
> though he reached out at each and every shadow and
> though he desired to say so much to her.

I was to remember these words vividly, years later, in the following circumstances, for I cannot leave the subject of Prince Norodom Sihanouk without a word about one of his Royal predecessors, a long-dead Princess, whom Monseigneur was accustomed to consult, through the vehicle of a 'medium' at the Court.

Just over twenty miles up the Mekong River from the town of Kratié, at a jungle village called Sambaur, there is a tomb of importance in the beliefs of the Cambodians. In it repose the ashes of the Princess Nucheat Khatr Vorpheak, who met a tragic death in 1834 while still of tender age. Bathing in the waters of the Tonle Sap near the then royal capital of Oudong, she disappeared. Some months later, her body, somehow preserved from decay, was discovered inside a crocodile killed many miles away in the river Mekong at Sambaur. The beast had evidently swallowed the child whole, and carried the body undigested for miles down the Tonle Sap to Phnom Penh, where the river flows into the Mekong, and then upstream beyond Kratié, a journey of around one hundred and ninety miles.

The Princess was duly cremated, as was and is the custom, and a stupa, or conical funerary tower, erected in her memory and over her ashes at Sambaur. She was high-born and beautiful, of royal

descent; she had died while still immature and hence, as the Cambodians see these matters, unmarked by sin; the recovery of her remains seemed little short of miraculous. These qualities, taken together, indicated the special favour in which she stood with the *Tevodas*, the mysterious divinities which presided over and protected the Kingdom of Cambodia. Tutelary spirits being widely believed in and revered, it was not long before the spirit of the dead Princess made contact with the living through the person of a *Hora*, or medium, at the royal Court.

Through clairvoyant astrologers, the Princess came to assert a benign influence on a succession of Kings and rulers. The most potent of all the human spirits of the realm, her special care was said to be the national survival and prosperity and – in that light – the conduct of Cambodian foreign policy. Princess Vorpheak was credited with having tendered sage advice throughout the trials and indeed near-extinction which threatened the country in the nineteenth century; while, in more recent times, she had predicted the success of the 'Royal Crusade'– the campaign against the French Protectorate conducted by the King of Cambodia which was to result in the grant of independence by France in 1953.

I was intrigued by the legend of the Princess when I first heard it whispered. I occasionally wondered about her when I made a move in my relations with the Cambodian Government. – What would she think and how would she advise? Would she look with favour on our efforts to patch up old quarrels and indirectly help Cambodia in the Kingdom's struggle for peace and survival?

Her presence was not widely spoken of. Few foreigners knew of her existence. No diplomats went to Sambaur. But I did decide, in September 1966, within a few weeks of the conclusion of my three-year mission to Cambodia, to visit her tomb. It was the season of heavy rains and dark grey clouds. I set out with two scholarly Australian friends across flooded rice fields, along muddy river banks and through foetid dark jungle, on an arduous seventy-two-hour round trip.

On the second day, we came to a halt where the laterite track disappeared under flood water. Here, we took a boat: a long *pirogue* with an outboard motor, plying as a sort of Green Line bus between riparian villages. Stopping here and there on our way, we slid up the Mekong, finally coming to a halt at Sambaur. We disembarked and we wandered along soggy paths between the wood-framed, rush-walled houses. Few people were about that afternoon: one or two

dark-skinned peasants loped by, wheeling bicycles; some Chinese shopkeepers stared blankly from their dark interiors; a group of children scampered along; dogs barked. I exchanged some Cambodian with those who would listen, but received only baffled smiles. Eventually, we came into an open space where a rather dilapidated and apparently deserted monastery stood in the clear grey light. The temple itself was a large wooden building and stood in the middle of the square, surrounded by lesser buildings of leaf and straw where the monks no doubt lived when they were at home – we could see newly-washed yellow robes laid out to dry. To one side stood the stupa of Princess Nucheat Khatr Vorpheak.

I chose not to approach the stupa at once, but walked into the temple and stood at the near end, looking down the length of the dim nave to the figures of the Buddha which stood elevated on their thrones at the far end. A few years later, the Cistercian monk, the late Robert Merton, in an identical encounter in South-East Asia, was to write, 'The silence of the extraordinary faces. The great smiles ... filled with every possibility, questioning nothing, knowing everything, rejecting nothing ...' It was to such serene but enigmatic figures that I mentally addressed my message, explaining why I had come. Having done so, in the empty and decaying temple, in that remote retreat from the world of my origin, I felt briefly at peace. The feeling was not to last long. Because it was then that – with a reluctance that came by instinct and was entirely irrational – I began to walk towards the stupa.

A tall conical structure, it stood, in a clearing apart, on a stone terrace of its own. Although restored in 1956, the tomb was already showing the erosion that time brings so speedily in its wake in tropical countries. The mosquitoes sang in my ears as I approached and the heat seemed the more stifling for there being no sun. Behind the stupa stood the dark green of the jungle and the khaki of the hutments. Above the stupa's needle point, the thick oily grey clouds sat overhead, heavy with more rain. A slight drizzle began to fall.

My mind felt blank, despite a quickening of the pulse. Perhaps I was screening it from self-conscious and superstitious melodrama or, worse still, from disappointment and bathos. But as I looked up from the foot of the stupa, I felt suddenly quite sad; it was not a distinguished edifice, being patched up here and there with cement, and covered by patches of light green moss; and I was struck by an emptiness, as of the tomb of Christ on the day of His resurrection, but without the triumph. Then something happened. My foot slipped on the wet steps of the terrace. I took this for the accident it was and

walked a step or two nearer. After I had looked about me for a few minutes more, my foot slipped again. I could see that the stones beneath my foot were wet with rain. And I knew that the rubber soles of the comfortable jungle boots on my feet were worn with long service. Yet I had been standing still when I slipped. Slipping and sliding a third time, I apprehensively backed down off the terrace, walked some distance away from the stupa and turned squarely to face it.

My mind then cleared. I felt rebuffed and resentful. Without either bogus reverence or Caucasian condescension, but certainly with an edge of reproach, I laid my thoughts calmly and consecutively before the Princess Vorpheak as if I had been speaking aloud.

I said that I was a foreigner who did not know the Khmer customs, who had lived for only three years in Kampuchea, and who would shortly leave for a destination at the further end of the earth (Paris), never to return to Sambaur. But I had come as a friend of the country and its people, and as one who respected the legend of the Princess. This legend was the property of Khmers and not of the British, and it was not for me to believe it or to disbelieve it. It was true that in the mental world in which I lived and had been brought up, I found it hard to see how a child, long since dead, could be active in the affairs of the living. Yet my civilisation laid no claim to all knowledge and to all wisdom and my personal scepticism could well be mistaken or, perhaps more probably, misplaced. In electing to visit the stupa, therefore, I had chosen to accept the legend as it stood, and I had had the presumption to offer the Princess, although I was an alien, some portion of the respect which was apparently her due from her living compatriots.

Her Highness, if she existed and could receive my thoughts, would know with what a heavy heart I had first come to Phnom Penh, to a mission which had proved no bed of roses. She would also know that I had laboured to understand and to help. I hoped that she would share my satisfaction that at least something had been done. I knew that there were tight limits to the action which my successors, as I myself, could take to advance the interests which it was the Princess's charge, under the *Tevodas*, to protect: the survival and happiness of the Khmer nation. But I asked her to be prepared to judge us fairly and generously, and to give us the credit of good intentions.

For a brief moment, I had the impression of contact, of a message not merely sent but received. Then the emptiness came back and the

everyday world once more took me in hand. I walked up to the stupa again – this time without slipping – and tried to decipher the inscription in squiggly Cambodian lettering on the base. My friends approached from the monastery and we exchanged one or two commonplace remarks. Then we strolled back to the riverside, in search of our boat.

After a few minutes, the pilot of the *pirogue* took us away for half an hour upstream to deliver a passenger and a bundle or two on the last of his rounds. The sun had re-emerged and we smoked and watched it set. Then the *pirogue* cast off for the last time and, turning into midstream, ran swiftly south with the current. It was dusk when we passed by Sambaur, silent in the shadow of the trees, one or two huts a-glimmer with lanterns. I stood on the roof of the cabin searching the skyline. Briefly, I glimpsed what I was looking for – the top of the stupa standing out in ghostly grey contrast to the black jungle beyond. Once again, the veil briefly lifted.

This time, a wave of gentle emotion seemed to reach me from across the water. It felt as if the Princess were sending me on my way with a message. For what I was, as such I had been accepted: a friend of Cambodia, within that wider discipline which made me before all else the servant of another country, the subject of another Crown.

As we shall see in the next chapter, not even the *Tevodas* were able to avert the fate shortly awaiting the Kingdom of Cambodia. But the country and its people have in the end survived; so Nucheat Khatr Vorpeak is not to be mocked.

Cambodian Coda

20

The Crash

Cambodia moved steadily towards disaster. This is, I think, how the crash came about.

The Americans started intensive carpet-bombing in Cambodia's frontier areas by B-52s in 1969 and continued it for four years (in what they called the 'sideshow'). Sihanouk, politically without options and emotionally on his uppers, progressively lost the plot, even immersing himself, in a mixture of vainglory and escapism, between 1966 and 1969, in a new hobby – the making of a series of appallingly bad romantic movies (in the earliest of which I was invited to take a walk-on part – I declined). In March 1970, in his absence on a private visit to Europe, Prince Norodom Sihanouk was deposed in a *coup d'état*. Sihanouk could have flown back from Paris or Moscow immediately to confront his critics and wrest back control, perhaps also making some judicious concessions. Indeed, he was urged to do just that, in Moscow, by Soviet President Podgorny, who had a plane waiting to take him directly back to Phnom Penh. The Prince, however, was exhausted and disillusioned. In any case, he had never in his whole life shown evidence of possessing actual physical courage. In July 1970, a military tribunal was to condemn the Prince *in absentia* to death for high treason. Meanwhile, the superstitious and not very bright Defence Minister, General Lon Nol, had taken over; he had invited the Americans back; and he had begun an attempt to throw the Viet Cong out.

As *Le Figaro* astutely pointed out, while Sihanouk could just about live with Viet Cong sanctuaries on Cambodian soil, if that were the price of peace, for General Lon Nol – a known Vietnamophobe – such sanctuaries were seen unequivocally as a martial provocation and an insult to Cambodian national honour. More of a policeman than a soldier (and long suspected by the British of being deficient

in military judgement anyway), Lon Nol immediately and most fool-
ishly addressed a bold ultimatum to the communists: all North Vietnamese and Viet Cong units were to be withdrawn from Cambodian
territory within three days. Simultaneously, Vietnamese civilians
began to be murdered in numbers and in cold blood – their bodies
floating down the Mekong for all to see. Vietnamese office staff and
domestic servants in Phnom Penh (including those employed in the
British Embassy) were rounded up and expelled from Cambodia.
Fighting duly broke out between the Cambodian army and the
North Vietnamese and Viet Cong forces in Cambodia, who – far from
clearing out – began to support elements opposed to the new
regime in Phnom Penh. Lon Nol appealed for help. On 30 April 1970,
in a televised address to the nation, President Nixon announced that
American and South Vietnamese forces were entering Cambodia to
drive out the enemy from their sanctuaries and destroy their supplies
(which, in the event, they failed to achieve). The Chinese, North
Vietnamese and Viet Cong broke off diplomatic relations with
Cambodia. Sihanouk was granted exile in Beijing. The creation was
announced of a 'Liberation Front of Kampuchea', composed of
patriotic and socialist forces, and dedicated to the re-establishment
of democratic and popular government in Phnom Penh – by means
of prolonged guerrilla warfare, if need be. The relatively few Khmer
Rouge followers, not battle-hardened like the communist Vietnamese,
were initially almost overrun by Lon Nol in Siemreap Province, and
forced to draw back to remote jungle and mountain lairs. But they
began to swell in numbers. The US B-52 bombing probably helped
recruitment; much more so, Prince Sihanouk's decision to set up a
government in exile in Beijing and – at Chinese instigation – to
confer some sort of royal legitimacy on the Khmer Rouge.

The US and South Vietnamese forces withdrew from Cambodia
in June 1970. Martial law was decreed from Phnom Penh. The
Kingdom was in the grip of open war. By 1971, Lon Nol's forces
were in difficulty. By 1974, the Khmer Rouge had secured the upper
hand. By 1975, they had taken Phnom Penh.

Back in 1970, in the broadcast referred to above, the US President
claimed that, over the preceding five years, North Vietnam had
occupied military sanctuaries all along the Cambodian frontier with
South Vietnam and that these occupied areas contained 'major base
camps, training sites, logistics facilities, weapons and ammunition
factories, air strips and prisoner-of-war compounds'. Prince Sihanouk
had himself been all too conscious of this growing, communist,

military presence over the previous few years. He admits in his memoirs to having closed his eyes to it. In January 1968, the Prince said to the visiting US emissary, Chester Bowles, that Viet Cong sanctuaries and facilities on Cambodian soil were not very extensive but that he didn't care if the US killed Vietnamese there, as long as they spared the Cambodians. (Sihanouk had intended, in what was an off-the-cuff remark, to indicate that he would not object to isolated, small-scale attacks, but Henry Kissinger used it to justify the B-52 offensive, the following year.) A full 12 months before his overthrow, in March 1969, Sihanouk had declared to the press that he was by then deeply worried at the extent of Viet Cong and Viet Minh infiltration, and had listed the provinces where they were to be found. His problem was to know what action to take: to attempt to see them off with the use of his small and ill-equipped army, or to run the risk that others would act where he did not. As late as 10 March 1970, in talking to reporters on the steps of the Elysée Palace after lunching with President Pompidou, Prince Sihanouk was to admit that the communist forces present in Cambodia had numbered as many as 40,000 in the preceding November. 'My country', he said, 'gets all the fall-out of the war in Vietnam and Laos'.

The reasons for the *coup d'état* of 18 March 1970 were complex. Some of them were rooted in purely internal considerations – the usual litany of unemployment, bourgeois impoverishment, government nepotism and corruption. More important, and as to foreign policy and the fight for national survival, Sihanouk had lost credibility with much of the country's 'Establishment' – including senior and respected figures such as my very discreet, very occasional contact Prince Sirik Matak – and he had forfeited the confidence of the Cambodian army. This was not in all respects the Prince's own fault. But after his deposition, a campaign quickly developed in Phnom Penh which lashed out at the Prince's economic and social policies, his personal style of government, his general political record, and even his private life and that of members of the Royal Family and others who surrounded him. True or false, these were harsh judgments.

Another view was expressed by the British Foreign Secretary, Michael Stewart, in answer to questions in the House of Commons on 5 May 1970. He said

> Whatever differences of opinion there may be, a very
> large number of Hon. Members in all parts of the

House must have felt great sympathy with the continued efforts of Prince Sihanouk to keep his small, peace-loving, kindly country at peace in the maelstrom of South-East Asia. This is certainly what I felt.

However, to do so, he had to pay a terribly heavy price, namely that considerable parts of his territory would be used by communist forces. He himself made it very clear when, on 13 March, 1970, on leaving Paris to visit Moscow and Beijing, he said: 'I intend to ask Moscow and Beijing to advise their friends in Hanoi and in the Viet Cong to put a brake on their interference in Cambodian domestic affairs'. Later, he said: 'I should like to affirm to my fellow countrymen that I will never tolerate either the infiltration of the Viet Cong and Viet Minh or their interference in our affairs, because ours is sovereign country. Yesterday, I informed the friendly Soviet leaders of this matter.'

This was the dilemma with which Prince Sihanouk was faced. Before anyone in the House criticises him, let us be fortunate that this country is not in the position that his was. I believe that, according to his best judgment, he tried to keep his country at peace. He was obliged to pay a high price for this, in allowing it to be more and more used as a base for communist forces.

Such was the British view in 1970. I share it still today and, as it happened, without Norodom Sihanouk, Cambodia was to be overtaken by disaster. As Senator Mike Mansfield (a sympathetic observer of Cambodia, well acquainted with Prince Sihanouk personally) said, in a debate in the US Senate, 'What was for a decade and a half the only oasis of peace in Indo-China has been turned into a bloody battlefield in the space of one month'.

But things were to get much, much worse. General Lon Nol failed politically; he was defeated militarily; he fled into exile in California in 1975, a broken and sick man; he died there in 1985.

In 1975 also came the 'Year Zero' of the Khmer Rouge, and the horrors of the notorious Pol Pot. Originally known as Saloth Sar, he was one of a group of disaffected Khmer Rouge who had taken to the *maquis* in Rattanakiri Province in the remote North-East in the early 1960s. Within a day or two of entering Phnom Penh on 17 April

1975, he began emptying the city of its entire population, including the elderly and those in hospital, for forced labour in the fields. Newspapers were closed down; private property, public transport and even the national currency were abolished.

Then came the purges. No one knows the exact figure; but, as noted in my Introduction, (page xii), a quarter of the population of the country may have perished, in the insane, Marxist/Maoist, genocide which followed – terrifyingly conveyed in the Hollywood movie *The Killing Fields*. We now know that, in order to purge the 'class enemies' of the 'Angkar' or 'Organisation' (as the secretive Pol Pot Government came to be known), 167 special prisons were set up, whose occupants, after interrogation under torture, were moved on to 343 killing fields, where (to conserve ammunition) they were usually clubbed to death. But the majority of Pol Pot's up to two million victims simply died of privation under forced labour and are buried in 19,440 mass graves, up and the down the country. In this process, the Khmer Rouge in effect annihilated almost the entire educated class. This wave of mass murder swept up virtually anyone who spoke French or English and all the Buddhist clergy (in his memoirs, Sihanouk reports that, touring central Cambodia in 1976, he saw only one Buddhist monk – and he was helping to dig an irrigation channel). I assume that it took all, or almost all, my own former Cambodian acquaintances, employees and personal servants who had not already fled the country. Some Cambodians managed to cross over to Thailand, where they occupied vast refugee camps in the jungle. Even as late as 1987 (when I visited these camps, in my capacity as the Director General in charge of trade and overseas development assistance in the European Commission), there were well over 300,000 of them.

Back in 1975, against his better judgement but on the insistence of Chairman Mao Tse-tung, Sihanouk had returned to Cambodia from exile. In effect, he then found himself trapped: he was the prisoner, under implicit sentence of death, of Pol Pot in Phnom Penh. Sihanouk was lucky to escape with his life back to Beijing three years later – unlike other members of the Royal Family, including his heir-elect. Altogether, the poor man lost three daughters, two sons and 14 grandchildren in the holocaust of Khmer Rouge rule from 1975–78; and he lost cousins, uncles and aunts, too. (Even in more gentle and less fanatical Laos, the Pathet Lao, when they came to power in 1975, promptly eliminated the King and Queen and their children; it must all go back to the precedent set by the Russian communists, with the last of the Czars.)

But Pol Pot, in his turn, soon found himself in deep trouble. He could not resist, for racist reasons, just like Lon Nol before him, antagonising and confronting the communist Vietnamese. Provoked beyond endurance, the latter entered Cambodia militarily in 1978, drove Pol Pot out of Phnom Penh, installed a Soviet-style communist government, and stayed on until 1989 (during which time, Cambodia remained largely closed to the world, under a pro-Soviet Government). Neither the Americans nor we approved of this new Stalinist regime in Phnom Penh. We went along – in November 1979 – with the Khmer Rouge being seated at the UN, possibly because we lacked full knowledge of the character of the Pol Pot regime. After the Soviet invasion of Afghanistan in December 1979, in order to reassure Thailand and discourage further Vietnamese adventurism, we began giving some small-scale, covert training and logistic support to the Khmer Rouge, as well as to other Cambodian resistance forces opposing the Moscow-backed set-up in Phnom Penh, (as we were doing in Afghanistan with the Taleban). All this availed little, until medical developments came to our assistance. Pol Pot, who visited Bangkok frequently for medical purposes, was diagnosed in 1983 as suffering from cancer. The monster eventually died miserably in a primitive retreat at Anlong Veng in 1998. His initially adoring and collaborative, first wife had, well before that, lost her sanity in the service of her husband's revolution, and been divorced and discarded.

Once the coast was clear and, following the Peace Agreement reached at the Paris Conference of 1991, Prince Sihanouk yet again returned to Cambodia after nearly 13 years of exile from his native land. In 1993, he consented to become once more the King. But the old magic had departed. He found himself no longer the all-powerful autocrat and popular leader of former years. He was upstaged, out-manoeuvred and rendered impotent by his youthful Prime Minister, Hun Sen – a man of mettle, ruthlessness and guile who privately mocked Sihanouk as an ageing tiger without claws or teeth. In 2004, King Norodom Sihanouk finally stood down, for a second and last time, from the Throne (but with many empty titles, and the promise of a comfortable retirement). He was succeeded as King by a ballet dancer son, Prince Norodom Sihamoni. Unlike his father, King Sihamoni has so far made no problems for his sponsors and appears content with a purely symbolic, constitutional role.

And Cambodia? The country has somehow survived, but it lives precariously.

On the plus side, the population (2005 census) has risen to 14 million, from eight million before Pol Pot. The magnificent temple complexes at Angkor, relatively little damaged by the fighting, are once again – and deservedly – an international tourist attraction. 'Eco-tourism' to unspoilt and exotic wildlife habitats and to scenic locations is under development. Visitors are expected to double in numbers, over the next three or four years. The capital city, mercifully still much less manic than Bangkok, has been rebuilt and greatly expanded. Oil has been discovered in Cambodian waters in the Gulf of Thailand. There is a booming market for the country's minerals and timber. Foreign investment has been attracted in.

But there are problems to be faced. Cambodia, today, is a different country from that which I knew, forty years ago. Dams built on the upper Mekong in China threaten traditional fisheries and riparian agriculture in downstream Cambodia. Despite massive, UN-sponsored aid programmes and the active assistance of almost every imaginable international charity and non-governmental organisation, the new economy is only slowly emerging to replace the old. Government corruption is widespread – and oil money, by the nature of things, can be expected to make that much worse. Privation and unemployment – little known in the immediate post-independence period – are now widely in evidence. HIV/Aids is endemic, infant mortality high, orphanages full. The Prime Minister is a former Khmer Rouge commander who had defected from Pol Pot to the communist Vietnamese in 1977. More or less democratic elections have been held. But the coalition of parties, interests and loyalties in government is fragile, the opposition very much present, even if divided and confined. While the excesses of the Khmer Rouge are exposed and deplored (notably in the Tuol Sleng Genocide Museum in Phnom Penh, and the local killing field outside town), the trial of those accused of having played a prominent role in the genocide seems deferred *sine die*, no doubt for fear of who might eventually be implicated among a powerful minority who have given themselves 'make-overs' and attempted to rejoin mainstream politics. (Pol Pot's most notoriously murderous lieutenant, Ta Mok, died – in detention, pending trial – at the ripe old age of 80 in 2006.) Altogether, war has left a mark on people and government, countryside and life-style, which blue-helmet peace-keeping, nation-building and lavish economic assistance have only partly erased. I have, very recently, been back to my old haunts in Phnom Penh and revisited Angkor. The latter was as it always had been. But, remembering

what was once the *douceur de vie Phnom Penhoise*, I did not always recognise the haunts now, incidently anglophone, not francophone.

For many years, even latterly in the somnolence of rural Shropshire, but in mind of everything I have heard of the evil and insanity of Pol Pot, I have suffered from a recurring nightmare. I am walking from my former Ambassadorial Residence, in the chic, ex-colonial quarter near the French Embassy towards the British Embassy Chancery, close to the Independence Monument. But the city is entirely deserted. The only noise is that of crunching underfoot – a crunching of human bones. So much for the efforts of the 'play-boy' Chargé d'Affaires, the 'Number One Twister of Cambodia'.

21

Epilogue on Indo-China

Sir Christopher Meyer, our Ambassador in Washington from 1997 to 2003, was one of a series of outstanding British diplomats in the post. In the general preface to *DC Confidential*, he writes: 'It is not to be blithely uncritical to say that the world is a far better place for the existence of the United States'. Is he right? The answer has to be 'Yes, but'. On US engagement in two World Wars, on the Cold War (including nuclear deterrence, the Berlin Blockade, and the response to the communist invasion of South Korea): 'Yes'. On the new war against international terrorism: 'Almost certainly' (but they must help get Palestine/Israel right). On global climate change: 'Don't know, yet'! But on Indo-China in the 1960s and 1970s: an emphatic 'No'!

Honourably, unselfishly but tragically, the Americans got it wrong in Vietnam. With hindsight these days, we can see the truth of the matter. We have witnessed the reunification of North and South, the new country's economic and commercial resurgence (largely regardless of former Marxist doctrines) and its opening up to the Western world. We have observed the cordial reception of the Vietnamese Prime Minister (a former red revolutionary) in Washington and even (in January 2007) Vietnam's accession to the World Trade Organisation. What is less well-known is that, from the outset, the British took a different view from the Americans.

The war fought in the Korean peninsula under US leadership and UN political auspices, to drive the North Korean armies back where they came from, was the right thing to have done. What went wrong was the subsequent American inference that Vietnam was a similar case for treatment. This, in the light of the disputable 'Domino Theory' formulated by the US National Security Council in 1952. According to this, if South Vietnam fell, Cambodia, Laos, Thailand

and other points West would follow in short order. President Eisenhower (nice, but not bright) 'bought' this thesis and recommended it to his successor in office. Khrushchev's proclaimed support, in 1961, for 'wars of national liberation' did not help.

But, if President Kennedy had escaped assassination, I do not believe that such an intelligent man, given to lateral thinking and with an ear to independent counsel from credible major allies (of whom Prime Minister Harold Macmillan was one) would have continued to 'bash on regardless' into the Vietnamese morass. Kennedy's successor, President Johnson, not merely continued JFK's policy of supplying the South Vietnamese with weapons and military advisers, but also made the fatal decision to commit US combat troops in large numbers to a guerrilla war in the paddy-fields and the jungles for which they were not well trained and which they could not win – even with massive air support and a prodigal use of fire power on the ground. As Dr Henry Kissinger subsequently wrote (*Diplomacy*, page 657), if J.F. Kennedy had lived long enough to realise that America had embarked on an unsustainable course, he would have had the authority and strength to reverse earlier decisions in a way which an insecure and hopelessly inexperienced L.B. Johnson was not to find possible.

I mentioned hindsight. The UK – which, in the 1950s, had some claim to understand South-East Asia from the ground up and even ex-French Indo-China better than the US – was unhappy from the outset about the escalating commitments in Indo-China into which the Americans were entering. Mr Dean Rusk, in an ironic remark about what he saw as UK pusillanimity, said that it would have been enough if we had committed only one battalion of the Black Watch – no doubt on the model of the compliant, token, Australian military commitment. But the fact was that the British did not think that Vietnam was the right place at which to draw a line, said as much, and had the self-confidence and independence of judgement to stay out of Vietnam and find better things to do.

When that francophile British Foreign Secretary and future Prime Minister, Mr Anthony Eden, brokered the Geneva Accords of July 1954, his objective was to get the French off the hook. By the time of their defeat at Dien Bien Phu, the French had been facing an insurgency and guerrilla war in Vietnam for nine years.

It was a cruel business – Ho Chi Minh was a ruthless communist dictator, his principal backer, Mao Tse-tung, likewise. But the insurgency was effective. The colonial power, even with modest US

logistic assistance, was confronted with political failure, military defeat and economic exhaustion. No one else was lining up, at the time, to fight the Viet Minh (even the Americans took a further ten years to get around to that). A fudged political solution was therefore called for. Kissinger was subsequently to admit that 'most of the time, ambiguous documents such as the Geneva accords reflect reality; they settle what it is possible to settle, in the full knowledge that further refinement must await new developments' (*Diplomacy*, page 635). Thus, the constructively ambiguous Geneva agreements did not establish a military border between one side and the other: the Seventeenth Parallel partition was an administrative boundary, and it left the way open to unification after internationally supervised elections. Eden would have had little doubt that these elections were likely to be rigged, and that the ultimate presiding power would be communist; but he and his advisers were pretty certain that there would be no drastic 'Domino' effect. As Kissinger was to again acknowledge, respectfully, Churchill and Eden 'believed that the best place to defend South-East Asia was at the border of Malaya'.

Of course, this was as much a matter of political judgement as of demonstrable fact.

On the one hand, we knew that the politburo in Hanoi was determined to seize all of Vietnam – and we suspected that its long-term plans were to secure some sort of ascendancy over both Laos and Cambodia. (In his excellent biography of Pol Pot, Philip Short writes that what originally turned Pol Pot against the Vietnamese was his perusal of the Vietnamese party's internal records – which made clear that Phnom Penh was to be made subservient to Hanoi.) And what of the potential capacity for trouble from the communist party of Thailand, whose guerrillas were to become a minor problem? On the other hand, China, we had good reason to suspect, had reservations about a reunited Vietnam. Of course, the world saw this, writ large, when China 'punished' Vietnam militarily in February 1979. But we had concluded, years before, that the Vietnamese were not trusted in Beijing. As – once again – the arch-realist Henry Kissinger has since conceded, China's perception of its national interest caused it to be 'deeply ambivalent' about having a major power, even a communist one, on its Southern border.

And Cambodia? The Kingdom was seen by the British as a credible buffer state. Chairman Mao had assured the Cambodians that the Viet Minh would not be allowed to trouble them.

Thailand? The new, American- and British-backed, SEATO Alliance would look after the Thai, whose security problems we knew about from our military efforts in Malaya, and whom we considered well able to see off communist subversion, with a little help.

As to Vietnam itself, the British came increasingly to suspect, at each phase of the escalation of conflict, that American support for Saigon was a 'no-brainer' and a non-winner.

Thus, in a guerrilla war in the equatorial forests, mountains and paddy-fields of Vietnam, with no classical 'front line', in which one Vietnamese would be pitched against another, the American forces would not have the advantage of distinguishing friend from foe (as the British had had in Malaya, fighting a mere ten thousand or so ethnic Chinese in the jungle in the defence of ethnic Malays, and also had in Borneo, fighting groups of Indonesian infantry who stuck out a mile in the jungle, among hostile, local tribesmen). While I was still in Singapore in early 1964, General William C. Westmoreland, the Commander of US forces in Vietnam, paid a visit to our Commander-in-Chief Far East, for a briefing on Sukarno's guerrilla 'Confrontation'. A Brigadier pointed out, on a large, marked-up map, where the Indonesian infiltrators were located on Malay-sian territory the day before. The visiting General's jaw dropped. 'How do you know this?' he asked incredulously.

More than that, the political regime in Saigon was corrupt; the civil administration in South Vietnam was ineffective (unlike the fairly well-administered and policed Malayan peninsula); and factions and war-lords complicated the act. Above all, there was a common frontier between North Vietnam and China, across which military supplies for the Viet Minh and the Viet Cong could be directed, which had not had to be taken into account when the UK won the guerrilla war in Malaya.

On top of all this, we thought the US armed forces terrifyingly credible, where all-out war, no-holds-barred, might be contemplated; but they were likely to be less effective, where 'hearts and minds' operations were concerned, in which Uncle Sam's hands would be tied inevitably behind his back. Apart from US 'special forces' and impressive airborne and marine units, US rank-and-file infantry battalions were totally inadequate; 'search and destroy' missions were led by junior officers, some of whom (like Lt. Charles Calley, of My Lai massacre notoriety) might have had difficulty getting into Sandhurst, let alone passing out of it. These incompe-tents were grudgingly accompanied by drafted 'grunts'; some of

them might not have succeeded in getting a job in any British employment exchange (even in conditions of full employment). Altogether, they were not capable of offering anything other than ill-directed aggression with the benefit of massive and indiscriminate expenditure of ammunition. As Calgacus said of Roman military methods in Britain, *Ubi solitudinem faciunt, pacem appellant* – it could be said of the US forces in Vietnam, 'they make a wilderness and they call it peace' (Tacitus, *Agricola*). The US air force was not all that much better. The US navy was OK – but it did not enter significantly into the Vietnamese equation.

To be blunt therefore, it was our general view that the war in Vietnam was unwinnable. So, the UK (quite rightly) declined to enter it militarily. A British government of today's stamp – Brown/Blairite or Cameronesque – might have found this refusal difficult. As Australia was then, we could have been swayed into making at least a token military commitment – and perhaps more – to the ground war in Vietnam. But Britain in the 1960s was more proud and more independent; our highly professional Foreign Office was not yet marginalised and undermined by a 'Presidential' Prime Minister and the associated 'political advisers' and 'spin doctors'. It helped that our forces East of Suez had enough on their hands (admittedly with modest Malaysian, Australian and New Zealand support), seeing off the attempt by President Sukarno to break up the newly created Federation of Malaysia. The new Federation was be seen by us as one of the last and greatest success stories of British de-colonisation. It may also have helped stiffen British pride in their independence of judgement over Vietnam that some people in Washington had looked askance at the British response to the undeclared war against Borneo and Sarawak, launched by President Sukarno in 1963. Sukarno was seen in certain US quarters as, on balance, a good thing: a bastion against Communism and barrier against falling dominos. Were the bumbling British going to somehow rock the boat? Finally, the UK had the excuse, as a non-combatant Co-Chairman with the USSR of the Geneva Conference on Indo-China, that our help would be better given indirectly, through diplomacy.

Not surprisingly, therefore, we did not have a smooth ride with the Americans over Indo-China. In my day, the (as it happened, personally very sympathetic, and ferociously anti-communist) British Ambassador in Saigon was kept at a distance by his powerful and Viceroy-like US colleague. Even if the Black Watch had been committed, and a heavier-weight Ambassador had been appointed,

it would have made no difference – no more than it did, recently, in Iraq. Was Paul Bremer, the US supremo in Baghdad – described by Lord Patten, in his *Not Quite the Diplomat*, as 'cocky, clever, confident' – open to any real influence from Sir Jeremy Greenstock, our high-powered Ambassador to the UN, made Bremer's British partner on the spot? (I eagerly await Greenstock's memoirs, apparently already written but still under official interdict.) The Australians – acutely aware of the disjunction between the line which their almost equally marginalised Saigon Embassy was being fed by the US authorities and the realities which their excellent troops on the ground were reporting – were scarcely better placed.

So the Americans chose not to respond to the Anglo-Soviet interest in 1963 (albeit London and Moscow each for their own reasons) in an attempt to count Cambodia out of the Vietnam war. It was only when it was too late – after they saw that they had lost and were going to have to negotiate their way out of Vietnam – that the Americans thought differently about Cambodia.

Would it, however, have made much difference if a Geneva Conference had convened in good order in 1963, and reached apparent agreement to respect Cambodia's independence, neutrality and territorial integrity? The debacle in Laos, the year before, was not too promising: agreements reached at Geneva were from the outset not respected by China and North Vietnam (the latter pretended to withdraw its forces and in fact progressively strengthened them); nor, thereafter, even entirely by the US (which launched clandestine B-52 bombing raids on parts of Laos, as well as on North Vietnam, in 1963 – and kept them going for ten years – as well as running deniable 'special forces' operations in the Kingdom of a Million Elephants).

One cannot know the answer to that question with certainty; but it seems likely that the Conference would have procured a better, even if confused, outcome, and calmed things down in neighbouring Laos in the process. A settlement in South Vietnam would then have been easier to reach. The more pragmatic and cautious Chou En-lai might have prevailed, for a time, over the more ideological and certainly the more reckless Mao Tse-tung – whose preference was for an escalation of the fighting within Vietnam's borders, and the further luring of the US into the Vietnamese meat grinder, all at no cost to China.

In the event, it was Mao's vision that prevailed. It took the political ruthlessness and skill of Henry Kissinger, and the massive carpet

bombing by American B-52s of Cambodian territory, to find an exit strategy. The Vietnam operation, from start to finish, probably involved the loss of five million civilians in Vietnam. Then there were the two million who were lost in Cambodia in the knock-on, Pol Pot genocide. Nothing, in comparison to the 70 million lives lost in communist China as a result of Mao Tse-tung's policies and decisions (perhaps half of them in the 'Great Leap Forward'). We must remember it was not the US, but Ho Chi Minh, who had started off the whole murderous process in Vietnam in the first place. He did so with deliberation and cynicism. This was not the end game which the US had envisaged when they originally decided to back South Vietnam against the North. If they had had hindsight – or at any rate had listened to others – they would most emphatically not have got involved in the way they did.

For us in the UK at least, there are difficult lessons to be drawn from the above story. In what is now, at least for the time being (pending the possible rise of a globally-powerful China, or conceivably even of a militant, fundamentalist, Pan-Islam) a uni-polar world, we need to work as closely as we always have with the US – a democracy and an ally of choice. America helped reconstruct Europe after World War Two, through the Marshall Plan. Their ground troops and strategic forces underpinned the North Atlantic Alliance during the Cold War. We get more than we give from them today, through our defence and intelligence co-operation. Economically, they are the top dog in the IMF, the World Bank, the WTO. They help drive global trade expansion and are the fount of high-technology innovation. The Americans are essentially a good people. We and they have tended to see the monsters of the modern world – Hitler, Stalin, Mao, Ho Chi Minh, Pol Pot, Milosovic, Saddam Hussein and the rest – for what they were. We are alongside them today, in the effort to tackle terror.

But we need to think what we are doing. The Americans can still get things wrong, as they may already be doing over climate change and global pollution, and as they apparently have done in Iraq, in their careless dismantling of police, security and defence forces immediately after the allied victory and their failure to enter Iraq with a credible exit strategy which took account of the realities of Iraq's society, ethnicities, politics and religious faiths.

As one of the greatest of French archaeologists (Bernard Groslier) once muttered to me, in Cambodia in the 1960s, US academic colleagues could usually be relied upon to have read everything and

understood nothing – a deliberately absurd paradox, yet one knew what he meant.

Me? I have travelled across the length and breadth of the US. I have been in and out of Washington and New York on official business more times than I can remember. I like the people and admire the country. I have worked closely with the State Department and (at one remove) with the Department of Defense, the CIA and the FBI on common causes. I found them fine enough fellows and sometimes even inspiring 'warriors'. But I have also negotiated eyeball-to-eyeball with them, on sordid trade matters, in a different spirit. They – the successive and often predatory 'Trade Representatives' and their teams of pushy lawyers and hungry economists looking for lucrative subsequent jobs in the private sector – the 'guys in the black hats'. Me – the detached, idealistic Foreign Office Mandarin with an eye more for political justice and economic common sense than for commercial banditry – the 'good guy'. (I have, personally, defused at least one trade war between the EU and the US. It was touch-and-go.)

Whence my personal ambivalence? We need the US as a friend and ally, but we also need others more like ourselves – of comparable size, common outlook and compatible experience of the world.

Hence, the hopes which I have always invested in a possible future Common European Foreign Policy, Trans-Atlantic in outlook, but Pan-European in inspiration. A touch of 'European Political Co-operation' would not have come amiss over Cambodia in the early 1960s. If the UK had already by then been permitted to join the European Community without a Gaullist veto, and if President de Gaulle had indeed been a genuine European rather than merely a Gallic messiah and a general 'throw-back' to the previous century, a powerful and convincing joint Anglo-French initiative in Indo-China might just have succeeded in lifting the US militarily off the hook, in restoring French national honour and self-respect after their defeat at Dien Bien Phu, in giving the British confidence in a less subservient transatlantic role, in saving the lives of many millions of human beings and indeed in turning the entire course of South East Asian history. Who knows? The Americans might even have ended up respecting and thanking the Europeans for it, instead of either learning to despise what Donald Rumsfeld has called 'Old Europe' or (worse) simply becoming largely indifferent to it. But this was not to be.

As to Cambodia, and the events described in this book, the British did do the right thing. Nice try. But they failed. What about the present, in Iraq (admittedly a very different crisis from Vietnam)? We must surely endure there as long as we are needed, for the sake of our single most important alliance, and to continue to help the Iraqis help themselves, wherever we are able. But, if toppling statues of Saddam Hussein did not look militarily too difficult, the political exit strategy was always going to be more of a problem. The formula for the latter proposed by the Pentagon and approved in the White House was innocent of local insight and understanding, and in the event proved disastrous to the allies and the cause they were seeking to advance.

Lord Hurd of Westwell has this to say, (see Select Bibliography):

> The post-war plan was based on assumptions in the Pentagon which quickly proved false. They ignored their own ignorance and trusted advisers who others knew were untrustworthy. The British Government subordinated its thinking so completely to the United States that no serious questions were asked about the plan and no attempt made to modify it in the light of British experience in Iraq or the Middle East .No attention was paid to those who predicted correctly that while most Iraqis would rejoice at Saddam Hussein`s overthrow, it did not follow that they would welcome foreign military occupation. The recklessness of these assumptions in the Pentagon passes belief. So does the failure of Britain to question them.

The sad reality is, therefore, that a Labour prime Minister, Mr Tony Blair, rubber-stamped a prospectus that a previous Labour Prime Minister, Mr Harold Wilson, would have examined and rejected. Of course, we need to remember that, as Douglas Hurd puts it in the same essay, "in the penny-farthing relationship which we now have with United State, the farthing is gradually getting smaller". But the British are still entitled to think of themselves as Allies, not Helots – as Free Yeomen, not Yes-Men.

There could be a lesson here, should Iran come to the boil. Let us stick, this time, to the letter and spirit of the UN Charter – and, if in doubt, simply stay out.

Meanwhile, what is the point of keeping a first class Foreign Ministry chained up in King Charles' Street, if Downing Street will

not let it bark? Major foreign policy issues – especially when they involve national security – are too tricky to be mostly the monopoly of the spin doctors, political advisers and romantic amateurs who have in recent years found their way into Number Ten. Parliament, and hard professionals ready to tell Truth to Power, must be fully brought back into the act.

With all this in mind from things past, I should like to send two memos for the future. The first is to Mr Gordon Brown : "Please give us back our FO – and a voice to the Foreign Secretary and Cabinet". The second is to the governments of the EU's other Member States: "Please get your act together – in tomorrow's troubled world, we may all have to do more than some of you have hitherto wanted".

At the Cambodian frontier with Thailand: the author teasing General Lon Nol, Head of Cambodian Armed Forces (and instigator of the subsequent coup d'état)

Confidential Annex – Not the Secret Service

Phnom Penh in the 1960s was not only a place (at least at the Royal Court) of necromancy and superstition; it was also commonly held to be a centre of international intrigue, espionage and secret intelligence gathering.

Was I an international intriguer? I hope so – that was my job. Was I myself a spy? Certainly not. Was I acquainted with 'the Secret World'? Only peripherally. But some chose not to believe it. Word went round the bars that I was some sort of 'spook'.

In August 1989, happily installed in Sussex as Vice-Chancellor of the University there, I received a letter from the Security Department of the Foreign and Commonwealth Office, alerting me to the publication, by some sort of oddball or anarchist group, of a 'Who's Who of the British Secret State'. It was, apparently, full of mistakes; but listed the names of some 1,800 officials and others who the publishers alleged were closely connected with, or actual members of, the Security Services – serving, retired, or (believe it not) in some cases actually deceased. One of the 1,800 was Fielding, Leslie, of 'MI6', whose last assignment was listed as 'First Secretary, FCO, 1970–'. I was told, as presumably the many other ex-Diplomatic Service recipients of the same round robin, not to attach too much importance to such rubbish, but to be alert and consult the local police if I had any anxieties, in the event that the publication attracted the attentions of investigative journalists, or of less well-intentioned individuals.

I was not, as Vice-Chancellor, or in any previous incarnation, whether as a member of HM Diplomatic Service or on the permanent staff of the European Commission in Brussels, a member of 'MI6' or what is more properly called the 'Secret Intelligence Service' (SIS). Of course, I would say that, wouldn't I, even if it were

not true – such are the supposed wheel-within-wheels of the Secret State? You can't win. Perhaps this is as it should be – although, in the twenty-first century, senior members of the SIS are as likely to be publicly declared as such, as they are to remain veiled from the public gaze. Nevertheless, the fact remains that I was a 'Dip' and not a 'Spook', all my life. The anarchists had registered yet another of their many and egregious errors.

Reflecting, at my desk in the University, I thought I could guess where all this nonsense went back to – namely, my three years as Chargé d'Affaires in Cambodia. Let me begin with professional eluci-dation, for the benefit of the innocent or un-informed.

As the British Government now openly declare, but formerly were reluctant to admit, there are at least three active secret intel-ligence-gathering organisations in this country. The first and best known is the Security Service, sometimes called MI5, accountable to the Home Secretary. The second, and necessarily the least known, is Government Communications Headquarters, (GCHQ), whose main office is in Cheltenham, and which is understood to engage in international electronic surveillance and code-breaking. The third is the SIS, whose impressive new headquarters on the South Bank in London are now a tourist landmark. Both GCHQ and the SIS are accountable to the Prime Minister and Cabinet and, more particularly, to the Foreign Secretary, whose Diplo-matic Service officials oversee the operations of these two organi-sations and furnish them with policy guidelines approved by Ministers. In addition, there are various other bodies concerned with intelligence, including – on the technical analysis side – a dedicated intelligence staff in the Ministry of Defence and – at a much higher and more general level – the Joint Intelligence Committee (JIC) in the Cabinet Office, on which all the relevant services and organisations are represented, but which is normally chaired, and supplied with a small secretariat of middle-ranking officials, by the FCO.

As regards the Diplomatic Service and the Secret Intelligence Service in particular, these are two distinct organisations which offer their members quite separate careers. Very occasionally, a young SIS officer will make a career switch into the Diplomatic Service. Perma-nent switches in the opposite direction, from the FO to MI6 are, I believe, virtually unknown. Occasionally, members of the Diplo-matic Service serving abroad may be invited to assist their SIS friends and colleagues, in some limited way or other. But the overlap (or

interface) stops there. The two organisations respect one another and work closely together, but 'each to his own last'. And there is a clear-cut distinction between ends and means. The ends of secret intelligence are determined by the FCO and No 10 and the means are, within given guidelines, the business of the SIS.

I joined the Diplomatic Service (then, before the merger with the Commonwealth Service, called the Foreign Service) in September 1956, on being successful in the open examination for entry to the Senior Branch, then called 'Branch A'. My subsequent, classically conventional career was copper-bottomed diplomatic.

After initial formation and language training in London, I was posted to the Embassy in Tehran. On completion of my language studies there, I was appointed to the Chancery, as Private Secretary to the Ambassador and general dog's body and hack. On leaving Tehran in 1960, I was posted back to London for a stint in the Western Organisations and Co-Ordination Department and as Resident Clerk. As recounted in my first chapter, I was then sent to Singapore, to the Office of the Political Adviser (POLAD) to the then British Commander-in-Chief Far East in Phoenix Park, as one of the two Foreign Office secretaries of the Joint Intelligence Committee, Far East.

In its usual, methodically professional, way the FCO had arranged, while I was still in London, for me to attend introductory courses – on what they did and how they worked – at the SIS and GCHQ, and with the Security Service. These were backed up by briefings from the Ministry of Defence and those directly concerned in the FCO with POLAD and South-East Asian and Far Eastern affairs. Much of this was rather new to me. While I was required to glance at the occasional intelligence reports from SIS and the GCHQ at the NATO/WEU desk in London, I had had no further 'need to know' and certainly no direct dealings with either organisation.

It was against this normal diplomatic background that I arrived in Phnom Penh in May 1964, and assumed charge of the Embassy the following month. I replaced both the departed Ambassador and my more immediate opposite number, John Shakespeare, the Head of Chancery (who had done a direct swap with me and gone to Phoenix Park). As explained in Chapter 4, the technical and clerical support staff numbered five, while the residual diplomatic staff consisted, apart from myself, of only two others. First, there was a Military Attaché in the rank of Lieutenant Colonel, recently transferred to the Intelligence Corps from the Royal Artillery as the result

of a flying accident. Second, there was a Vice Consul concerned with visas, administration and accounts. The political Second Secretary in the Chancery had been withdrawn without direct replacement, as the Ambassador had been, and as other staff had earlier on, including the commercial and information Second Secretaries.

This new profile provoked a certain interest, among communist bloc Embassies, and the omnipresent, proprietorial and ever-inquisitive French. Had British Intelligence turned its back on Cambodia, where it was assumed still to have secret agents and 'assets'? Or was Intelligence Colonel Robson, or that odd Monsieur Fielding, the new master spy? After all, our French allies reasoned, over their evening glasses of Pernod, Fielding was clearly some sort of Military Intelligence Officer, because he had been sent direct to Phnom Penh from the British base in Singapore. (The French, in particular, have always been slightly baffled by the way the British Government machine works; and, since no one branch of the French Government will ever operate entirely smoothly with another, a simple enquiry of the Chancery of the French Embassy in London – with whom I had had weekly dealings on diplomatic business, when still in the Western Organisations Department – was presumably never attempted by French Intelligence.) The 'Deputy Defence Attaché' in the French Embassy in Phnom Penh therefore came sniffing round me, to the point of requiring active discouragement.

Even in the Chinese Embassy, with whom we had paradoxically very correct working relations, mainly over Hong Kong, people were similarly exercised. At Chinese receptions I was pressed, in an arch sort of way, by someone I took to be their senior intelligence officer, about the nature of my duties – When had I last been based in London? Which Department had I served in? Was it 'PUSD?' (The 'Permanent Under-Secretary's Department', then the FCO liaison office with the Ministry of Defence, the Chiefs of Staff and the SIS.)

But it was the French who strongly most suspected, on what they considered their 'patch', SIS operations in Cambodia directed (and perhaps dramatic new intelligence initiatives undertaken) by person or persons not only unknown but – worst of all – also undeclared to *les services français*. In what was still, in some respects, a village as well as a capital city, the buzz went on for some months in the bistros, cafés and bars, among the cannier journalists as well as the *barbouzes* (intelligence and security officers) and the military types. Whenever conversations edged that way, I myself offered arched

eyebrows and a puzzled stare to all comers, until I finally perfected a Gallic shrug and a sphinx-like facial expression. But I continued to be closely observed. The image of the 'play-boy' Chargé d'Affaires, seemingly somewhat out of kilter with the normal comportment of a British Head of Mission, served only further to fuel suspicion. My not infrequent excursions up-country and to the border regions were assumed to be part of a sleuth-like professional search for military secrets and clandestine Viet Cong bases, or for clearing 'dead letter' boxes, or for placing cunning transponders or fiendish tracking devices.

And so, to my surprise and initial embarrassment, the 'walk-ins' began. A well-placed resident French journalist sought me out, offering to sell me privileged inside information about domestic Cambodian politics. Someone from an Eastern Bloc Embassy indicated that he was toying with the idea of defection to the West. Unexpected intermediaries popped up, with suggestions for the negotiated release by the Viet Cong of hostages and prisoners, through clandestine channels. Somebody else altogether had yet something else to offer or suggest. What did I want? What would I pay? Much of this, I could not begin to evaluate, let alone handle. But other people, I imagined, could, who were competent in these matters. So I learned to cope as best I might, with a word here and a nod there, and advice from somewhere else. The Australians, among others, were helpful and discreet. Very occasionally, senior SIS officers from London would take a swing through Phnom Penh, for a stroll in the open and a private chat; or asked to meet me elsewhere in South-East Asia. But I did all this without personally engaging in activities incompatible with my status as Envoy.

After nearly three years of such, I settled down to routine diplomatic life in the Paris Embassy. To any sane observer, I was visibly and fully responsible, with another First Secretary (initially, Kenneth James, then the late Michael Simpson-Orlebar, both later Ambassadors and Knights of the Realm), for classic across-the-board work with the Quai d'Orsay on foreign policy issues. But, for some Frenchmen, this could only be a blind. Fielding must be up to something deep and undeclared. (One only had to look at his night life: all those bars, night clubs and discotheques. An expensive man to 'tail'. Who was he meeting? What were his targets?) Even the expatriate press corps got wind of these suspicions. The late Sam White (gossip columnist extraordinaire of the *Evening Standard*, long-serving Lunch Time O-Booze at the Crillon Bar and self-designated

Doyen of the Western Press in Paris) once found himself unjustly threatened with libel proceedings by a particularly unsavoury *barbouze*. It was therefore to me, over a pig's trotter lunch in the Marais, that the savvy Sam (ever, he believed, 'in the know'; but, as always, somewhat confused) carried his loud complaint. I naturally reported this. Rubbing his hands with glee, the SIS Head of Station told me to carry on the good work.

But 'give a dog a bad name'. My (totally, non-) career, as an alleged SIS officer, lingered on, by reputation, for years, after assignment to other equally transparently orthodox official duties, whether as Deputy Head, from 1970–73, of the FCO 'Planning Staff' think-tank, or as a 'Eurocrat' in the European Commission, from 1973–87. (I still wonder why, when Jacques Delors became President of the Commission, he was initially so circumspect in his dealings with me as his Director General for External Relations. Was it that I had just won the EC Rifle Championship? Or was he the recipient of a solemn warning from *les services* in Paris about 'Danger Man Fielding'?)

At the University of Sussex, however, despite its left-wing reputation, absolutely no one cared a fig about their Vice-Chancellor's past 'form'. For leading officers of the Students Union, much of the time, and even for a few members of Academic Faculty, some of the time, anyone not a neo-Marxist, post-Maoist, Deconstructionist, Feminist Socialist was an obvious secret agent of Western Capitalism, anyway. So, what else was new? Seemingly equally indifferent are the congregations to which I, as an Anglican Reader, have subsequently preached at Matins and Evensong in the Welsh Marches – like all my former students, they have more important things to worry about.

Chronology

Wider developments affecting Cambodia are in bold

1859	French naval force seizes Saigon.
1864	France imposes a Protectorate over the Kingdom of Cambodia.
1930	Nguyen Ai Quoc ('Ho Chi Minh') founds Indo-Chinese Communist Party.
1941	Prince Norodom Sihanouk is crowned King of Cambodia.
1942–45	**The Japanese overrun South-East Asia.**
1949–50	**The triumph of Mao's Communists in China.**
1953	King Sihanouk wins Cambodia's independence from France.
1954	France is defeated in Vietnam (Dien Bien Phu). The Geneva Conference on Indo-China recognises Cambodia's neutrality and orders the withdrawal of the communist Viet Minh and Khmer Rouge to Hanoi.
1955	King Sihanouk abdicates the throne in favour of his father, Norodom Suramarit, and reverts to Princely status. (Nevertheless, as Prime Minister, he becomes the country's principal political leader.)
1960	On his father's death, Prince Sihanouk becomes Head of State, leaving the throne vacant.
1962	Prince Sihanouk requests the convening of a Geneva Conference to guarantee Cambodia's neutrality.
1963	Leaders of the communist opposition to Prince Sihanouk leave Phnom Penh for the 'maquis'.
	Prince Sihanouk renounces American aid.
	Failure of the first British initiative to convene, and Co-Chair with the USSR, a Geneva Conference, to guarantee the independence, neutrality and territorial integrity of Cambodia (mainly due to US and South Vietnam's objections).
	The CIA's 'Secret War' in Laos begins.

1963 (cont.)	British Prime Minister Harold Macmillan resigns and is succeeded in October by Lord Home; Lord Home is in turn succeeded as Foreign Secretary by Mr R.A. Butler.

US President John F. Kennedy's assassination in November. He is succeeded by Vice President Johnson.

1964	The British and American Embassies in Phnom Penh are attacked by Cambodian mobs.

The British Embassy is reduced in size, its dependants evacuated, and finally the Ambassador withdrawn in April, to be replaced by a junior Chargé d'Affaires brought up from Singapore.

A Labour Government comes to power in October under Prime Minister Harold Wilson, with Mr Patrick Gordon Walker as Foreign Secretary.

1965	**Mr Michael Stewart succeeds Mr Patrick Gordon Walker as British Foreign Secretary. The United States announces 'continuous limited airstrikes' against North Vietnam. The first US Marine Infantry (3rd Battalion, 9th Marines) lands in South Vietnam.**

Occasional attacks on Cambodian frontier villages by South Vietnamese and American forces.

Failure of renewed effort, under Mr Harold Wilson, to convene a Geneva Conference on Cambodia (US and South Vietnam consent, but China and North Vietnam veto project). Mr Patrick Gordon Walker's peace mission to Indo-China leads nowhere.

Cambodia breaks diplomatic relations with the United States; but relations with the UK begin to improve.

1966	Failure of British attempt to secure international agreement for the strengthening of the International Control Commission in Cambodia, to monitor Cambodia's neutrality and territorial integrity. (USSR lukewarm; China and North Vietnam opposed.)

Cutural Revolution breaks out in China, in May.

An improvement in Anglo-Cambodian relations leads to accreditation of a new British Ambassador in Phnom Penh in October, and departure of previous Chargé d'Affaires in November.

1967	Prince Sihanouk's armed forces crush a left-wing peasant revolt in Battambang Province.

More left-wingers flee from Phnom Penh to the 'maquis'.

Prince Sihanouk is compelled to turn a blind eye to Vietnamese communists using the border areas of his country adjoining South Vietnam and landing supplies at the port of Sihanoukville. South Vietnamese and American forces mount more frequent raids across the Cambodian border.

1968	In January, US Ambassador to New Delhi, Mr Chester Bowles, visits Cambodia to explore restoration of relations between Cambodia and the United States and ways to limit communist use of the border areas.
	In November, Mr Richard Nixon elected US President.
1969	US B-52 bombing attacks on communist base camps inside Cambodia begin, in March.
	In June, Prince Sihanouk announces that Cambodian–US relations will be restored.
1970	In March, an estimated 20,000 Cambodians demonstrate against Vietnamese communist presence in the country and sack the North Vietnamese and Viet Cong Embassies in Phnom Penh.
	Prince Sihanouk is deposed as Cambodia's Head of State while on a trip to Moscow and Beijing. Power is seized by the Prime Minister, General Lon Nol, supported by Prince Sirik Matak.
	In Peking, Prince Sihanouk announces that he has formed a National United Front of Kampuchea (later, a Government in exile) with his former enemies, the Khmer Rouge, to fight a guerrilla war against the Lon Nol Government.
	In April, General Lon Nol makes an international appeal for aid. President Nixon announces that American and South Vietnamese troops have crossed into Cambodia to attack communist bases. (US forces withdraw in June.) Initial success for the General, against the Khmer Rouge.
1971	General Lon Nol's 'Chenla II' expeditionary force to drive out the Viet Cong is heavily defeated by North Vietnamese troops. B-52 bombing continues.
1972	**President Nixon visits China.**
1973	**Paris Agreement to end war in Vietnam signed in January.**
	US B-52 bombing of Cambodia ends in August.
1974	Khmer Rouge forces in Cambodia make real progress.
	US President Gerald Ford succeeds Mr Richard Nixon in August.
1975	General Lon Nol goes into exile in Hawaii.
	Phnom Penh falls to Pol Pot's forces in April (Prince Sirik Matak and other senior Government figures executed, as well as all captured Cambodian servicemen, by the Khmer Rouge).
	Saigon falls to the North Vietnamese.
	The Communist take-over of Laos is completed. (Laotian royal family 'disappear' – in reality, put to death.)
	Prince Sihanouk returns to Phnom Penh from China, but promptly becomes prisoner of the Khmer Rouge. (In early 1979, he is allowed to return to Peking at Chairman Mao Tse-tung's request.)

Pol Pot's purge of opponents begins, leading eventually to the extermination (by execution or privation) of up to a quarter of the population of Cambodia.

1976 **The death of Mr Chou En-lai, Prince Sihanouk's friend and confidant, in January.**

The death of Chairman Mao Tse-tung, in September.

1977 Growing tension between communist regimes in Cambodia, Vietnam and China.

Pol Pot's provocation of communist Vietnam provokes a large-scale Vietnamese invasion of Cambodia in December

1979 Pol Pot is toppled in January and takes refuge in remote area near Thai frontier.

A puppet regime (under Mr Heng Samrin) is established in Phnom Penh by Vietnam.

China's 17-day invasion of Vietnam in February.

Cambodia becomes largely closed to the outside world, under influence of Vietnam and USSR.

Khmer Rouge guerrillas continue to exist, but are ineffective.

Soviet invasion of Afghanistan, in December.

1989 Vietnamese forces finally withdraw from Cambodia in September.

1991 The Paris Peace Agreement ends Cambodian Civil War in September.

1992 UNTAC (United Nations Transitional Authority in Cambodia) is deployed.

1993 'Free' Elections in Cambodia result in a contested outcome, with power divided between the royalists, the former communists and the liberals. Mr Hun Sen (a former Khmer Rouge commander who later defected to Vietnam) becomes second Prime Minister, in a coalition government.

Outwitted and un-nerved, Prince Sihanouk agrees to re-ascend the throne; he plays a diminishing part in public life.

1997 Mr Hun Sen overturns elected Cambodian government; engineers own mandate.

1998 Pol Pot dies in the 'maquis' at Anlong Veng.

Fresh elections, but Mr Hun Sen this time gains the upper hand.

2000 **US President Clinton visits Hanoi.**

2004 King Sihanouk finally abdicates in favour of one of his sons, Prince Norodom Sihamoni, a mild monarch acceptable to Mr Hun Sen. King Sihanouk, in failing health, spends his time thereafter mostly in Beijing.

2006 Ta Mok, Pol Pot's lieutenant, dies (in detention, awaiting trial) in Phnom Penh.

US President Bush visits Hanoi, in the latest stage of a steady improvement in relations.

2007 **Vietnam accedes to the World Trade Organisation.**

Select Bibliography

The Earlier History of Cambodia

For a general account of Cambodian history

Dannaud, J.P., *Cambodge,* Lausanne, 1956.

Giteau, Madeleine, *Histoire du Cambodge*, Paris, 1957.

Hertz, M.F., *A Short History of Cambodia*, Phnom Penh, 1957. Written by an American diplomat formerly serving in Phnom Penh; the book has, however, been roughly handled by B.P. Groslier in the *Bulletin de l'Ecole Française d'Extrême-Orient*, Volume I, (1960) pp. 209–16.

Migot, André, *Les Khmers,* Paris, 1960.

For a closer look at the earlier centuries

Briggs, L.P., *The Ancient Khmer Empire*, Philadelphia, 1951.

Coedes, Georges, *Les peuples de la péninsule Indochinoise,* Paris, 1962. (An English version is available from Routledge and Kegan Paul, called *The Making of South-East Asia*, 1966.)

Coedes, Georges, *Les états hindouisés de l'Indochine et de l'Indonésie,* Paris, 1964.

Hall, D.G.E., *A History of South-East Asia*, London, 1955.

Osborne, Milton, *Southeast Asia: An Introductory History*, St Leonards NSW, 6th edition, 1995. (This distinguished Australian academic and ex-diplomat is currently the foremost writer on Indo-China.)

For translations of reports of Chinese, Arab and Iberian travellers, see

Ferrand, G., *Voyage du marchard arabe Sulaymân,* Classiques de l'Orient VII, Paris, 1922.

Groslier, B.P., *Angkor et le Cambodge au XVIe siècle, d'après les sources portugaises et espagnoles,* Paris, 1958.

Pelliot, P., (Translator), *Mémoires sur les coutumes du Cambodge par Tcheou Ta-kouan,* Paris, 1951.

de Saint-Denys, Hervey, (Translator), *Ma Touan-lin,* Méridionaux, 1883.

Cambodia in the Nineteenth Century

Some of the principal authorities include

Cady, J.F., *The Roots of French Imperialism in Eastern Asia*, Ithaca, 1967.

Osborne, Milton, *The French Presence in Cochinchina and Cambodia, Rule and Response (1859–1905)*, Ithaca, 1969. (A first-class piece of scholarship which is also very readable.)

Osborne, Milton, *River Road to China: The Mekong River Expedition 1866–1873*, St Leonards NSW, 2nd edition 1996.

Keay, John, *Mad about the Mekong: Exploration and Empire in South-East Asia*, London, 2005.

Anyone interested in getting close to the original sources for this period, but with little time to spare in which to do so, should turn to the following admirable compendium of commented extracts from contemporary French writers, state papers, *etc.*

Taboulet, G. (editor), *La geste Française en Indochine: histoire par les textes de la France en Indochine des origines à 1914* (2 vols), Paris, 1955.

The Victorian explorers and colonisers make interesting reading. They include

Bouillevaux, C E., *Voyages dans l'Indochine 1848–56*, Paris, 1858.

Delaporte, L., *Voyage au Cambodge*, Paris, 1880.

Forrest, E.F.J., *Journal of the Royal Geographical Society, Vol XXX* (Edited by J. Campbell), London, 1860.

Garnier, F., *Voyage d'exploration en Indo-Chine, effectué pendant les années 1866, 1867* (2 vols), Paris, 1873.

Mouhot, H., *Voyages dans les royaumes du Siam, du Cambodge de Laos: Le Tour du Monde*, Paris, 1863, pp. 219–352.

Then there are the following additional French sources

Aymonier, E., *Notice sur le Cambodge*, Paris, 1875.

Bouinais, A. and Paulus, A., *L'Indo-Chine française contemporaine, Cochinchine, Cambodge, Tonkin, Annam* (2 vols), Paris, 1885.

Branda, P. (real name P. Reveillère), *Ça et là: Cochinchine et Cambodge: l'Ame Khmère: Ang-Kor*, Paris, 1887.

Collard, P., *Cambodge et Cambodgiens: metamorphose du Royaume Khmêr par une méthode française du Protectorat*, Paris, 1925.

Delvert, J., *Le paysan Cambodgien*, Paris, 1961.

Doumer, P., *L'Indochine française (souvenirs)*, Paris, 1905.

Hess, J., *L'Affaire Iukanthor: les dessous d'un Protectorat*, Paris, 1900.

Leclère, A., *Recherches sur le droit public des Cambodgiens*, Paris, 1894.

Lemire, C., *L'Indochine: Cochinchine française, Royaume du Cambodge, Royaume d'Annam et Tonkin*, Paris, 1884.

Moura, J., *Le Royaume du Cambodge* (2 vols), Paris, 1883. (The first major documentary work on Cambodia, compiled by a French Government representative in Phnom Penh.)

Cambodia as Seen in the Twentieth Century

The following are suggested

Armstrong, J.P., *Sihanouk Speaks*, New York, 1964. (A study of the political speeches of Prince Sihanouk, written with sympathy and insight.)

Field, M., *The Prevailing Wind: Witness in Indo-China*, London, 1965.

Lacouture, S., *Cambodge,* Lausanne, 1963.

Lancaster, D., *The Emancipation of French Indo-China*, Oxford, 1961. (By a British scholar and former diplomat, who later served as an adviser to Prince Sihanouk – see also Zasloff and Goodman below.)

Leifer, M., *Cambodia: The Search for Security*, New York, 1967.

MacDonald, M., *Angkor,* London, 1960. (By the former British High Commissioner for South-East Asia.)

Pym, C., *The Road to Angkor,* London, 1959.

Pym, C., *Mistapim in Cambodia*, London, 1960.

Smith, R., *Cambodian Foreign Policy*, Ithaca, 1965.

Steinberg, D.J. (editor), *Cambodia, its People, its Society, its Culture*, New Haven, 1959.

Wilmott, W.E., *The Chinese in Cambodia*, Vancouver, 1967.

On the original Geneva accords of 1954, there are useful insights, *passim*, from one of the principal architects

Eden, Anthony, *Full Circle*, London, 1960.

See also two important sets of documents published by the British Government. First on the Co-Chairmanship of the Geneva Conference generally; second, on Cambodia

Documents Relating to British Involvement in the Indo-China Conflict 1945–1965 (December 1965) Cmnd. 2834

Recent Diplomatic Exchanges Concerning the Proposal for an International Conference on the Neutrality and Territorial Integrity of Cambodia (June 1965) Cmnd. 2678.

The narrative from 1966 is taken up in

Osborne, Milton, *Before Kampuchea*, Sydney, 1979 (2nd edition, Bangkok, 2004).

The commentaries of two of Prince Sihanouk's former foreign advisers are to be found in

Meyer, Charles, *Derrière le Sourire Khmer*, Paris, 1971.

Zasloff, Joseph J. and Goodman, Allen. E. (editor), *Indo-China in Conflict: A Political Assessment*, Lexington, 1972, Chapter 4: 'The Decline of Prince Sihanouk's Regime' by Donald Lancaster.

The best biography of Norodom Sihanouk (although offering a slightly less flattering portrait than I would have painted myself) is

Osborne, Milton, *Sihanouk, Prince of Light, Prince of Darkness*, St Leonards NSW, 1994.

The Prince's own three-part biography, starting with *Chroniques de guerre ... et d'espoir* and *Souvenirs doux et amers*, concludes with the riveting

Sihanouk, Norodom, *Prisonnier des Khmers Rouges*, Paris, 1986.

See also, in English, edited and translated by Ambassador Julio A. Andres

Shadow over Angkor, Vol. One, Memoirs of H.M. King Norodom Sihanouk, Phnom Penh, 2005.

From the pen of the controversial communist Australian journalist, I will mention

Burchett, Wilfred, *My War with the CIA: The Memoirs of Prince Norodom Sihanouk as Related to Wilfred Burchett*, London, 1973.

Finally

Osborne, Milton, *Phnom Penh: A Cultural and Literary History*, Oxford, 2007.

The Cambodian Tragedy

The broadest sweep is probably to be found in

Chandler, David P., *The Tragedy of Cambodian History: Politics, War and Revolution since 1945*, New Haven, 1991.

On the Pol Pot pogrom, readers will have seen Haing Ngor's Oscar-winning performance in *The Killing Fields*; but should also read his book

Ngor, Haing S. with Warner, Roger, *Surviving the Killing Fields*, London, 1988.

On Pol Pot himself, we now have the authoritative

Short, Philip, *Pol Pot, The History of a Nightmare*, London, 2004.

And also the spine-chilling

Dunlop, Nic, *The Lost Executioner: A Story of the Khmer Rouge*, London, 2005;

plus
> Bizot, François, *The Gate*, London, 2004.

To which should be added, as essential reading, two eloquent and magnificent philippics
> Shawcross, William, *Sideshow: Kissinger, Nixon and the Destruction of Cambodia*, London, 1979.
>
> Shawcross, William, *The Quality of Mercy: Cambodia, Holocaust and Modern Conscience*, London, 1984.

Which, in turn, point to the relevant passages, *passim*, in
> Kissinger, Henry, *Diplomacy*, New York, 1994.

A French perspective is furnished by
> Ponchaud, François, *Cambodia, Year Zero*, New York, 1978.

On an important aspect of the modern Cambodian economy
> Osborne, Milton, *The Mekong, Turbulent Past, Uncertain Future*, St Leonards NSW, 2001.
>
> Osborne, Milton, *River at Risk, the Mekong and the Water Politics of China and Southeast Asia*, Double Bay NSW, 2004.

On UN intervention
> Goulding, Marrack, *Peacemonger,* London, 2002, see Chapter 14.

A well-observed novel about this period is
> Donald, Elsie Burch, *A Model American*, New York, 2007.

Cambodian Art and Architecture

I recommend the following
> Boisselier, J., *Tendances de l'art Khmèr*, Paris, 1956.
>
> Boisselier, J., *Le Cambodge, manuel d'archéologie d'Extrême-Orient: Asie du Sud-Est: Vol I*, Paris, 1967.
>
> Coedes, G., *Pour mieux comprendre Angkor,* Paris, 1947.
>
> Glaize, M., *Les Monuments du Groupe d'Angkor,* Paris, 1963.
>
> Giteau, M., *Les Khmers : Sculptures Khmers, reflets de la civilisation d'Angkor,* Biblothèque des Arts, Paris 1965.
>
> Groslier, B.P., *Angkor, Hommes et Pierres,* Paris, 1962.
>
> Groslier, B.P., (Translated by Lawrence G.), *Indochina: Art in the melting-pot of races*, London, 1962. (Both these are standard works.)
>
> Jacques, C. and Lafond, P., *The Khmer Empire*, River Books, Bangkok, 2007.

Loti, P., *Un pélérin d'Angkor,* Paris, 1912. (An early touristic narrative of great charm.)

Thierry, Solange, *Les Khmers*, Paris, 1964.

Wening, R., *Angkor: La cité des temples retrouvée dans la forêt vierge,* Zurich, 1965.

British Diplomacy in General

Patten, Chris, *Not Quite The Diplomat: Home Truths About World Affairs*, London, 2005.

Meyer, Christopher, *DC Confidential*, London, 2005.

Ziegner, Graham (editor), *British Diplomacy: Foreign Secretaries Reflect*, London, 2007. Douglas Hurd's contribution is entitled : "After Iraq - what future for humanitarian intervention?", pp. 83–96.

Parallels with Iraq

Polk, William R, *Understanding Iraq*, New York, 2005.

Bremer, Paul, *My Year in Iraq: The Struggle to Build a Future of Hope*, New York, 2006.

McGovern, George and Polk, William R, *Out of Iraq: A Practical Plan for Withdrawal Now*, New York, 2006.

Chandrasekaran, Rajiv, *Imperial Life in the Emerald City, Inside Baghdad's Green Zone*, London and New York, 2007.

Index